D0770850

SING
ENGLISH
SONG

a practical approach
to the language
and the repertoire

Stephen Varcoe

Foreword by Dame Felicity Lott

Thames Publishing
Distribution by William Elkin Music Services

First published in 2000 by Thames Publishing
Station Road Industrial Estate, Salhouse, Norwich, Norfolk NR13 6NS

Text © 2000 Stephen Varcoe
First printing © 2000 Thames Publishing
Reprinted 2002

No part of this publication may be reproduced in any form
(photographic, mechanical or electronic), or for any purpose,
without the prior written permission of the publisher.

Library
University of Texas'
at San Antonio

Printed and bound in the United Kingdom by
Thanet Press Limited, Margate, Kent

Contents

To Gerald Finzi for his music,
to Wilfred Brown for his guidance,
and to Melinda for her encouragement

Foreword

BY DAME FELICITY LOTT, DBE

Reading this fascinating book fills me with guilt at having neglected so much of my native repertoire in favour of Lieder and Mélodies! Stephen, with whom I have had the pleasure of collaborating on a number of occasions, not least as members of The Songmakers' Almanack, excuses me a little by writing that 'there are many more songs with a specifically male viewpoint than a female one'; and, in my defence, I have loved singing songs by Maude Valérie White, Lisa Lehmann and Madeline Dring, to choose a few of our fine women composers. But English song, with perhaps the exception of Britten, has for years been rather the poor relation in the concert hall.

This book, written by one of our foremost interpreters of the native repertoire, rightly places tremendous importance on clear enunciation of the text, and provides excellent background information on the most frequently set poems and poets, as well as on their composers. How marvellous to have all this in one volume, complementing the helpful and thoughtful suggestions based on Stephen's very extensive performing experience.

I hope that many more singers – experienced as well as students – will be encouraged to delve into the neglected realms of English song. There are many treasures to be found in the various Thames Publishing volumes, as well as collections – alas, less numerous than they used to be – from other publishers. With Stephen's book as guide, and the wealth of factual information about availability to be found in Michael Pilkington's *English Solo Song* (Thames, 1998), let us take up his challenge, and fill the concert halls and recital rooms with words and music in our own great language.

Introduction

English is thought to be a difficult language to sing, and this is an opinion held by most English-speaking singers. Far better the simpler sounds of Italian, they say, than the messy complications of diphthong, neutral vowel and clipped consonant which so get in the way of good tone. Italian was made for singing, it seems, and every pizzeria has a budding Pavarotti on its staff, eagerly awaiting the call from La Scala. Through beautiful Italian vowels the voice can resonate freely, producing lovely cantabile lines unencumbered by too many distracting consonants. If this is the best language for allowing the voice to flourish, then the logical conclusion is that we should make the English that we sing into a version of Italian. In fact, this happens so regularly that there is a recognisable dialect of English which might be called 'singer-ese', bearing only a passing resemblance to the real language. Unfortunately, if the listener wishes to understand the meaning of the text, a certain amount of translation back into the original is needed. In a work as familiar as Handel's *Messiah* this probably doesn't matter much; 'Evree vahlee shahll be exolted' will pass off quite happily. What about less well-known texts, though? 'Ah weedaw bahd sat marning for har lahve ahpona weentree bah' (A widow bird sat mourning for her love upon a wintry bough), or 'Tek, aw tek therz leeps aweh' (Take, o take those lips away). Those who think I'm exaggerating should try listening to singers without being too generous with their translating skills, especially when they are hearing a sung text for the first time. Don't get the idea, however, that I'm suggesting that every singer mangles the language like this, and indeed our best singers are capable of wonderfully true and just diction.

If we are to get away from the strange sounds of this 'dialect' and approach something more like the true language, we need to learn how to do it, because there is no doubt that Italian is indeed made of fewer, simpler sounds. But if English is our native tongue we at least know what it ought to sound like, so the first and most important rule is to learn how to listen, not just to ourselves but to others. We must continually ask ourselves questions about what we are hearing: do I accept what I hear simply because that is the way it always seems to be sung, or do I wonder whether there is another, truer way to make the language more like the one we are used to hearing spoken? When compromises are made to accommodate the requirements of vocal production and technique, are they entirely necessary, or can they be made in such a way as to minimise the damaging effects on intelligibility? How much of what we hear sung is due to convention or laziness, and if there is a choice between a conventional, sung sound and a normal conversational one, can the conversational version be used without getting into a vocal tangle? In this book I hope to show ways in which our sung language can be made more like the spoken word without ignoring the needs of the singing voice, and I want to stress how fascinating the process of discovery and refinement can be.

There is another purpose to this book aside from reclaiming our language from the misuse it has received for so long, and that is to reclaim the reputation of English song. Henry Purcell flourished at a time when English music could boast a glorious history of achievement which had lasted more than a century from the golden age of Queen Elizabeth. After his death our native musical genius seems to have fallen asleep, and we developed an irreparable inferiority complex in all things musical. German musical traditions and ideas became all-conquering, and it is quite obvious that we are still in thrall to their musical culture. Anybody's list of the great composers of the eighteenth and nineteenth centuries would be dominated by Germans and Austrians, and theirs is the music which still dominates today. We pay reverential respect to the wonderful repertoire of nineteenth-century Lieder, and take a great deal of trouble to study and learn it. So we should, for it is undoubtedly art of the highest quality, but because of our feeling that English music is inadequate and unsatisfactory in comparison, we ignore the songs in our own language. The truth is that a singer only comes fully alive when singing in his or her native tongue. If someone were to say to me 'Ich liebe dich', I would of course know what it meant, but the message would come to me via a process of translation. I'm certain that if someone said to me 'I love you' instead, my hormones would start jumping around before I knew what was happening. The message would hit me instantaneously. In a similar way, no amount of careful translation of a foreign text can give the singer the same opportunity to express and communicate meaning as can be found in his own language. I am not talking about correct stress, accentuation and mood: that can all be learnt. I am talking about subtle nuances of feeling, about gut-reaction and what is in the mind's eye, and if an English-speaking singer wishes to learn about the masterpieces of Lieder and of the great French Mélodies, the best place to start is with English song. Discover the possibilities of emotion and how it affects the voice through the words that are in daily use. Feel what it is like to sing 'I love you' by including personal experience of that hormone-rush, and be prepared to find some hitherto unknown musical treasures.

* * * * *

Michael Pilkington's knowledge of English song is encyclopaedic, and I am very grateful to him for giving his time to ensure the accuracy of my dates and other facts. In fairness to him, though, I should point out that the opinions expressed in these pages are my own.

* * * * *

Thames Publishing was founded in 1970 by John Bishop and his wife Betty Roe to publish English music and books on English music and musicians. It was a great loss to the musical life of the country when John died in September 2000. His enthusiasm for the subject seemed to know no bounds, and without him this book would not have been written.

1 – Whose English?

When I write of the attempt to sing language in a way that approximates as closely as possible to the spoken word, I am begging the question of whose spoken word it might be. Is it someone from London? From Bristol? From Newcastle, Liverpool or Glasgow? From Dublin, New York or Sydney? The number of ways of speaking correct educated English is legion, and we have a tower of Babel all to ourselves. How do we decide which to use when singing? We might, if we are looking for an 'authentic' approach, choose an accent to correspond to the way the composer or the poet spoke, or we might perhaps consider how the composer or the poet expected the text to be spoken or sung, though for those that lived before recordings were available, that is largely a matter for conjecture. Shakespeare may have spoken with a Midlands accent, but surely in four hundred years the Stratford speech has altered, probably a great deal. Was there an accent of the Court which aspiring courtiers and hangers-on might adopt, a kind of posh English of the day? Even if there were, would the aristocracy of Northumberland or Devonshire or other far-flung parts have recognised it, or expected their house-musicians to sing in it?

There is a clue to resolving this question of accent, albeit a negative one, in the work of Percy Grainger. Grainger was deeply involved in the collecting and arranging of traditional folk-songs from the British Isles, and he developed some unusual ideas about performance. Here he is writing a preface to his setting of *Bold William Taylor,* collected by him in 1906 in Lincolnshire: 'To sing a Lincolnshire folksong such as *Bold William Taylor* without the folksinger's dialect and without the nonsense syllables and other details of English folksong traditions is as inartistic as it would be to sing Wagner with Italian operatic traditions, or to sing *Rigoletto* with Wagnerian operatic traditions. Singers should wake up to the fact that such a folksong as *Bold William Taylor*, shorn of its local dialect, loses its charm as surely as would *Kathleen*

Mavourneen, Comin' through the Rye or an American-Negro spiritual if sung in "Standard Southern English".

'The greatest crime against folksong is to "middle-class" it – to sing it with a "white collar" voice production and other towniefied suggestions. Whether it be true, or not, that the ballads originated in the knightly and aristocratic world, one thing is certain: they have come down to us solely as an adjunct of rural life and are drenched through and through with feelings and traditions. To weaken any characteristics of this rusticness – in collecting, arranging and performing folksongs – is, in my opinion, to play false to the very soul of folksong.'

It is quite clear that Grainger is railing against the way his (and others') arrangements were being sung; that is, with 'middle class' tones. These are presumably the tones in which all English song was being sung, not just folksong, and these are the tones, with modifications due to the passing of time, which we hear to this day. It seems, therefore, that unless a composer specifically requests otherwise, or the text is written in a dialect style, English song has to be treated in a 'middle class' way. The same is generally true in opera, where, for instance, Britten's Peter Grimes, a Suffolk fisherman, is usually portrayed with a standard singer's English accent. An actor in a play of the story would probably find this quite unacceptable, and at least make an attempt at a regional sound in order to give life and realism to the character. As far as opera is concerned, this option does not seem to be available at present unless, as is the case with Grainger's folksong settings, the piece is written in dialect. Vaughan Williams's *Riders to the Sea* has just such a libretto, where the strong Irish brogue is an essential element in the story-telling, and as I write this I note that Deirdre Gribben's opera *Hey Persephone* has been premiered at the Aldeburgh Festival with the successful use of Glaswegian accents. Incidentally, German opera follows the same kind of convention whereby unless the libretto has specific indications of dialect, the singers are expected to use *Hochdeutsch* pronunciation.

The consensus nowadays for those of us living and working in Great Britain is that we use Received Pronunciation, or RP, and that is the assumption I am making when writing this book. Another term for this accent used to be BBC English, though that is now out of date and misleading, since the BBC no longer suppresses regional accents in favour of the Alvar Lidell school of speech. Perhaps Grainger's 'Standard Southern English' is a more accurate term, but I shall use RP for brevity's sake. Just as language itself has developed over time, so have ways of pronouncing it. Many Americans from different parts of the USA and with different regional accents claim to have a monopoly on 'pure' English, either in their dialect expressions or in the sounds they use. Certainly the pronunciation of English as spoken by Elizabeth I would have been very unlike that spoken by Elizabeth II, whose accent, incidentally, is not RP but a distinct upper-class sound. The British, and I think especially the English as a nation, are able and willing to make fine judgments about a person's class and background through listening to the way he or she speaks. The present Queen and Prince Charles have to a certain extent altered the sound of their speech, either as a natural process or possibly as a deliberate attempt to appear less remote from the rest of us, but the change is minimal, and the upper-class tones remain unmistakeable.

Spoken English in England, and possibly in the rest of the British Isles, is horribly enmeshed in snobbery of all kinds. So much information about class and education comes through in the way we speak, and the snobbery cuts both ways. Accent can be used as a weapon in the class war to establish one's credentials as a member of a particular social group. Much is made by many politicians of their working-class roots, for example, when they have left behind those roots for a jet-setting, chauffeur-driven London life-style. The accent, though, remains as an affirmation of origin, just as clipped, upper-class tones might belong to somebody struggling to support a family on inadequate pay.

Setting aside the undertones of class-consciousness and snobbery, the people of the British Isles speak in an enormous variety of different accents, all of them perfectly acceptable and 'correct' in their own way. One of the advantages of RP lies in its being non-regional. This may be as a result of the old public school (that's private school to an American reader) boarding system, a kind of common denominator amongst children brought together from far and wide. When those children became parents themselves they would perpetuate the speech-patterns they learned by passing them on to their own children, even in the face of the regional sounds around, perhaps unconsciously showing their separateness and 'superiority'. Provided we can escape from such feelings of class distinction that may lurk in the background, then RP seems a useful standard.

For those readers who are unfamiliar with RP I recommend listening to actors like Juliet Stevenson, Derek Jacobi or Sam West. Listening to recordings of various singers should also help, though if that were all that's needed to sing English correctly, there would be no point in writing a book about it. There are several reasons why it is not enough simply to listen to a few recordings. Firstly, we rarely listen with our full attention, either to others or, more particularly, to ourselves – we often do not know what to listen for. A Spaniard, for instance, can find it extremely difficult to differentiate between the sounds of the words *ship* and *sheep*. His ears have not been accustomed to the short *i* of *ship*: for him in his own language it is always a long *i*, and so it sounds to him like *sheep*. Another example is the problem that English-speaking people have with Italian consonants. Many English words end on a consonant, and the way we say them gives a rather clipped, staccato effect. Italian words, on the other hand, almost all end on a vowel, and unless a double consonant is written (as in *mamma*, *otto* etc), Italians expect to hear an unbroken line of sound. Stopping on the *n* of *pani* (loaves) changes the sound to *panni*, and the meaning to cloths. I had an unfortunate experience with an Italian coach who was trying to get me to say *amo*, and each time I obliged he became crosser and crosser: 'It's not *ammo*, it's *amo!*' and yet I was convinced that I'd said exactly the same as he had. Listening carefully is in reality much more difficult than might be imagined.

Secondly, all singers make mistakes, and many otherwise fine artists are apparently not very bothered about the intelligibility of what they are singing, so long as the voice is heard to good effect. The major thrust of individual singing lessons is to train the voice as a musical instrument which projects well and without strain. The result of this in many cases is that the sound is carried on the most comfortable vowels, modifying the less comfortable ones to suit, and avoiding the awkward consonants as much as possible. Some kind of compromise is indeed necessary in order to accommodate the conflicting demands of voice production and language, but my contention is that more can usually be done to improve the quality of the latter without adversely affecting the former.

Thirdly, music colleges rightly emphasise the importance of the correct pronunciation of foreign languages, and devote much effort to teaching the sounds of Italian, German and French. Opera companies employ language coaches to ensure the right nuances of foreign accent, likewise recording companies. Our foreign colleagues are only too happy to respond to requests for help in this way, and all this can result (if we have a facility for mimicry and a decent memory) in near-faultless diction. The same is not at all true with singing in English, and there seems to be little interest in teaching the sounds of our own language, perhaps because it is assumed that we will know what to do anyway. English-speaking colleagues would probably be terribly offended by any suggestions for improving the quality of their diction. Conductors can do it for choirs (who tend to be treated like children anyway), but even they, with all the power which they wield over the performance, seldom make any comment about soloists' pronunciation. Just as we can always polish up our German or French, I'm convinced that we can do the same for our English provided we listen to ourselves and others, and, crucially, provided we believe that it is necessary and worthwhile in the first place. An example which was a real ear-opener to me was the singing of Dietrich Fischer-Dieskau in Britten's *War Requiem*, near the end of the work, where there is that wonderful line 'I am the enemy you killed, my friend'. That whole section is full of words ending in '-ld' or '-lled', like *wild, world, distilled, spoiled* and *walled.* Dieskau really relished the 'l' sound, in a way that I have never heard an English-speaker do, and it is wonderfully effective. The point is not that his English is perfect, although it is very good, but that he has learnt the English sounds as a German, just as we might learn the sounds of the German language as foreigners.

Fourthly, and this is really connected with the previous point, elements of foreign pronunciation spill over into the way we sing English. I do not mean such things as Fischer-Dieskau's '-ld' which I mentioned above, because that is a case of a foreigner teaching an Englishman how to sing his own language correctly. An example of what I have in mind is the often-heard encouragement for us to use Italianate vowels when we sing in English, and that seems to be the basis for the queer sounds of 'singerese' which I mentioned in the Introduction. In addition to the vowels coming out with the wrong colour, the English diphthongs lose their native character; either the closing of a diphthong is lost altogether or the subtle gradations between the sounds disappear. Foreign pronunciation also spills over into English unconsciously in the colour of certain consonants. 'L' is a problem in this regard, being often given the bright sound heard in the German word 'Held'.

We singers have a great advantage over other musicians because we have words to enunciate. The vowels offer us more than a dozen different tone-colours for a start, more than any instrument apart from the organ can manage. Then we have the variety of attack and decay that the consonants give us, either percussive or stroked, hummed or hissed, with moments of silence or strings of unbroken tone. The voice can be made to convey joy, sadness, anger, pleading, triumph or detachment; any of a myriad of emotions, in fact. And yet, with all this treasure-chest of wonderful noises at their disposal, what is the singer's standard complaint? It is that the words get in the way of the vocal line, and if they are British, they wish they were singing in Italian instead (some of them sound as though they are, without realising it). Singers are desperate to sing an uninterrupted musical line like an instrument, while instrumentalists envy the singers their great range of expressive options.

I want to show that words should be an integral part of a singer's music-making, not a necessary and unfortunate problem to be overcome. Furthermore, I want readers to feel that as well as communicating meaning, the sounds of a language are fascinating in themselves. This is not to suggest that our aim should be an exaggerated precision and clarity of enunciation. Clarity is a relative term, implying what is necessary in a given context to make meaning clear, and at all times it should stem from what sounds most natural. W B Yeats is supposed to have walked out of a concert sung by John McCormack, complaining about the 'damnable clarity of the words'. Listen to a recording of the great man and see if you agree with Yeats; his English diction does sound extraordinarily un-English, and it doesn't sound Irish either, though his defenders might well say that he was only pronouncing it in the manner expected of the singers of the time. Certainly the pronunciation of English is continually changing, and from recordings of seventy years ago we can hear things which are long out of fashion, such as the two rolled r's in 'evermore' which people were then expected to sing. Doubtless the future will bring more new fashions, and the norms of today will sound quaint and outdated. Indeed, I have recently been hearing students sing unrolled r's ('fricative', technically) where we would usually hear rolled ones, as in the word 'praise', for instance. This sounds oddly disturbing to me if only because I am not used to it, and it serves to underline the fact that what I am offering in this book is a snapshot of sung English at the turn of the millennium, which in another fifty years will in many ways be superseded. But in the quaint museum-piece which it is bound to become, there may remain some principles that will last a while longer, especially the principle that there is nothing wrong with English as a singing language if you know what you are doing.

2 – The Vowel Continuum

Shut the door, open your mouth, and make the loudest noise you can. The chances are that someone will knock on your door to ask if you're OK, but assuming you can reassure them on that score, I expect you came out with something like 'Aaaaa!', possibly with a B or a D at the beginning for emphasis. The sound of your voice carried on the vowel Aa, or whatever other vowel you might have chosen. The vocal cords set up a vibration like a reed in a woodwind instrument, and the shape of the throat, mouth and nose amplified the rather feeble initial sound and projected the noise that you and your friends consider to be your unique voice. That's all simple stuff and pretty well known, but think for a moment about what it is that distinguishes the various vowels from each other. Those of us who do not suffer from impaired hearing have all been familiar with speech since before we can remember, and it has probably never occurred to most of us to wonder why 'hat' sounds different from 'heat', or 'bowl' from 'ball'. How are these sounds made, and how does the ear perceive their differences? We can sing all the vowels on one note and make them distinct, so it must be something other than the pitch of the voice that comes into play. As we sing or speak the vowels we notice that our mouths take up different shapes and our tongues alter their positions, and it is these changes in the shape and size of the mouth cavity which affect its resonating capacity and produce the distinctive qualities of each vowel. What, though, is happening to the basic sound of the voice as it is modulated by these various mouth-shapes?

Experts in phonetics distinguish more than seventy separate vowels throughout the world's languages, of which thirteen are to be found in English (with some more if one accepts distinctions between words like 'fir' and 'fur', though I do not know anyone who pronounces those two words differently). Whether the true figure for the purist is thirteen or fifteen or twenty, it seems to me that in reality we have an infinite number of vowel sounds available to us. Anyone who has been involved in decorating a house knows the bewildering array of colours offered by the paint companies. Each one produces a colour chart with hundreds of shades and tones, varying subtly and almost imperceptibly from one to the next; and yet for convenience we talk of there being seven colours of the rainbow – red, orange, yellow, green, blue, indigo and violet. This division of the spectrum into seven colours was suggested by Sir Isaac Newton, specifically in order to equate with the seven notes of the diatonic scale. With the addition of reddish-orange, yellowish-green and greenish-blue we find ten perfectly sensible rainbow colours instead of the conventional number. Another example of an arbitrary choice of numbers is that of the twelve semitone intervals which make up our musical scale; in reality, every frequency between one note and its octave can be heard. So it is with the thirteen vowels of English; we can move subtly and imperceptibly from one vowel to the next through an uncountable number of barely distinguishable sounds, and that is why I have called this chapter *The Vowel Continuum*. I hope to make clear why I think that this as an extremely important idea, and I trust that the reader will have patience with the rather dry technicality of some of what follows.

At this point I need to assume that the reader is familiar with the sounds of the English language, since I cannot imagine a system of written instructions which would result in the perfect reproduction of those sounds, notwithstanding the existence of the international phonetic alphabet. There is a large element of mimicry involved, and in this sense I recommend that students listen attentively to a range of modern recordings. But it is true to say that we cannot mimic every nuance of what we hear without the presence of a knowledgable and understanding coach who can guide us towards correct and idiomatic pronunciation.

The continuum

The list of English vowels, assuming standard RP, is as follows: 'Do Put Paul's Pot Plants Under Pat's Best Fig Tree'. That makes eleven, but the more perceptive readers will have spotted that I mentioned there being thirteen vowel sounds in all. The eleven here are all 'pure' vowels, meaning that they are made with the mouth and tongue held in one position for each. Another kind of sound is the diphthong, which is a combination of two vowels, and the list of diphthongs is 'Oh Boy, Wow, I Say', and four more in a group: 'Sure', 'Shore', 'Share' and 'Sheer'. 'Sure' is close to 'Shoo-er' (but with the first element nearer the short u of Put than the long oo of Do), 'Shore' is like 'Shaw-er' (Paul, -er), 'Share' is 'Sheh-er' (Best, -er) and 'Sheer' is 'Shi-er' (Fig, -er). 'Oy' is made up of 'Aw' and 'Ee' (as in Paul, Tree), 'Ow' is approximately 'Ah' and 'Oo' (Plants, Do), and 'I' is 'Ah' and 'Ee' (Plants, Tree). 'Oh' and 'Say' are approximate combinations respectively of 'O' and 'Oo' (Pot, Do) and 'Eh' and 'Ee' (Best, Tree), but the first element of each of these two diphthongs is modified to such an extent that they rightly take their places in the spectrum of distinct English vowels, being added to the other eleven. The amended list, therefore, is 'Do Put Old Paul's Pot Plants Under Pat's Best Great Fig Tree', or, as my old teacher Arthur Reckless used to have it: 'Who would know aught of art must learn and then pay his fees', though most singing teachers make it a sensible habit to insist that you pay up beforehand.

Now that we have our list, the next thing is to whisper those thirteen syllables, with or without their consonants. Most of us whisper by tightening the throat and using the resulting weak, unvoiced sound to carry the resonance of the words. For this particular exercise don't do that, but keep the throat entirely free and force the air past the tongue, in much the same way as a German pronounces the 'ch' in 'Ach', or a Scot in the word 'loch'. If this is done correctly, the list of syllables will give a sequence of thirteen rising notes. Next, try flicking with a finger the area where the throat and mouth meet, preferably at the side, and in order not to hurt yourself, place a finger of your other hand against the spot, and flick that instead. If this all goes according to plan, then the list of syllables will give another sequence of much more resonant notes which rise at first up to 'And' and fall rapidly for 'Pay His Fees'. These two sequences give a pair of notes for each vowel, and when Sir Richard Paget did this in the 1920s he discovered that it is the same pair of notes for a given vowel irrespective of who is speaking and what the pitch of the voice might be. One of these notes was found to be produced by the resonating effects of the part of the mouth behind the tongue, and the other by the part of the mouth in front of the tongue.

Our ears, then, are tuned to analyse the pitches of these two combined notes in order to decide which vowel we are hearing, and this suggests that it is the absolute pitch which counts, not just the relation between the two. Other authorities state that the spectrum of these vowel notes, or formants, varies according to the length of the vocal tract (from vocal cords to lips), and that our perception of vowel colour depends upon the relation between the formants, not on their absolute pitch. Either way, it means that anyone who can distinguish the sounds of language has the ability to discriminate between different pitches in a very precise fashion. This suggests that such a person who can communicate normally through speech, even though he or she might be the most awful growler at the back of the school choir, cannot possibly be tone deaf.

The quality of each vowel, therefore, is determined by the resonant frequencies of the two parts of the mouth, one behind and one in front of the tongue, and the two elements which control this, the shape of the mouth and the position of the tongue, are themselves controlled automatically and unconsciously as a response we learned when in early childhood. This may be true for ordinary speech, but the aspiring singer should know that he or she can and must learn to bring the process at least partly under conscious control, and the only way to do this is to practise and to listen. Intone the vowels and feel where the tongue is; move the tongue fractionally and listen to the effect it has on the sound; try changing the mouth-shape as you intone the series, and then try not changing it. The more you do this while listening and observing the effects of anatomy on sound, the more you will gain knowledge and mastery of what is involved. I have noticed with so many singers that they often do not seem to have listened to themselves enough in order to gain that mastery, perhaps because they have not realised how important it is.

Long and short

In speech, the eleven 'pure' vowels are either long – who, aught, art, learn, fees – or short – would, of, must, and, then, his. When we sing, we are required by composers to fit words to long notes and to short notes, and this would be no great problem if the long notes were given to the long vowels, and the short to the short. In the real world of music, however, this is not what happens; we are expected to sing short with long and long with short. 'Rule', Britannia, Bri<u>tann</u>ia, rule the <u>waves</u>, <u>Bri</u>-<u>tons</u> never, never, never <u>shall</u> <u>be</u> <u>slaves</u>'. The longer notes in Arne's famous setting are here underlined, and some of them have long vowels (Rule, waves), while some have short (Bri-, shall). Similarly, the shorter notes have long vowels (-ver) and short (-tann, ne-). Most of us are so familiar with the piece that we wouldn't give a second thought to the length of these vowels, and those who aren't familiar with it, but who are familiar with the English language, would likewise have no problem with this. Consider, for instance, the first syllable of 'Britons'; make the sound as in 'fig' and prolong it, taking care that you do not alter the quality of the vowel at all. That's fine, except that many singers, without thinking, and without listening to what they are doing, actually produce the sound 'Bree-' as in 'fees'. That is naturally a long vowel, and perhaps their voices have more carrying power on that sound.

This lengthening of short vowels is such a common fault that I want to give examples of all six of them. First, from *Dover Beach* by Matthew Arnold, comes 'The tide is <u>full</u>, the moon lies fair . . .'. 'Full' has a short vowel, yet how often we hear the same sound as that of 'moon', giving a ludicrous 'fool'. Second, from *Messiah*, we have 'and though worms destroy this <u>bo</u>dy'. We are so accustomed to hearing 'bawdy' that it doesn't strike us as being horribly inappropriate. Third, from *Dover Beach* again, there is 'let us be true to <u>one</u> a<u>n</u>other'. The short u becomes a long ah, giving 'wahn anahther', which, apart from looking very strange in print, is not the required sound. Fourth, from *Songs of Travel* by Robert Louis Stevenson, comes 'and far on the level <u>land</u>', where the sound is altered to 'lahnd' as often as not. Fifth, from A E Housman's *A Shropshire Lad*, we find 'Now of my threescore years and <u>ten</u>', which can come out as if it rhymes with 'fern' or 'burn'. The sixth example, the lengthening of the short I, has already been given above with 'Bree-tons'.

Much of this kind of difficulty can be overcome if we understand that what is true of speech is not quite true of singing, namely that vowels are not to be thought of as either long or short, but as taking their unique places in the continuum. All are capable of being curtailed or extended according to the demands of the musical setting, but each maintains its individual quality. If you were successful in the attempt, you will earlier have seen how the syllable 'Bri-' could be prolonged indefinitely while retaining its normal colour. Conversely, a 'long' ee can be clipped to almost nothing, eg, 'Or let autumn fall on me/ Where afield I linger' from Vaughan Williams's *Songs of Travel*, where the syllable of 'field' is set to a staccato quaver. All the other 'long' vowels can simply be clipped in a similar way if necessary, and all the 'short' ones can easily be prolonged. The problem that I mentioned earlier, when a composer sets a long vowel to a short note and a short one to a long note, is therefore no problem at all, provided we abandon thoughts of long or short and think only of the particular sound of each vowel.

Light and shade

'Who would know aught of art must learn and then pay his fees'

Singers often describe vowels as being 'dark' or 'bright'. In the above list the dark ones are towards the left, while towards the right are the bright sounds, becoming progressively brighter until the brightest of all, **Ee**. Why we should talk of darkness or brightness in this context I'm not sure; it seems intuitively correct, somehow, just as when we describe the pitch of a note as high or low. As a matter of physics, however, pitch cannot properly be described as low or high; the frequency of vibration is the variable element of pitch, the slowest frequencies giving the 'lowest' notes, and the quickest frequencies the highest. The fact is, though, that everyone seems agreed on the high/low convention, and this high/low convention in pitch is equivalent to the bright/dark convention in vowels. As you may have found earlier when you hissed the vowels, they are intimately related to pitch, with **Oo** having the lowest upper formant (the hissed one) and **Ee** having the highest. Large cavities resonate at slower frequencies, and therefore lower pitch, than small cavities, whose frequencies are quicker, giving higher pitch. The larger the cavity, the larger the object, which is also heavier and slower, whereas the smaller cavity is associated with something lighter, higher and quicker.

This association of size and weight with pitch and vowel tone or colour has implications for singing, specifically for choosing a suitable colour of vowel for a particular voice or a particular song. A bass singer should generally choose darker vowel colours to correspond with the depth and weight of his voice, and a high soprano should choose brighter ones to correspond with hers. In addition, a melancholy song requires darker sounds than a joyful one, and even certain words or phrases within a song may call for sounds that are darker or brighter than the generality of that song. I remember clearly a recording of the Finnish bass Kim Borg in *Trepak*, from Mussorgsky's *Songs and Dances of Death,* where the singer has to portray the roles of Death and a child. The lugubrious Russian tones he used for the part of Death were wonderfully offset by the bright, high resonance he managed for the child. How could he achieve this darkening and lightening?

For practical purposes the darkest vowel is **Aw**, near the left of the list, and to darken the sound of the other vowels it is necessary to shade them towards this one. In other words, the vowels to the right of **Aw** are shifted leftwards to a small extent. Unfortunately the process is sometimes exaggerated, leaving the listener with the unnerving impression that he has stumbled on some hitherto undiscovered language. If **Aa** is to be given something of the colour of **Aw** it does not mean that it actually becomes **Aw**. Similarly, 'must' should not come out as 'mast', 'fern' should not become 'farn', and 'head' should not become 'heard'. Each of these examples has gone so far that it has become a distortion. The secret lies in the subtlety with which it can be done, and moreover it should be either a conscious choice or a natural property of the individual voice, and it should be something consistent and not an occasional habit. The best bass singers can produce beautiful English, preserving in their chosen dark spectrum of sound the distinct qualities of each of the thirteen vowels.

Lightening is achieved in a similar manner, but this time the shading is towards the lightest of the sounds, **Ee**. All the other vowels are shifted subtly to the right to give the required effect, and again the process should be a conscious choice or a natural property of the voice, and again it should be consistent. Distortions can often be heard, but this time in the opposite direction from the dark travesties. If 'Lord' is made to sound like 'Lard', the result is not only ludicrous but possibly blasphemous. In an operatic context, Susanna from Mozart's *Marriage of Figaro* would normally be sung by a light soprano, probably with these brightened vowel sounds, while the Countess would have a heavier soprano voice, probably using dark sounds. In the context of English music, Finzi's *Let us Garlands Bring* has the dirge *Fear no more the heat o' the sun* where dark sounds would be appropriate, followed immediately by the bright vowels of the love song *O Mistress mine.*

Neutral vowels

There are some sounds which are hard to categorise within the normal vowel continuum because they are usually so short that they hardly register at all. Two examples are the first syllables of 'above' and 'behind'. These are not too difficult to place: '**a**bove' lies somewhere between 'must' and 'learn', while 'behind' is close to 'his'. Other vowels of this neutral type are rather more problematical. Try the second syllables of 'basket', 'mistress', 'movement', 'quiet', 'family', 'enemy' and 'the' (neutral, before a consonant), and imagine that you are singing them all on sustained notes. Somehow you need to decide what colour that neutral vowel will have when it is brought out of hiding and is no longer over in a flash. The trouble is that the vowel chosen may be too near a normal continuum vowel. 'Basket' is wrongly given a 'kit' on the end, with a true **i** sound. 'Mistress' is given a real 'tress' to finish, 'movement' gets 'meant', and 'quiet' gets either 'ert' or 'ett'. The truth is that 'bask**et**' has a slightly slacker, darker sound than the usual **i** of 'his'. 'Mistr**ess**' is mostly the **e** of 'then' mingled with a hint of the **a** of 'above', while 'move**ment**' is marginally different: it has the **a** of 'above' mixed with a touch of the **e** of 'then', and 'qui**et**' has the sound of the **a** of 'above'. 'The', being such a common word, is one most often wrongly pronounced, usually as 'thaa', whereas the neutral sound of '**a**bove' is the one to aim for. The second syllable of 'family' is probably one that is undergoing a change at this moment, because although most people say 'fam-uh-ly' as if the second syllable were as in 'above', and although most children even sing 'fam-uh-ly', the best version of that syllable for singing is still the plain **i** of 'his', at least for the time being (I can believe that it may sound precious soon if the spoken form remains 'fam-uh-ly'). 'Enemy' usually gets the same treatment ('en-uh-my'), but here the best approximation is probably the neutral **e** of 'mistress'.

The neutral vowels especially show how extraordinarily narrow the differences between sounds can be, and the student could argue that these differences are so minute that they will not be picked up by the listener and can therefore be ignored. Perhaps that is true of some of them, but there is great satisfaction to be had from making the attempt and succeeding. I must make the point here, however, that all this navel-gazing about the precise nature of each vowel might seem like death to singing as a natural human activity, and I want to emphasise that, as with so many things we have to learn, they will become second nature. During a performance such considerations of detail are consigned to the practice room, and the creative artist gets the opportunity to communicate with the listeners.

In the chapter on consonants (Chapter 3) I describe the process of *lateral plosion* in words like 'hidden' or 'bitten', where in speech the **d** or **t** is modified. The final '-en' of such words is an example of a vowel that is completely swallowed, as the **d** or **t** is released directly on to the final **n**. The syllable therefore does not have a vowel at all, not even a neutral one. Since **n** is a nasal consonant which is voiced, it might be thought that we could sing the second syllable of 'hidden' entirely on the **n**, in much the same way as we can on the second syllable of 'people'. In the future this may indeed happen, and in folk singing it already happens, but for 'serious' music at present the convention is that we choose a neutral vowel (the **a** of 'above') and close it with an **n**.

Vowel modification

We have seen how the vowels are formed by a combination of two resonant frequencies, which may possibly differ between individuals, but which for a specific person are fixed for any vowel whatever the pitch of the voice. Therefore, when I sing an Aa, the pitches of the two vowel formants are the same whether I sing on middle C or the octave below. Each voice creates a unique and complex mix of harmonics or partials which gives it the character that we instantly recognise as belonging to a particular individual. Out of this mix of partials the two necessary frequencies to create a certain vowel are enhanced by the shape of the two mouth cavities, and the listener hears the expected sound. As the voice rises in pitch, there are physiological actions connected with the shortening of the vocal cords and the increased pressure of the breath which alter the balance of the cavities and make a true vowel sound more difficult to create. Moreover, the problem becomes greater for a soprano in her upper register because the partials needed to excite the formant resonances are too high to be effective. All singers find that if they wish to maintain a certain quality of tone-production, the colour of the vowels will alter appreciably at the top of their register, and for sopranos more than others the vowels become progressively less distinct as they rise above the treble stave.

Having admitted that there is a physical cause for the modification of vowels at the top of any singer's register, I must plead that this should not be taken as an excuse to give up on the attempt to create just and true sounds for as long and as high as they can be comfortably and sensibly maintained. Hiding behind excuses about technique and beauty of tone is a tempting proposition because it exonerates the singer from making the effort to achieve intelligibility. Audiences are unfortunately accustomed to hearing language garbled by singers, and for many of them it is perhaps not a great concern provided they get the general gist of what is being sung. Similarly, singing in tune may not be a high priority for some listeners, but that is no reason for a singer to assume that nobody cares about it. For the musician, tuning is crucially important, and for the lover of song, with an ear for the poetry or prose that the composer has so carefully chosen and set, the text is an integral part of the total experience.

3 – The Consonants

Consonants are often considered by singers to be a terrible nuisance: they interrupt the flow and get in the way of the beautiful sounds made by *La Voce*. In my student days I remember hearing a well-known Lieder coach suggesting that when you learn a new song you should speak the text first, next sing the notes to 'Aa' without any consonants, and then sing to the relevant vowels (still without consonants), before attempting to sing words and music together. I imagine that, in general, the composer came to write a song having read or heard a certain poem, although I believe that Richard Strauss often had ideas for a song before he had found a suitable text. The singer, however, comes to the poem of a song through the song itself, and the music has to be the singer's starting point. For this reason I can see why running through the music wordlessly might be a good plan, but in that case why read the poem first? The big problem that I see in this wordless learning technique is that it serves to reinforce the fear of what the consonants might do to the vocal line. The vowels are the main means of carrying the voice's sound, and the consonants thwart our *cantabile* ambitions by forcing us to stop the vibration of the vocal cords from time to time. This can cause all sorts of problems, and the biggest problem of all is our fear that we will have problems. Not only is it possible to overcome this fear, it is possible and even desirable to relish the partnership between consonant and vowel. We singers are uniquely blessed in having words to articulate, whereas other musicians have to make do with a much more limited repertoire of sounds. Yes, I know that they bring a heap of difficulties with them, but by understanding how they work through feeling and listening we can positively use them to our advantage. Here, then, is the list of basic consonant sounds in English.

   Plosive – when the passage of air is stopped under pressure and then released. Plosive consonants are **p**, **t** and **k** (all unvoiced), and **b**, **d** and

g (all voiced). I include also the **glottal stop**, which has the effect of a voiced plosive, and we shall see later where it occurs.

Fricative – produced by the friction of air passing through a narrow opening between two speech-organs. They are **th, sh, s, f, wh** and **h** (all unvoiced), and **th, ž** as in barra*g*e or plea*s*ure, **z, v,** and **r** when not rolled (all voiced).

Affricate – when the passage of air is stopped under pressure, like a plosive, and is released through a narrow opening like a fricative. They are **ch** (unvoiced), and **j** as in *j*am (voiced).

Rolled – when two speech-organs touch and release several times to make a continuous sound, ie, **r** (voiced). Cats use the unvoiced one to purr with, but I don't think they do it in English.

Flapped – as with the rolled **r**, but the touch and release occurs only once.

Nasal – when the mouth is completely blocked and the soft palate is lowered to allow air to pass through the nose. They are **m, n** and **ng** (voiced).

Lateral – when the middle of the air passage is blocked by raising the tongue to the roof of the mouth, and the air escapes around the sides, ie, **l** (voiced).

Semi-vowels – the two most closed vowels 'oo' and 'ee', when they move quickly on to another vowel, become **w** and **y** (voiced).

In order to go into more detail about these sounds and about some of the problems they can bring, I propose to deal with them in groups.

M b p, then **n d t** and **ng g k,** are the first groups on my list. With the lips together hum **mm,** then release with a little extra emphasis on **b.** Here's our first problem: too many singers have the habit of humming before an initial **b,** giving 'Mblow, mblow, thou winter wind' for example. Now try placing the tip of the tongue on the upper teeth-ridge and make the sound **nn,** following it with an emphasised release on **d.** Here's another recurring problem, similar to the first, that is, the habit of humming before an initial **d,** giving 'Ndown by the Salley Gardens'. Next, raise the back of the tongue to meet the soft palate and make an **ng** sound, following it with an emphasised release on **g.** Here's problem number three, rather like the other two: 'Nggo not, happy day'. With **p** the lips are brought together, pressure builds up, and when the lips part they make a pop, while **b** follows the same procedure but that the vocal cords are made to vibrate at the moment of release. With **t** the process takes place further back in the mouth, with the tongue behind the teeth-ridge allowing pressure to build up, **d** being the voiced version. With **k** the process is even further back in the mouth, the release taking place at the soft palate, and the hard **g** is the voiced version. You will have seen above that the affricate sounds **ch** and **j** start off like plosives, but are released more slowly; this is our next besetting English sin, where **p**, **t** and **k** are made to sound like affricates. **P** is made to sound as if a candle is being blown out, **t** becomes something like 'tss' and **k** resembles the sort of wet sound which babies sometimes make when they are pleased.

The **glottal stop** is not normally included in the list of plosive consonants, but for a singer I think it should be. The pressure for this builds up even further back in the mouth than the soft palate where **k** and **g** were formed. In fact it is not in the mouth at all, but behind the glottis, which is in the throat. This 'consonant' is used as a means of attack for words beginning with a vowel where additional emphasis is required. The vocal cords are made to sound initially by bringing them together and passing air through to set up a vibration. If you try singing 'aa' very softly, you will find that the note starts at a certain breath pressure, which if you are lucky will be very low and very soft. Nonetheless, below that threshold pressure nothing happens because the vocal cords cannot be brought together to start vibrating. There are many singers, especially those who have regularly sung heavy operatic roles, whose vocal cords will not start to vibrate until the air pressure has become quite high, meaning that their initial attack on a note is always comparatively loud. This loud form of attack can be made instead by deliberate use of the glottal stop, but although it is invariably used before an initial vowel in German, in English it should be used quite sparingly. In Finzi's *The Clock of the Years* the line 'let her stay thus always' asks for the glottal stop on 'always', and in the same song 'but alas for me' probably needs one on 'alas' in order to avoid the listener imagining 'butter lass' instead.

In addition to using the glottal stop in the above example for clarity of meaning, it should be considered when a word ending in r is followed by one beginning on a vowel, eg, 'For ever'. Spoken Southern English elides the words with a fricative **r**, which sounds quite normal and acceptable, but in singing it doesn't sound right at all, not because there is anything intrinsically wrong with it, but because it is simply 'not the done thing' at the present time at least. The alternatives are either to run the two words together with a single flapped **r** between, or to make a break with a glottal stop, which has the usual effect of giving emphasis. Another example is 'Sure on this shining night', the beginning of a song by Samuel Barber. Here the choice is complicated by the fact that Barber was American (even though the poet was English), and he would have used the standard American fricative **r** in speaking rather than missing it out altogether as in Southern English speech. American singers that I know would sing it also with a hint of the fricative **r** eliding the two words together, but I believe that this would be a mistake for a British singer unless he or she were prepared to go all the way with singing the whole song in an American accent. A better solution for us is to elide the words with a gentle flapped **r** and maintain an English diction throughout.

While on the subject of elision, there is an often-heard peculiarity of speech which involves an intrusive **r** where none exists. This is to be found in words like 'drawing', or between words like 'saw an' ('I saw an unusual sight today'). Rather than moving smoothly and cleanly from 'aw' to 'in' or 'an', the speaker lets the tongue rise to the roof of the mouth and insert a fricative **r**: 'aw-r-in'. Needless to say, this is bad enough when spoken, but when sung it sounds truly awful. The future may bring acceptance of the practice, but my bet is that it will not be for a long time yet.

S, sh, ch and **z, ž, j** are made up of fricatives and affricates, and they are my next two groups. By saying these in sequence you will discover how they are related, and how the second group of three is a voiced version of the first group. In **s** the sides of the tongue touch the roof of the mouth and the air escapes through the narrow gap between tongue and teeth-ridge. **Sh** has the tongue higher, forming a longer channel against the hard palate for the air to escape through, and the lips are often pushed forward as well. **Ch** has the tongue stopping the air by resting against the teeth-ridge, and then releasing gradually with the **sh** sound. Make these three sounds in sequence and notice how they vary in pitch: you will probably get the highest sound on 's', while the 'sh' and the 'ch' will be at nearly the same pitch as each other because the tongue is virtually in the same place for both. This may not seem to be a particularly important property, but the 'pitch' of consonants can be used to colour what we do in the context of different songs. For instance, speak the word 'miss' and maintain the bright quality of the vowel as you hiss the 's'. Then say 'remorse' and maintain something of the quality of the dark vowel on the hissed 's'. The first has a higher pitch than the second, and although I am not saying that the one should always have a bright 's' and the other a dark one, nevertheless you do have the choice, and it is a choice which you should exercise consciously to enhance the impact of a given passage of singing.

F and **v**, a fricative pair, are formed by air escaping between the upper teeth and the inside of the lower lip, one being voiced, the other not. The unvoiced and voiced **th** are made by the escape of air between the tip of the tongue and the upper teeth. We all know what problems these two sounds give to foreigners, but it seems strange to me that rather than struggling with 'that', for instance, and coming out with 'zat', they don't go straight for the easy option of 'vat', which is really a much closer approximation to the original. Anyway, assuming that you, the reader, do not have that difficulty, I would like to point out a common failing in the singing of the voiced **v** and **th**, which is that they are often hardly voiced, and sometimes not voiced at all. The opportunity which good voicing of these consonants gives for colour and expressiveness should not be missed.

Wh is included here among the fricatives, and some readers may wonder why, since for many English speakers the words 'where' and 'wear', for instance, sound identical. If they listened to a Scot saying those words they would immediately notice the difference. The **wh** as spoken by a Scot starts with air escaping between pursed lips to make a weak hiss, followed by a standard **w**, and this is traditionally used in formal speech. The fact is, though, that this sound is disappearing from South of the border, and I know few English people who say 'what, which and whether' in the formal manner. Singers are still using the formal version, and although I like to hear it, I am not especially upset if it is missing, and I expect that before long it will be dropped in favour of the straight **w**.

H presents us with the sorry fact that it is pretty well inaudible even in speech, while in singing, which is expected to carry much further, it is all but useless. I have heard choir trainers exhorting their singers to give it all they've got, and the result has been not much more than a wheeze; this sets up a cough amongst the smokers, and gives away at least half the lung-capacity in one go. Oddly enough, the listener's ear is best served by what is effectively a moment of silence. In the example above (*The Clock of the Years*), 'let her stay thus always', it is the tiny stop between 'let' and 'her' which prevents it coming out as 'letter'. Indeed, I think that to make a big thing about putting a sounding 'h' on the beginning of the word would be a mistake, leading to a gross over-emphasis on 'her'. Naturally, these decisions always have an element of taste in them, but the essential thing is that it should be conscious taste that dictates rather than an unknowing and unthinking approach which treats these subtle distinctions as if they don't matter. If emphasis is required on the **h**, for example '*h*ere shall he see no enemy but winter and rough weather', then 'ch' as in German *ich* gives a very good approximation. Before a dark vowel (a, o or u) the emphatic form would be close to 'ch', as in Scots *loch* or German *ach*: eg, 'the *h*ouse with open door'.

    R, as we have seen above, can be either fricative, rolled or flapped, and whichever is used depends to some extent upon the context. Before the Second World War the **r** was always rolled quite heavily, often when we now don't sound an r at all, eg, 'everrr-morre' for plain old 'evermore', and this strikes us as quaint and old-fashioned. However, when we are presented with a wonderful opening to a song like 'Bright is the ring of words when the right man rings them', the **r** in 'Bright', 'ring', 'right' and 'ring' cries out to be rolled with relish. A Scot (and Robert Louis Stevenson, who wrote these words, was a Scot) would doubtless roll every other **r** in the piece, including 'worrrds', but since the poem is not written in dialect, and since there is at present general agreement to use standard RP, we needn't go down that road. The next line, '<u>Fair</u> the fall of songs', has a silent **r** whose presence is deduced from our subtle use of diphthong, while 'still they are <u>carolled</u> and sung' is probably best with a single flapped **r**. The fricative **r**, the one most commonly used in ordinary speech, is not often used by singers at the time of writing, but who's to say how long that situation might last? Certainly if the text is deliberately colloquial or folky, or if it is American, then this form of **r** might be suitable, but not for formal speech (but see above for the use of **r** in eliding). Some people have an impediment which makes them unable to say their fricative **r** properly, substituting something like a **w** instead, but that is not really a problem for a singer, who hardly uses the form anyway. But when this is allied to an inability to roll the **r** either, then things can become quite awkward. I have heard a guttural French **r** at the back of the mouth to get around this difficulty, but better would be to approximate a flapped **r** by substituting a very quick **d** (try it!).

L, the lateral consonant, seems at first sight to be fairly innocuous, and unlikely to raise obstacles and difficulties, but it does in fact need a certain degree of care. The sound is formed by raising the tongue to the roof of the mouth and blocking the central part of the airway. Try making this sound, but as you do so, imagine making the vowel 'ee' at the same time. Then, while continuing to make the **l** sound, change your imagined vowel to 'aw' and listen to what happens. The quality of the sound alters, and the tongue, which was lying along the roof of the mouth for the imagined 'ee', moves downward, while still maintaining contact with the teeth-ridge. There is therefore a range of **l**'s available to us, and the one we choose tends to be the one which fits with either the preceding or the following vowel. 'Please' has a bright **l** corresponding to the following 'ea', whereas 'implore' has a dark **l** which goes with the dark sound of 'ore'. 'Pleasant' can be given something in between. A similar effect can be observed with the words 'bill' (bright **l**) and 'ball' (dark **l**), with 'bell' lying in the middle.

Phonemic modification

This alteration of the precise sound of **l** when it is preceded or followed by various vowels is something which occurs across the whole range of speech sounds or *phonemes,* as they are known, and I mentioned an example earlier with the **s** of 'miss' and 'remorse'. The phonemes of ordinary speech are modified by their context, and we make these subtle variations quite naturally if English is our native tongue. Problems can arise when it is not our native tongue and the phonemes are modified in a non-English way, or when, in singing, we ignore the usual conversational sounds and assume a 'fundamentalist' kind of diction which treats each sound as if it exists in isolation rather than within real language. The variations we have just seen in l have their counterparts in other consonants, notably **k**. Observe the different quality of **k** (or hard **c**) in 'core' and 'keen', the first further back in the mouth than the second, giving it a harder, drier effect. Now speak the words 'kick' and 'quick'; the implied presence of the **w** in the second word means that the lips are rounded for the initial consonant, whereas in 'kick' they are not. The result is a difference of quality between the two.

Consider next the phrase 'Comfort ye my people' from Handel's *Messiah*; how is the last word to be sung? The correct way to speak it would be to release the plosive **p** directly into the lateral **l** without any vowel in between, modifying both phonemes in the process. For singing, if the **l** is given a dark colour, as though it were part of the word 'pull', then the whole of the second syllable can be sung on the **l** *without any vowel sound at all*. But for heaven's sake, don't do as a former Home Secretary, Michael Howard, did, and make the **l** bright, brighter indeed than anything found in normal speech; I've heard it sung like that, and it sounds horrible. If it doesn't feel comfortable singing the whole note on the **l**, then a very carefully managed 'pee-pull' can be tried, colouring the vowel to suit the context.

An even trickier word is 'little', as in Britten's *Songs and Proverbs of William Blake,* where the phrase 'Little Fly' is set on a semi-quaver, dotted quaver and crotchet (or sixteenth note, dotted eighth note and quarter note). The second syllable of 'Little' is relatively long, and ideally it should be sung like 'people' on the consonant itself, though with a slightly lighter colour. The real trouble lies in the phonemic variation of the **tt,** because in speech it doesn't sound like **t** at all unless the speaker is from Wales, for instance, or from South East England and anxious to avoid the cockney glottal stop. Say the word 'little' to yourself and observe the position of your tongue on the '-ttle'; if all goes according to plan you should be releasing the plosive **t** with the tongue already in place at the roof of the mouth for the lateral **l**. The sound which the **t** makes like this is half way to becoming a **k** because the tongue is half way further back in the mouth than usual. I say half way, and not, heaven forbid, all the way to becoming a **k**; that would sound ridiculous and childish. But the children do have a point, since 'lickle'

37

is their approximation to the adult version of the word. When we sing such a word, the nearer it can be to this halfway house the better, since the intention should be always to be as close to speech as possible.

Convention

The above example can be described as *lateral plosion*, where the consonant is modified by the presence of the lateral l after it. Another example in speech is of *nasal plosion*, where the consonant is succeeded by a nasal consonant, as in 'hidden' or 'bitten'. The tongue stays put behind the teeth ridge on the d or the t, and the release is through the nose when the soft palate is lowered for the n. The effect is not only that the phoneme d or t is modified, but that the second syllable of the word consists solely of the nasal n with no vowel at all (cf. 'people' above). With 'people' we can achieve this when we sing the second syllable on l, but with nasal plosion it doesn't seem to work. In Gilbert and Sullivan's *Yeomen of the Guard*, Phoebe sings: 'Unbidden teardrops fill her eyes'. I suppose there's no very good reason why we should expect her to sing 'unbidd-en' with a normal, unmodified d and a neutral vowel following, rather than the natural spoken version where the d is modified and the following vowel is missing, and yet that is what convention requires. Maybe this is another case where the future will bring a change in practice, but for now we ought to sing it conventionally as if there were no modification.

I cannot think of a song in which the word 'associate' occurs, but there is a chance that if it hasn't happened yet, it might in the future. In everyday speech it is quite likely that the soft c in the middle is altered to sh, giving 'ass-o-shi-ate'. Present convention, however, requires that there should be no such drastic modification in singing, which has to follow formal speech with 'ass-o-ci-ate'. Oddly, 'association' is less likely to modify the c, possibly because of the presence of a sh sound later in word on '-ti-'. 'Tune' is another word where the colloquial modification doesn't sound right in singing, probably because our laziness in speaking results in something like 'ch-yune'. Nevertheless, even in formal speech a certain alteration of the t takes place, and this more subtle phonemic modification is what we should aim for when we sing. Like 'tune', 'nature' is generally altered in speech, this time approximately to 'nay-cher'. If we were to formalise this to the correct 'nay-t-yooer' it would sound unbearably precious, perhaps because we are so accustomed to the word in its conversational version. Here, then, is a case where I think that the formal sound needs to be degraded into something nearer the colloquial, and 'casual', 'usual' and 'righteous' are others in this category.

A word in which this degradation has become fully assimilated into formal speech is 'pleasure'. At some point in its history I believe it was 'ple-z-ure', which then underwent a transformation into 'ple-ž-ure', with the ž of 'barrage'. For a time it may have been thought proper to correct the modification, but time and usage have sanctioned the form which we now know. 'Ple-z-ure' would not seem precious, it would be positively weird. 'Occasional' is another such word, 'substantial' yet another.

Double consonants

In English, the doubling of a consonant has the effect of defining the vowel preceding, but it has no effect upon the duration of the consonant itself. We do not hiss any more on 'essay' than we do on 'say'. 'Fitting' has no more t to it than 'fit in'. This is not true of many foreign languages. My difficult Italian experience with 'amo' and 'ammo' is a case in point. German makes much of the doubled consonant, such as the **tt** in 'Mutter', or the **nn** in 'brennen'. Nevertheless, even though we do not do the same on 'essay' or 'fitting', try saying 'that dog' or 'eccentric character' or 'chief fire officer'. For 'that dog' the tongue touches the teeth-ridge after 'tha-' and pauses there for a moment before releasing a voiced d on 'dog'. Similarly, the back of the tongue rises to the soft palate after 'eccentri-', pauses briefly and then releases on the hard c for 'character'. The 'chief fire officer' does something of the same sort, but hisses gently as he pauses after 'chie-'. This is the natural way of speaking, and generally, if the pause is properly observed, it is the most effective way for singing unless a special emphasis is required. I can imagine that if you were wishing to make a distinction between a dog and a cat you might well say 'that dog', making a complete release on the t before articulating the d in order to make it clear that it is a dog you are talking about rather than a cat. This distinction can be useful in singing from time to time.

A similar effect is heard between words when the consonants are not the same. For instance, 'that cat' in normal speech has the tongue pausing behind the teeth-ridge on t before it moves back and releases from the back of the mouth on c. The t, then, isn't really there at all, but is replaced by an interruption in the sound. There are countless examples of this kind of elision, for instance 'Trip no further, pretty sweeting', or 'And stands about the woodland ride', and the singer needs to use discretion when choosing whether to treat them in a formal or a more colloquial fashion. Indeed, the deeper you delve into the minutiae of the real language, the more you discover anomalies and inconsistencies, and the more taste and discrimination come into play. That discrimination will only be truly effective if you are prepared to listen to yourself and to others, and are willing to question what you hear and to change things if necessary.

4 – Phrasing

English is a stressed language, one in which longer words carry a 'tonic accent' on one or more syllables. *Tonic*, for instance, is stressed on the first syllable and unstressed on the second, as are *English, language* and *accent*. Not all words have this type of emphasis: *because, admire* and *report* have their tonic accent on the second syllable. Words of more than two syllables can have one tonic accent, as in *syllable, emphasis* and *accentuate*, or they can have more than one, as in *accentuation* or *prestidigitation* (not that we're ever likely to sing either of these). As with most things in the English language there do not appear to be many hard-and-fast rules. Why are *emphasis* and *emphatic* stressed differently? *Therefore* and *thereby* refuse to see eye to eye, while *present* changes its mind depending on whether it is a noun or a verb. In this respect at least French has the edge over English because it is unstressed and does not require that the accentuation of each word be learnt separately. As a result it creates a very different music when spoken. It does not bump along like English, with its endlessly varying rhythms, but glides in long melismatic phrases.

Not only do individual words in the English language possess tonic accents but strings of words occurring in phrases and sentences possess additional accentuation. This property of the language allows for the rhythm of poetry.

> Trip no further pretty sweeting;
> Journeys end in lovers' meeting,
> Ev'ry wise man's son doth know.

Some words of one syllable like *Trip, end* and *wise* are here stressed, and others like *no, in* and *doth* are unstressed. It is difficult to say whether such a word on its own is stressed or not, because there is nothing to measure its one syllable against. Only when it is in the company of other words can we say which it is. Prepositions like *in, on* or *up*, pronouns like *you, me* and *it*, and conjunctions like *and, when* and *but* are normally unstressed in context, but when emphasis is

41

required they can change: 'Exceptions to the rule? There are <u>no</u> exceptions'; 'You took it out of context, I prefer to take it <u>in</u> context'. The rhythm of English poetry normally alternates stressed and unstressed syllables in pairs to make a 'foot' either as iambic verse (di-dum di-dum) or trochaic verse (dum-di dum-di). Exceptionally there is dactylic verse (dum-di-di dum-di-di) or anapaestic verse (di-di-dum di-di-dum). From Shakespeare's *A Midsummer Night's Dream* comes:

<u>I</u> know a | <u>bank</u> where the | <u>wild</u> <u>thyme</u> | <u>blows</u>

Later in the same play comes:

Over <u>hill,</u> | over <u>dale,</u>
Thorough <u>bush,</u> | thorough <u>brier</u> . . .

When there are two stressed syllables in a foot the result is called a spondee ('<u>wild</u> <u>thyme</u>').

If there is any doubt about the stress of a word, a musical setting indicates the composer's choice by having stressed syllables on stressed beats. From the above three lines of poetry ('Trip no further . . .') we can see that a simple musical setting could be made with a long note for stressed syllables and a short note for the unstressed ones, giving a dum-di dum-di rhythm throughout. This works for our three-line extract, but does it work for the three lines which make up the first half of this same verse?

O <u>mis</u>tress <u>mine,</u> where <u>are</u> you <u>roaming</u>?
O, <u>stay</u> and <u>hear;</u> your <u>true</u> love's <u>coming,</u>
That can <u>sing</u> both <u>high</u> and <u>low:</u>

It seems to fit for the first line, and if we make 'roaming? O' into three short notes we can get through to the end of the second line. Unfortunately, if 'coming' is on a long note followed by a short note it does not tally with 'roaming', which is on two short notes; but if it is made of two short notes to match 'roaming' there is a hiatus before 'That can sing' on the next line which ruins the rhythm. When declaiming a poem, this kind of thing does not present too much of a problem since a metronomic rhythmical style is rarely appropriate unless as a special effect. Our simple dum-di dum-di musical setting, however, looks as though it has broken down irretrievably and is destined for the bin, which is definitely the best place for it.

Let's look at Finzi's setting of the poem to see what solution he came up with:

> O mistress mine, where are you roaming?
> O, stay and hear; your true love's coming,
>   That can sing both high and low:
> Trip no further pretty sweeting;
> Journeys end in lovers' meeting,
>   Ev'ry wise man's son doth know.

One of the words with tonic accent ('mistress') seems to have lost it altogether, and in the first line 'O' and 'mi-' have swapped stresses, as have 'where' and 'are'. Otherwise the stresses are the same as if the poem were being read, and are closer in length to good declamation than the discredited dum-di dum-di version. Quilter in his setting altered things rather more:

> O mistress mine, where are you roaming?
> O, stay and hear; your true love's coming,
>   That can sing both high and low:
> Trip no further pretty sweeting;
> Journeys end in lovers' meeting,
>   Ev'ry wise man's son doth know.

I have exaggerated a little in removing so many accentuated syllables: 'mistress', 'journeys', 'pretty' and 'ev'ry' should still retain fractionally more emphasis on the first syllable than on the second. However, the general thrust of a phrase like 'O mistress mine' as Quilter set it is definitely three short notes leading towards the main stress on 'mine', and in that sense I feel justified in describing all three of them as unstressed. The result of removing these stresses has been to lighten the beginning of each line, and the text, read in this way, seems to move on much more swiftly than before. Even so, of the two songs under consideration, it is the Finzi setting which comes closer to the rhythmic values of the spoken word.

So far the discussion has been about the stress of the language, either in its spoken form or when modified to suit a musical setting. How does this connect with phrasing, which is, after all, the title of this chapter? The primary meaning of the word 'phrase' is a grammatical one: it is a number of words grouped together to form a single idea,

43

usually as part of a sentence. For example, 'O mistress mine' is itself a phrase signifying the person addressed, and it is part of the sentence 'O mistress mine, where are you roaming?' of which it forms the subject. A secondary meaning of the word 'phrase' is when it is applied to music, where it signifies a fairly small group of notes which form a relatively independent part of a longer musical passage. In a song, a musical phrase can either be spoken of in terms of the notes themselves or in terms of the words which go with those notes. Since a song composer starts off with a verbal phrase which he sets to music, there is usually some correspondence between the verbal and the musical phrases, though, as we shall see, it is not necessarily an exact correspondence. 'Phrasing' describes the process of expressing the musical phrases.

If we return to the Quilter example above, where so far we have been dealing with the word-stresses, we can begin to see the musical phrases appearing. We have seen how some single-syllable words lose their stress to create the poem's basic rhythm. Then we saw how, in a musical context, some more single- and double-syllable words lose their stress. Now we can ask whether some of the remaining stresses are more important than others and, if so, which ones. 'Mine', 'roam-', 'hear', 'com-', 'sing' and 'low' are the best candidates for taking precedence, and it is no coincidence that these are the ones that Quilter chose to place on the first beat of the bar, since that is the beat with the strongest accent. Even now, though, we have not gone quite far enough to discover the phrasing, because some of these first beats are more important than other first beats, and there is often a degree of judgment and experience involved in deciding which ones to choose. 'Mine' is on the highest note and is therefore the most prominent, but the first really important note is on 'roaming' for reasons which I will put forward later, and which are to do with just that judgment and experience I mentioned. After 'roaming' comes a full stop in the form of a question mark, and in parallel with this short opening sentence we have at last found the first musical phrase, and it coincides with the first line of the poem. One could suppose that the next two lines of verse would have two separate musical phrases, but the way Quilter's music connects them suggests that they are really one. First of all, the sense of these two lines runs quite smoothly over the comma after 'coming', and secondly Quilter moves the music quickly on through 'That can' to the final word 'low'. We regather our forces for the next phrase up to 'sweeting', quickly build to the high note on 'end' and fall back gradually to the end of the verse.

The phrasing pattern of the first verse now looks like two halves made up of: first line, one phrase; second and third line, one longer phrase of two subsidiary parts; then the fourth, fifth and sixth lines, three phrases which together make up one long phrase, and this long phrase has its climax near its middle. The second verse shows the same pattern, with 'kiss' at the climax. This time, by lengthening that note compared with the same note on 'end' in the first verse, and by marking it *forte*, Quilter clearly intended it to be the climax of the whole song. Each verse of this song runs on without a break, other than that which is needed for breathing, and this invites the singer to go further in his quest for the most effective phrasing and to treat the whole verse as a single elongated phrase of two halves or six sixths.

The pattern of Finzi's song is at first sight rather different. There is an upper counter-melody in the piano part signifying the girl, which demands the listener's attention. There are also definite breaks in the vocal line, especially after 'roaming' and 'sweeting' and, to a lesser extent, after 'hear'. It looks as though this song has to be chopped up into short phrases: one line, half a line, one-and-a-half lines, one line, one line and one line. That is certainly the pattern of the individual subordinate phrases of the verse, but in reality the singer should still treat the whole verse as if it were one long arching phrase, in much the same manner as with the Quilter song. The trick is to maintain concentration and intention through the breaks, connecting the shorter phrases in the mind. The great French singer and teacher Pierre Bernac used to suggest breathing immediately after the note before a rest and holding the breath until the next note. An example in this song would be to sing 'where are you roaming', breathe immediately, hold it, then sing 'O, stay and hear'. The listener, being aware of the quick intake of breath (without any noise, I hasten to add) expects a new vocal entry then and there, and in a way has already started hearing the next phrase before the singer has uttered a note. This may sound slightly fanciful, but I can assure the reader that it works, and I think that there is an important principle inherent in this example, which is that as performers we should make every effort to engage the listeners' minds in the process which we are instigating. We must truly nurture a partnership with our listeners, otherwise they are quite likely to lose the thread and switch off.

Another effective ploy for connecting two separate strands of vocal line, and again one involving the listener's mind in the process, is to make a *crescendo* on the note before a break, in this case through the long note on the second syllable of 'sweeting'. The listener then assumes that there is something more to come, because the traditional shape of a phrase is up and down, *crescendo* and *diminuendo*. If the *diminuendo* is missing we seem to be programmed to wait until it appears. Meanwhile, the phrase has been perceived as continuing through the silence. It requires rather more care and experience to achieve this single arching phrase in the Finzi than in the Quilter, but it is worth remembering that this should be our aim in the great majority of songs: we should always be looking for the longer phrase. If we keep dropping our intensity and concentration at the end of each short subsidiary phrase we will lose that essential impetus which helps to convey the full meaning of the complete song and not just small disjointed images and ideas.

If the long phrase is an important element in singing a song, so too is the internal shape of the phrase. I mentioned in passing that the standard musical phrase contains a rise and fall, a *crescendo* and *diminuendo*. Phrasing marks in any piece of music, vocal or instrumental, are long curved lines looking like flattened arches, and they give a clue to how phrases should sound. There is usually one 'high point' in a phrase which represents the moment to which that phrase is leading and from which it falls away. This high point can often be the highest note in a phrase since that will naturally have prominence because of the way our voices and our ears function. But the highest note is not necessarily the most important, and there are certain clues to finding the high point if we know what we are looking for. The most obvious clue is in the sense of the poem itself, but that is not necessarily the final arbiter in making our decision. There may be more than one important word in a phrase, and the composer may have chosen one above another in order to underline some particular aspect of the song. A clue to the composer's intentions can sometimes be found in the harmonic treatment of the music on a crucial word.

In order to help explain the matter, we shall now look at the second song of Vaughan Williams's *Songs of Travel*:

> Let Beauty awake in the morn from beautiful dreams,
>> Beauty awake from rest!
> Let Beauty awake
> For Beauty's sake
> In the hour when the birds awake in the brake
> And the stars are bright in the west!

Vaughan Williams's phrasing marks stretch over each line of verse, telling us where the phrases occur, but the question still remains concerning the high points of those phrases. There are several options available in the first line: one or more of 'Beauty', 'awake', 'morn', 'beautiful' and 'dreams'. Generally, but by no means always, we should aim to put the peak of a phrase of music towards the end of that phrase rather than near the beginning, and that is why, when I was discussing the first line of Quilter's *O mistress mine*, I suggested making the peak of that line on 'roaming' even though it is not the highest note. The reason for this seems to me to be that in this way the music is continually moving forward through each phrase and carrying the listener's attention onwards with it. If the phrases fall away each time from an early climax, the music keeps on losing its tension, and the listener feels somehow let down and disappointed. This general rule applied to the first line of this song suggests that the peak of the phrase should come on 'beautiful' or 'dreams'. Now if we look at the harmony at this point we can see that Vaughan Williams has an ordinary six-four triad of A major on 'beautiful', but a G sharp dominant seventh on 'dreams'. The tension in the dominant seventh, a discord which insists on being resolved into the subsequent C sharp minor chord leads me to assume that Vaughan Williams wanted the peak of the phrase on that chord with the word 'dreams'. The next task is to find the peak of the second phrase, that is 'Beauty awake from rest'. The syllable '-wake' on a G sharp is placed over a spread chord of A major, and this discord suggests the second-phrase peak. However, if we take the first two lines as a whole, remembering our rule of thumb about going for the longer phrase, we find that there is a discrepancy between the key signature and the key of the song's opening bars. Four sharps indicate E major or C sharp minor, and yet the song opens in F sharp minor and does not reach the home key of E major until the chord on 'rest'. This is such a relief to the ear that 'rest' probably represents the peak point of the elongated first phrase.

Another reason why I think that 'rest' is the crucial point of the phrase lies in the structure of the first two lines of text. The poet writes 'Let Beauty awake' in the first line and repeats it in the second line with an additional qualification: 'Beauty awake from rest'. We know that he wants Beauty to awake, because he has already told us so, and to stress 'awake' a second time would be pointless unless he were symbolically shaking Beauty out of her sleep because she has not heard his first command. The poem as it stands is telling us the second time how or why Beauty has to awaken: she must awaken from rest, and because 'rest' is the new piece of information, it is 'rest' which has the main stress.

The two short third and fourth lines have both been given their own phrase-marks, but if we look at the melody of the fifth line we see that it is almost identical with that of the third and fourth combined, which seems a good reason to treat them as one phrase. Whether that phrase should go to 'Beauty's' or to 'sake' is open to question, but I will make a suggestion based upon the following fifth line. I have already made the point that the melody is repeated here, with one changed note. Vaughan Williams tells us to make the peak of the fifth line on the C sharp of '-wake', even though instinct might suggest 'brake' instead. The equivalent place in the earlier line would be the first syllable of 'Beauty's', but to sing a repeated melody twice in the same fashion would be uninteresting and unimaginative, so I would make the peak of the first of these phrases on 'sake' instead. With the final line's climax marked on the middle of 'bright' we now have the shape of the verse: one opening phrase in two parts over two lines; one phrase of two short lines followed by an answering phrase on one long line, leading into a

48

final resolution on the last line, effectively giving one long final phrase of four lines. Incidentally, having said that the key signature of this song indicates E major or C sharp minor, I have to confess that it is not really in a major or a minor key at all, but in a mode, specifically the Dorian mode, based on the note F sharp. This is almost the same as F sharp minor, but with a flattened seventh, in this case the note E. Our ears are so attuned to expecting major or minor keys that we hear E major as the home key in the earlier part of the song. It requires some repetition of the modal F sharp before we finally accept that as the proper key.

This chapter on phrasing opened with a discussion of stress in the language, and we have seen how musical phrases in a song are built up from those individual word-stresses. Another way of looking at this would be to picture a set of Russian dolls. The stresses of single words are represented by the smallest doll, which is nested inside the doll representing the stresses of the musical barlines. This is then nested inside the one giving the major stresses of the poetic lines, which is nested inside the one giving the major stresses of the verses. The doll for the major stresses of the verses is nested inside the one representing the major stress of the whole song to create the complete over-arching phrase of that song. The metaphor of the Russian dolls continues even after this. Within a group of songs there is usually one that can be regarded as the high point of that group, so each song is nested within its group. Furthermore, within a recital there is usually one group which constitutes the high point or the main fare of the concert, so the final Russian doll is the concert itself.

I know that it is unusual to speak of phrasing in these terms, suggesting that one 'phrasing mark' covers the whole of an evening's music-making. Nevertheless, I feel that the longer we can maintain our energy and concentration, the more satisfying it will be for an audience. This is not to say that there should be no let-up or light relief in a recital, far from it. Such relief is essential for giving new impetus to the proceedings, but it needs to be part of an overall vision and structure with many colours and interesting features along the way. The designing of a good programme requires the skill of a sort of musical architect, balancing all the elements you want to incorporate into something that is satisfying to perform and to hear. Graham Johnson

49

is a master in this field, and his programmes for The Songmakers' Almanac have been published by Thames (ISBN 0 905210 42 5). This should be compulsory reading for serious students of singing, giving as it does so many different ways of putting songs together. There is generally a theme to each of these concerts, and that is something which may not always be desired; even so, the reader can see how songs can be placed together in the most surprising ways to create all kinds of fascinating effects. One of the very interesting results is how a song can radically change in character when it is put in a new or unusual context, and this gives the programme-planner an opportunity to enter the world of the composer and re-interpret his work. Enjoy the feeling!

5 – Tempo

Thank heaven for the composer who writes 'crotchet = 72' at the top of a song, or 'minim = c.58'. We can breathe a sigh of relief at not having to make the decision about tempo ourselves, and if it seems too fast or too slow we can blame someone else for it. A marking like *andante* or *lento* requires that we choose a speed and take responsibility for it, and this can be a daunting prospect. How do we translate *con anima, vivace non troppo* or *moderato* into a specific speed? These and all the rest of the tempo markings are very difficult to define even if we know what they mean, especially since they often indicate mood as well. *Molto teneramente* or *andante espressivo* are markings which ought probably to be deduced from the style of the poem and the music anyway, being mood markings more than anything else. In order to make informed decisions about the speed of a song we need to consider several elements: first, metronome markings; second, experience of other songs; third, indicators in the music itself; fourth, vocal requirements and limitations; fifth, pianistic requirements and limitations; sixth, environmental factors..

Metronome markings should be a foolproof way of deciding the issue: if the composer has asked for a certain speed we must do just that. After all, it is the composer's creation, and the composer must know what speed best suits that creation. Or perhaps not. The performer shares in the creative process, making a new and unique entity at each performance, and most experienced musicians will admit that the duration of a piece changes from occasion to occasion even when a metronome marking is involved. Besides the different variables which come into play each time, singers and players do not carry metronomes within their heads even when they have practised with a real one ticking away. These markings should be taken as an indication of the ideal speed for a song, but they should not be taken too seriously if the performers cannot feel comfortable with the result. To stray too far from that speed may make for a rotten performance, but there are plenty of rotten performances anyway, many of them at the 'correct' speed.

The second element in our tempo decision-making process is experience of other songs, a wretched Catch-22 for the young singer. In order to gain experience you need to perform, but without the experience in the first place you will find performing difficult. The solution available to most singers is to use the experience of a teacher or coach to suggest suitable tempi, and this use of other people's ears is something which singers can benefit from throughout their careers. No-one has a monopoly of all the best tempi and no-one is too perfect to be in a position to spurn help and advice from another musical intelligence. After some time you will perhaps have gained enough background knowledge to be able to make most of these judgments for yourself, and there is some danger in relying too much and for too long on the judgment of another. There is a difference between taking someone's advice on a matter in order to reach a decision, and following every aspect of that advice to the letter. The greatest legacy a teacher can give is to enable the pupil at last to stand on his or her own and give a performance that expresses what the pupil wishes to convey rather than what the teacher wishes.

The third element is what the music itself is telling us. If the beats are subdivided into quarters, for instance, the music will sound busier than if they are whole or in halves, and the song will sound more hurried anyway without doing anything to the basic tempo. The tempo marking usually refers to the mood of the vocal line, which is supported and confirmed by the accompaniment, but the voice and the accompaniment can appear to be at odds with each other, most often when a sustained and possibly slow-moving vocal line is underpinned by a much faster-sounding piano part. Quilter's *Love's Philosophy* is a good example of this. When in doubt the accompaniment needs to accommodate itself to the needs of the voice part, and this can make quite heavy demands on a pianist if the ideal vocal speed is faster than is comfortable for the player (but see the fifth element below). Another musical tempo indicator is the speed with which the harmony is moving. If the harmony is changing quickly, and particularly if there is much chromaticism in the process and not simply chord progressions within the home key, then the ear seems to demand that things slow down so that the changes can be heard. Warlock delighted in writing 'wrong-note music' which continually surprises us with strange sounds. His song *Sleep* is marked 'rather slow', which not only allows the weird harmonies to be heard but also fits the feeling of the poem. *Sigh no more, ladies,* on the other hand, though it is marked 'fast and in strict time', requires a steadier tempo than I would normally expect 'fast' to mean. It is so packed with chromatic harmonies that it needs to be slower than the vocal line alone might suggest.

The fourth element in choosing a tempo, vocal requirements and limitations, is illustrated by this same Warlock song. The vocal line might well be quite happy jogging along at a fairly fast speed with its mixture of crotchets and quavers, but suddenly the singer is presented with a frantic 'hey nonny nonny nonny' in semiquavers. Certainly with practice one can improve the tongue's agility, but there is probably a limit to the number of nonnies that can be fired off in a given time. My own best efforts come up with about three per second, which gives me a maximum tempo for the song of something like dotted crotchet equals sixty. Finzi's *It was a lover and his lass* has fast semiquavers on 'ding-a-ding-a-ding' which I can manage at only a little more than four 'ding-as' per second, which is somewhere near the metronome marking of 'minim = c.72'. This method of finding an upper limit to a tempo often comes in handy, and it is even useful for finding a comfortable speed and not solely a maximum. A further indicator of suitable tempo occurs in songs which use the rhythms of speech: Ireland's *Sea Fever* and Butterworth's *The lads in their hundreds* come into this category. By simply reciting 'I must go down to the seas again, to the lonely sea and the sky' we find a natural rhythm and speed which correspond quite closely with Ireland's rhythm and tempo of 'about crotchet = 52-56'. *The lads in their hundreds* has no metronome marking, but by using the same method as with *Sea Fever* we reach a tempo of between sixty and seventy beats to the minute.

The fifth element, pianistic requirements and limitations, has a cause and effect similar to the fourth element, that is the problem of excessive speed. Warlock is a major culprit in this regard because he writes accompaniments that do not lie easily under the pianist's fingers. *Spring* is an example of such a song, where the marking of 'very fast and light' might spur the singer on to wild extremes and leave the poor pianist in a complete tangle. The sixth element in choosing a tempo I have termed 'environmental factors', a catch-all phrase which includes the acoustics of the performance space and decisions based on other artistic matters. For example, the mood and tempo of a song immediately before or after might affect this song's tempo, or the overall shape of a programme may influence a song and draw out of it some unusual nuance.

After a basic tempo has been chosen, the question arises whether a song should continue in that tempo or whether there are moments when it should alter. The first consideration here is what the composer has marked in the score. *Rall., rit., allarg., ten., sost.* and so on tell us to slow down or wait, and *animato, string., accel.* and the rest tell us to press on and go faster. So much is clear, and we are told exactly when to do it, but by how much we do it is a matter for us to choose. A danger in slowing down a lot is that a song can lose its impetus and narrative drive if the process goes too far, while speeding up too much can produce a ridiculous gabble. In order to deal with some of these points, let us look at Parry's song *And yet I love her till I die.* The marking at the top, *andante,* indicates a moderately flowing tempo, somewhere in the region of sixty to seventy beats to the minute. The first marked change of tempo comes at the *lento* on 'till I die'. *Lento* is usually taken to mean slow, but not as slow as *adagio* or *largo*, and here it does not signify a slowing down but a new speed entirely. If we were to take this literally, the piano would be forced into a very unnatural and sudden pull-up in the middle of its short phrase. To avoid this, we have to put in a short period of slowing down before briefly establishing the new slow speed, and this is not precisely what the composer has indicated. This kind of interpretation of a composer's apparent wishes is something we are continually faced with, since he himself would have written his songs expecting a certain style of performance and would not have marked every single nuance of that style, and we bring to our performances all the changes in taste and aesthetics which have occurred since his day. The balance between our taste and the taste and style of a past era is a very difficult one to strike, and is always open to debate and reinterpretation.

Returning to Parry's song, I now want to deal with how slow the short *lento* section should be. There are three verses to this song, and three appearances of the phrase 'till I die', each of them with the *lento* marking. Are those three phrases to be the same? Straight away, if we look at the third 'till I die', we can see that this one is not the same, because Parry has written *colla voce* under it. *Colla voce*, 'with the voice', seems a strange instruction to give an accompanist, because we should expect him or her to be 'with the voice' all the time. It has, in fact, become a conventional marking to show that the singer is expected to slow down at this point, and it could easily be replaced with *rallentando* or the like. The implication is that the singer has a certain freedom to stretch the time as he wishes here, and therefore the third 'till I die' is clearly different from the others. As for the first two, there is a general rule that if a phrase or musical idea is repeated, it should not be treated in exactly the same way as that which went before. A phrase repeated nearly always carries a subtly different nuance anyway, and moreover the listener's attention is maintained through constantly varying material. In this case, although I acknowledge that it is a matter of opinion, my choice would be to make the first 'till I die' the least slow, the second slightly slower and the third slowest of all. Since I do not want to make the last one so slow as to become *largo*, I must choose tempi for the first two which prevent this from happening, and which will be only marginally slower than the song's basic tempo.

A tempo in this song tells the performers to return to the opening speed, but that is not always its meaning. Finzi's *The Phantom* has an initial speed of about 88 beats to the minute which changes after two pages to 76. At the top of the third page comes *A tempo,* which does not in this case mean the first tempo of 88, but the second of 76, and we do not return to the original tempo until we see *Tempo I* later on. This may seem fairly obvious, but it is something which can easily be overlooked. Parry's song has no problem of that sort, and just before the *a tempo* at the beginning of the third verse there is a short *ritenuto* which helps to give space for the new modulation into B minor. *Animando* means animating or becoming animated, which implies an on-going process, rather as *crescendo* means getting louder, whereas *animato* means animated, the result and not the process. *Accelerando* might be an alternative for *animando*, though for Parry's purposes here there cannot be very much speeding up. *Allargando* two bars later describes another on-going process, this time getting slower (and louder), but Parry does not tell us when to stop the process. Plainly the music does not get continually slower and louder because there is a *diminuendo* and then a *piano* marked before the final *lento*. The performer's judgment now needs to come into play to decide when to stop slowing down and whether or not to return to the opening tempo before the *lento* bar. My own suggestion would be to have two bars of the broader tempo followed by two bars which almost return to the original tempo before the slower *lento*. The piano postlude then comes in at the first tempo, with a slight *rallentando* on the last three beats or so.

At the end of this song the pianist is expected to do something which has not been written in by the composer, namely to slow down on the last few beats. This is a convention which applies to most Western music from very early times, even though the extent and degree of such a slowing-down varies according to style and period, and it has the effect of rounding off a work or part of a work in a way which prevents it from being an abrupt cut-off. We saw another similar moment when I suggested preparing the *lento* passages with some previous slowing down. This song, and others like it, requires a flexibility in tempo which goes beyond the occasional *rallentando*, and which needs to be applied throughout. The word which describes what I mean is *rubato*.

Rubato is the Italian word for robbed, which in normal usage communicates the idea of taking away without returning. Society would be all the happier if the normal meaning were like the musical meaning of the word, which implies a taking-away followed by a restoration, expansiveness followed by compression, slower and then faster. This ebb and flow of tempo is an essential part of a song such as this, breathing life into the notes and bringing off the page many of the feeling-qualities of the poem: the passion, yearning and joy which Parry's music encapsulates. Giving a simple definition of *rubato* is one thing, but describing in words how it is applied in a particular song is quite another. One of the problems is that if I am too prescriptive about what should be done at each moment in the song, the result could be as mechanical as if I advocated strict rhythm throughout.

Before giving an example of flexible tempo, I want to mention two other important factors. The first is a rhetorical device which involves bending the rhythm and which is intimately connected with *rubato*; it is the dramatic pause. In order to draw attention to a word an actor waits for a split second before that word. Listeners, who are attuned to the underlying rhythm of the speech, are aware of a momentary break in that rhythm, forcing them to focus on the reason for the break, which is the word immediately following. 'I was . . .' Well, what was I? Happy, sad, twelve, out, swimming, or what? '. . . livid.' Ah, at last. This device for heightening the impact of words in speech can also be used for heightening their impact in singing, and for heightening the impact of a purely musical point. The second additional factor is taking time out to breathe. This is something we encounter in all forms of singing, whether it be Bach, Brahms, Stravinsky or Tavener, and there are many occasions when the composer has given us insufficient time to breathe properly. Sometimes, as often in Bach, the tempo marches on inexorably, forcing us to shorten notes or (dare I say it) to leave out notes altogether. At other times it is stylistically quite acceptable to broaden the tempo for a moment to allow the intake of breath, and we can use this practical necessity to our advantage by making it into an expressive device. The one thing in common through every style is that the singer should not have to gasp or sound uncomfortable and rushed (unless that is in itself appropriate to the sense of the piece).

My first example of *rubato* and dramatic pause is the piano introduction to this same song, *And yet I love her till I die*. There are four rhetorical moments in this passage which coincide with the first beats of the bars. The first two and the fourth are suspensions while the third is not only the highest point of the phrase, it is a D major chord rather than the A minor which we are being led to anticipate. Each of these moments is designed to cheat our expectations of simple harmonic structure, although admittedly not in a way that shocks us greatly. Each time, then, we could delay the first beat in order to draw attention to these moments, but the danger would be of making the effect stale through repetition. If we delay the first because of the crescendo which is marked, we can by contrast make very little of the second, make the most delay on the third at the climax, and wind down to hardly any delay on the last. Having worked on a pattern for the dramatic pauses we are now in a position to make some effective *rubato*. Accelerate a little on the opening three notes in parallel with the crescendo, relax the tempo for the next bar and a half, then accelerate again through the three notes leading up to the climax before again relaxing the tempo through the bar.

The other example I want to give is the opening and first verse of Butterworth's *Loveliest of Trees*, which I also use in the chapter on Meaning. The marking at the top is *Molto moderato, sempre rubato e con espressione*, which translates loosely into 'Very moderate speed, always *rubato* and with expression'. That hardly counts as a translation since I have left one word in the original language and the meaning of the rest is either opaque or too obvious to mention. *Rubato* we have already discussed, and I justify leaving it in because it stands for so much more than simply 'robbed'. 'Very moderate speed' is a tricky one, akin to describing something as 'very average', and it only says 'neither too fast nor too slow, tending towards the slow side'. 'With expression' is a quality which we hope to hear in every piece of music provided it is appropriate to the inherent feeling. A composer presumably writes such an instruction in order to encourage the performers to heighten the expressive nature of the song, and one of the ways to achieve this is to pay particular attention to its rhythmic flexibility.

The piano figure at the start hangs there without at first showing any rhythmic impetus. Not until the fourth note can the listener begin to calculate the tempo or the note-length relationships. The movement is arrested again on the fifth note to hang once more before rolling downwards and gathering momentum until the tempo relaxes for the final few notes of the melisma. There is a free, timeless quality to the phrase which the pianist must dare to exploit fully. The singer, on the other hand, should not use so much freedom even though the phrase is quite similar: the rhetorical gesture has already been made by the piano, and to repeat the gesture is redundant and unartistic. The song is now under way, and it needs only an infinitesimal acceleration through the vocal phrase until the *poco rit.* at 'along the bough'. The singer then speeds and slows a little through the next short phrase before the piano returns to the opening *espressivo* figure and gives an echo of that figure's freedom. My choice for the next phrase is to have a slight acceleration through 'Easter' to accompany the *crescendo* at that point and to prepare and connect with the following piano section. The piano loses impetus at the end of the *fortissimo* phrase and becomes again free and timeless, anticipating the timeless nature of the voice part at the beginning of verse two.

Attempts of this sort to describe *rubato* and rhythmic flexibility are a poor substitute for the real thing, and I recommend listening as much as possible to first-rate performances so as to make the use of *rubato* into something almost instinctive. I have used words like 'slight', 'a little' and 'infinitesimal' to qualify the amount of change in tempo needed for a well-made *rubato*, but these words are as vague as the Italian terms *molto moderato, colla voce* or those two gems which Handel often used: *tempo giusto* and *tempo ordinario*. The very vagueness of these words is in fact their strength, because they allow a freedom of interpretation which is essential if music is to come alive. But that freedom must always be tempered by a knowledge of and feeling for the style which the composer assumed his performers would adopt. There are songs with clear rhythmic drive, like Vaughan Williams's *The Vagabond* or Ireland's *The Encounter*, which need an inexorable and invariable tempo. Otherwise, to sing an English song from the late nineteenth or early twentieth century without paying attention to *rubato* is as unstylish and unacceptable as playing Bach as if it were Chopin.

6 – Meaning

Most vocal music differs from instrumental music in that it comes with a text, and the traditional purpose of a text is to convey meaning. Where the work is an opera or an oratorio the chances are that the words set are in the form of prose, whereas in the song repertoire the texts which composers choose to set are nearly always poems or parts of poems. I want first to consider aspects of meaning connected with poetry, and later I shall return to prose and recitative. The song composer's choice of a particular text probably depended on a variety of factors; a commission for a specific occasion, perhaps, or the requirements of a publisher. The composer's state of mind may have entered into it; joy or sadness, confidence or self-doubt, or, as with Schumann in 1840, the state of his love life. Whatever the reasons may have been, we can assume that the text touched upon the appropriate nuances of thought and feeling at the time. We can also assume that if the resulting composition possesses sincerity and originality, the composer has understood and absorbed its meaning, and has expressed this understanding in the song. But that meaning which the poet may have intended to convey is now overlaid with the composer's understanding and intention, which may to some extent be at variance with it. The music is at least likely to emphasise certain qualities of the poem and to play down or ignore other qualities, thus enhancing or diminishing its original impact, and perhaps contradicting the listener's own interpretation of it. Furthermore, just as the listener's understanding of a poem can be aided or hindered by the abilities of a reader, so the listener's understanding of a song can be affected by the abilities of the singer and accompanist. There is a succession, then, of carriers of the 'message' in a song: poet, poem, composer, song, performers and listener.

For the completest possible picture in our search for meaning, it seems sensible to start at the beginning of this succession: the poet. Does his or her life-story have a bearing on the subject of the poem, either at the time of writing or before? If the poet concerned is Thomas Hardy, the answer is an emphatic yes. What are the ideas and feelings expressed in the poet's other works? If the poem under consideration is one of a set, how does it stand in relation to its companions, even if those companions have not been set to music? The composer may have been aware of all of these elements or possibly some of them, or even none at all, and it can be fascinating to try figuring out whether any of them entered his or her mind, or whether the composition was a spontaneous response to a naked set of verses. Be that as it may, for brief summaries of a selection of poets' lives and works I refer the reader to chapter eight.

After the poet we have the text itself, and I want to start with A E Housman's *Loveliest of Trees*:

> Loveliest of trees, the cherry now
> Is hung with bloom along the bough,
> And stands about the woodland ride
> Wearing white for Eastertide.
>
> Now, of my threescore years and ten,
> Twenty will not come again,
> And take from seventy springs a score,
> It only leaves me fifty more.
>
> And since to look at things in bloom
> Fifty springs are little room,
> About the woodland I will go
> To see the cherry hung with snow.

The three stanzas of this poem show three distinct stages of development. Verse one sets the scene, which is simply a cherry tree in bloom at Easter. This is a straightforward description of a natural phenomenon, with the poetic embellishment of an Easter garment. Verse two introduces an entirely new idea, unconnected with verse one except that spring is mentioned. The poet is conscious of the passing of time, and now that he has reached the age of twenty, his expected life-span of three score years and ten gives him only another fifty years. In verse three the ideas in the first two verses are now joined. If he only has fifty more years to live, then he should be sure to go and see the cherry blossom while he can.

Now we have the bare bones of the poem, the surface meaning; what about the underlying meaning, if any? The white cherry blossom is a symbol of renewal and growth; like Easter, it holds the promise of life to come. A tree without blossom would not serve so well, nor would one whose flowers were any colour other than white, since white stands for unmarked purity, the unwritten page whose potential is limitless. Verse two introduces the idea of mortality, life's end after the allotted seventy years, and this is an end which does not seem to be redeemed by the Easter promise of resurrection. Verse three has the poet determined to enjoy the beauty of the earth while he may, but this time he describes the cherry blossom not as a white Easter dress signifying the hope of summer and life, but as a covering of snow, a portent of winter and death.

There is an element here which does not quite fit in with our knowledge of the world; why is a young man of twenty worrying himself about death? At such an age he thinks of himself as virtually immortal, and fifty years stretch away into an unimaginably distant future. Such intimations of mortality are far more likely when the numbers are placed the other way around: the fifty-year-old contemplating the realisation that he may only have twenty more years of life. In 1895, the year of this poem, Housman was aged thirty six, so his personal circumstances do not seem to be directly involved here. To try to resolve this paradox we might look at some of Housman's other poems, and for this purpose I want to consider those which George Butterworth set.

Loveliest of Trees is the first of *Six songs from A Shropshire Lad*, published in 1911. All six, as might be inferred from the title, describe aspects of a young man's life and feelings. The second and third songs, *When I was one-and-twenty* and *Look not in my eyes*, are concerned with love and the pain associated with it. The next, *Think no more, lad,* comes nearer to giving a clue to our paradox, since it ironically extols the tendency of the young to avoid any thought for the morrow. A still stronger clue comes in the fifth song, *The lads in their hundreds*, where mortality is given prominence:

But now you may stare as you like and there's nothing to scan;
And brushing your elbow unguessed-at and not to be told
They carry back bright to the coiner the mintage of man,
The lads that will die in their glory and never be old.

Finally, *Is my team ploughing* is a stark story of death and betrayal. Now, perhaps, the meaning of *Loveliest of Trees* has become clearer. Beneath the surface the poem is not about a cherry tree nor a twenty-year-old worrying over how short a time there is until he reaches seventy. The lad may not be conscious of it, but his real concern is about whether he will survive beyond tomorrow. This is a realisation that slowly dawns as Butterworth's six songs unfold, but in Housman's original the tone is clear from the outset.

Loveliest of Trees is the second of sixty-three poems entitled *A Shropshire Lad*. The first, *From Clee to Heaven the beacon burns*, describes Queen Victoria's golden jubilee:

> Because 'tis fifty years tonight
> That God has saved the Queen.

But there were many who were not there that night because they gave their lives in the wars that helped to ensure that Her Majesty would indeed be saved:

> It dawns in Asia, tombstones show
> And Shropshire names are read;
> And the Nile spills his overflow
> Beside the Severn's dead.

With an opening like that, *Loveliest of Trees* possesses a much more obvious connection with doomed youth, and I am sure that Butterworth knew all sixty-three of the poems. They were some of the most popular verses of the day, and Butterworth did set a further five in another set, though he would not have guessed that he himself was to be one of the countless young men who died to 'Save the King' in the trenches of the Western Front.

Our first reading of this poem gave a superficial understanding of it, but thought and study have given deeper insights. If it were prose, it would be designed to be understood by the rational mind in a step-by-step series of statements or logical deductions. This book, for instance, is written in that way, and although a psychologist could probably read into it all kinds of neuroses and obsessions, hidden meanings are not part of my intention as the author. Poetry, on the other hand, is intended to have layers of meaning which can be absorbed by the emotional or irrational mind, and some of those layers can never be fully rationalised and explained. My attempts to do so are bound to fail, since those attempts are themselves aimed at the rational mind. The beauty of a musical setting in this respect is that music itself largely appeals to the irrational, feeling mind, and we thus have a musical 'explanation' of the poem in terms which complement its non-intellectual side. Our perception of the meaning is sharpened by the music. This, I think, helps to explain why songs are usually settings of poetry and not prose. Words, when used in prose, are truly 'prosaic', that is, plain and matter-of-fact. They should be read and understood at their face value, so that a rose is a rose is a rose, for example, the flower of a spiny shrub. This is not to say that prose is necessarily dull and prosaic; anyone who has read a thrilling novel can refute that. The drawback with prose is that it usually requires a large number of words to transmit its message if that message is at all complicated. Poetry, on the other hand, uses words in a different way, one where they are assumed to carry all sorts of symbolic and referential meanings. A rose, in a poetic sense, can convey ideas of love or beauty, for instance, or stand as a symbol for the beloved, perhaps. As soon as we understand that the word is being used in a poetic manner our minds are flooded with a whole array of images and feelings which can spring from our own personal experience or from our indirect experience of poetic language and custom. For this reason poetry can carry an enormous amount of meaning in a very small number of words, and it is this economy which makes poetry ideal for song-writers.

To illustrate how music can enhance our comprehension, let us take Butterworth's song *Loveliest of Trees*. It begins in E major, a key suggesting strength and confidence; yet the opening is a long falling melisma, first on the piano, then in the voice. This is not a confident start, but one that paints a picture of descent and decline, and it may refer to the imminent fall of the blossom. 'Wearing white for Eastertide' by contrast has nobility and grandeur, a feeling continued in the piano with its E-major fanfare. This dies away into the yearning quality of a pair of thirds (from G sharp to E) which takes us into the relative minor of C sharp for the second verse. Again at the end of verse two the piano has that fall from G sharp to E, this time not to find rest in C sharp minor but to run through a swift progression of keys to a climax on 'woodlands' in A major. There is another climax for the piano in E major before the song settles, after three bars of bitonality, on the final soft E major chords. This progression of keys in verse three suggests to me a sense of restlessness and a desire to be making up for lost time. The bold A major and subsequent E major transmit a feeling of decisiveness, but this is followed by three bars of hesitation and uncertainty until at last we reach a quiet acceptance in the final two bars.

The emotional implications of the music in Butterworth's song follow quite closely the narrative of the poem. There is a clear musical structure to mirror the verbal structure, which is not at all the case for every song, and for that reason I want to consider Arthur Somervell's *Loveliest of Trees* as a contrast. This is the first of ten songs entitled *Song cycle from A Shropshire Lad*. The setting is much simpler than Butterworth's, being perfectly strophic apart from the end of the third verse. In such a song there does not exist an opportunity for individual word-painting since one melody and harmonisation has to serve for all the verses (cf. many of Schubert's Lieder). Clues to the song's meaning have to be found, if at all, in features of that tune and harmony.

The key is E major, like the Butterworth, with a brief modulation into B major (bars 4 and 5), and even briefer moments in C sharp and F sharp major (bars 6 and 7). There is not much to go on here in our search for musical meaning. The opening bar of piano introduction, with its rising pairs of quavers, draws the ear in to the vocal entry, and perhaps draws the mind's eye towards the tree standing above. The two long phrases of the vocal melody, with their satisfying internal structure, the second mimicking the first but a tone higher, have a pleasing ebb and flow, but they do not of themselves indicate an obvious mood. The piano interlude, with its repeated falling phrase, might bring the mind's eye back to earth, but without much emphasis. The only alteration in the strophic form is the doubled length of the notes on 'hung with', where the suspension of time imitates the suspended blossom.

This song is therefore a straight lyrical narration, and in this respect it follows Goethe's dictum that his own poems ought to be set strophically, for he thought that through-composition was 'thoroughly reprehensible, since the general lyrical character is thereby completely destroyed and a false interest in detail is demanded and aroused'. Whether one agrees with Goethe or not, these two songs show quite clearly two different approaches to setting the same poem. Butterworth uses the music to indicate salient points in the text, while Somervell allows the text to speak for itself through an appropriate lyrical melody. Later in Somervell's cycle the ninth song, *Into my heart an air that kills*, takes the melody of *Loveliest of Trees* as the pattern for that 'air' (using the word to mean a heart-wrenching melody and not a poisonous atmosphere, you understand). The result is wonderfully effective, not only because the music is beautiful in itself, but because we recognise it from the earlier song and associate it with the purity of that earlier picture.

Again, I have been attempting the impossible, to explain the inexplicable in rational terms. All I can do is to hint at the real understanding which comes through hearing the music. One of our problems as inheritors of rational Western culture is that we absorb so much through our eyes and our intellects that we have in many ways lost touch with our ears and our feelings. Left-brain rationality has overwhelmed right-brain intuition. Because of this I suggest an alternative approach to singing a song; rather than starting with the text, why not try starting with the music?

We shall now look at the first song of Finzi's *Let us garlands bring* without first considering the text, or perhaps imagining that it is in an unknown foreign language where words like 'death' and 'weep' do not make any sense to us. The marking at the head of the song is *Lugubre*, and the lugubrious piano introduction, low and slow in B minor, portends a serious song. In bar 9 the opening chord on 'cypress' has an A against a B flat at a major seventh, followed by a B natural false relation in the bass, while in the three bars 9 to 11 the vocal line and the middle voices in the piano are being dragged along harmonically over the bass line in a series of heavy appoggiaturas. Consequently, a simple progression of chords (E minor, D major, E minor, G major and F sharp minor) becomes a complex web of tension. The falling sevenths

('Come away, death' in bar 7, 'Fly away, breath' in bar 15 and so on) add to this mood of heaviness. In bars 24 and 25 'stuck all with yew' has C sharp against D natural followed by B against C natural and C sharp against D natural again. There is another false relation in bar 33 on the second beat of 'true', where the E sharp is against an E natural and both are contending with the F sharp in the voice.

There are many more such examples in both verses of this modified strophic song, with more chromaticism and more dragged appoggiaturas, especially in the melisma on 'weep' (bars 70 to 74). This is the only word in the song, incidentally, which Finzi writes with more than one note to a syllable, and the melisma is a reference to St Peter's reaction in Bach's *St Matthew Passion* when he 'wept bitterly' at having betrayed Jesus. I cannot pretend to deduce from all this exactly what the poem is saying, but I can be sure that the underlying context is one of heaviness, grief and anguish. The message in this song is quite unequivocal and the mood is consistent throughout, like Somervell's *Loveliest of Trees*, but unlike Butterworth's, where the 'feeling tone' of the music varies to suit the details of the poem.

The rational analysis here is intended to hint at something which communicates so much more to the human mind when it is directly experienced, that is assuming that the human mind in question is reasonably well attuned to Western serious musical traditions. There is much to be said for undergoing the experience without the analytical preparation, but once the singer has had that experience, then if he or she wishes to develop further as a performer, the rational and analytical should be brought to bear on the intuitive to create an ever-deeper insight into the meaning of a song, and enable an ever-fuller communication with an audience.

When I characterised poetry as being full of hidden significance and imagery, and prose as a matter-of-fact conveyor of facts or processes, I was using an over-simplification. The truth is that the distinction is not as clear-cut as this, and there is poetry which serves a rather prosaic, descriptive purpose, and prose which is full of inner meaning. It is important to be aware of this when singing, and to know the nature of the words being sung. Goethe's condemnation of through-composition as arousing false interest in detail can be applied more generally to singers interpreting songs where individual words are highlighted according to a mistaken need to 'get the meaning across'. Words should rather be allowed to stand in their context of overall meaning, not as a series of brightly-painted concepts lined up in a row. The thrust of that meaning may well alter through the progress of a song, especially if the poet travels along some inner journey at the same time, but that is rarer than one might think. *La Belle Dame Sans Merci,* a narrative ballad by Keats, set to music by Stanford, takes us on such a journey as the Knight describes his entrapment by the Lady of the title. De la Mare's *King David* is another poem of incident and discovery, and although Howells's treatment of the text is less overtly dramatic than Stanford's is of the Keats poem, the power and importance of individual words and phrases still require a certain amount of careful colouring. The majority of songs, however, are concerned with one central idea, from which the whole takes its colour. *Loveliest of Trees*, for example, needs the subtlest possible shading of expression between pleasure at seeing the blossom on the tree, and anxiety at not having enough time left to enjoy the sight. Make too much of either and the result will be hammy, overdone and embarassing.

Recitative is a form of singing which requires more attention to the meaning of separate words since it is generally concerned either with story-telling in some way or with expounding ideas or describing feelings. The singer has more freedom to express his or her understanding of text through accentuation, variation of speed, dynamic contrast and quality of diction than is possible in a song or aria. The narrative moves on, and the narrator's mood changes to coincide with the thoughts being expressed. There is a danger, however, that by emoting too well through each word and line of the story, the inner journey can be overlooked. The singer needs to express the thoughts and feelings as if they are present in his or her mind at that very moment, not things which have been prepared and memorised beforehand. This is unfortunately not always as easy as it sounds. Everyone working on the stage has experienced that ridiculous moment when they find that they cannot perform some perfectly straightforward, everyday task simply because they have been asked to do it at rehearsal. Likewise, knowing what it is that you are about to sing, but pretending that it is only occurring to you at that moment, can keep you almost tongue-tied. The secret seems to be to maintain a focus of intention through each idea so that it lives in the forefront of your mind and becomes clearly communicated to the audience. If the idea is generalised or allowed to pass the lips without the energy of mental concentration, the listener will lose the thread of reality which you are trying to create. A problem of another sort can occur if you, the performer, have not committed the work to memory sufficiently, in which case, being in the moment in this way during a performance means that you can lose the thread of what you are saying and forget what comes next. A further difficulty can appear if you are too deeply bound up in the emotional turmoil of the character you are portraying. You are looking for tears in the listener's eyes, not your own, and it's an unnerving feeling when you lose control of your diaphragm. A tearful wobbly voice doesn't work very well.

The concentration required for the majority of songs is more single-minded than we usually find in recitative. The arch of meaning stretches much further, often over the whole of a song, because a unified poetic and musical idea is unfolding. Search for those arches of meaning in the poem and in the music to become aware of the length of that 'moment' of focussed intention, and do not be afraid of allowing the moment to encompass the complete song if necessary.

7 – A Short History

The history of song must be as old as the history of Homo Sapiens, and theories of its origins in pre-verbal cultures make fascinating reading. But for the purposes of a book on English solo song a rather later starting date can be chosen, and because so little material survives from earlier times I shall start with the Tudor kings and queens of England. In 1485 Richard III, the last of the Plantagenets, was defeated at Bosworth Field by Henry Tudor, who became Henry VII. Thirty years of civil war came to an end, allowing the country to recover and grow in power and prosperity. The king's retinue included the usual complement of professional musicians who played and sang for the entertainment of the court. During the reign of Henry's son, Henry VIII (himself an accomplished amateur musician), the role of music and musicians grew in importance. Composers at court wrote for a wider audience and a growing number of gifted amateurs, especially for those who had taken up the fashionable lute. Church musicians produced partsongs and consort songs for singers outside the ecclesiastical context, and music became a thoroughly acceptable pastime for leisured gentlefolk.

The great majority of the songs from the sixteenth century have not survived; though there are books of poems clearly intended for setting to music, the music itself has largely disappeared. A major breakthrough occurred in 1597 when John Dowland (1563-1626) published his *First Booke of Songs or Ayres*, establishing a new genre – the lute song. Dowland was the foremost lutenist of his day, acknowledged as such by his fellow musicians. He had lived in France for four years and had travelled widely in Germany and Italy, and his music brought together the many influences he had absorbed. There were elements from the earlier English partsongs and consort songs, and from the French *air de cours* tradition, which used simple strophic settings for several voices or for single voice with lute accompaniment. Dowland's songs achieved immediate popularity, being reprinted four times at least, and he published two more *Bookes of Songs* over the next six years. Many other composers followed suit with their own collections, but in a relatively short time the fashion passed, the final volume of this kind being published in 1622 by John Attey. The lute song declined in popularity as the lute itself was gradually superseded by keyboard instruments, and as lute tablature was replaced by the figured bass.

Meanwhile, another strand of music-making was developing for the stage. Shakespeare at The Globe theatre followed the normal practice of the time by using music extensively in his plays to underline dramatic moments and changes in mood, to increase dramatic tension or to allow for scene-changing. Songs were also included, especially in the later comedies, the texts of which have furnished countless settings over the intervening years. Robert Johnson (1583-1633) wrote for Shakespeare's company, The King's Men, and a good number of his songs survive from *The Tempest* and *A Winter's Tale*, Webster's *The Duchess of Malfi*, and plays and masques by Jonson and Beaumont and Fletcher. William Lawes (1602-1645) also wrote for The King's Men in the 1630s, providing songs and instrumental music for at least twenty-five plays and masques. William and his brother Henry Lawes (1596-1662) both wrote songs which were intended for non-dramatic use, setting the work of contemporary poets like Herrick, Suckling and Lovelace. In this field of courtly or domestic song Henry was the outstanding master of the time, and the various manuscripts and published sources contain 434 of his settings. The dramatic context of so many of these compositions created a need for a dramatic style of declamation, for which Italian monody provided the ideal pattern. Dowland's earlier songs had sparingly used a declamatory style as an expressive tool, but his use of declamation increased with time as he became involved with dramatic presentations and masques. By the time of the Lawes brothers the style of the songs being written was either fully declamatory or was that of a simple melodic ballad.

When the Puritans defeated the Royalists and beheaded Charles I in 1649, a period of austerity was introduced which was only fully lifted by the restoration of the monarchy in 1660. At first all theatrical productions were banned, which naturally meant the end of the music associated with the stage, and Church music was similarly proscribed except for metrical psalm-singing. An unlooked-for result of all this prohibition was a great increase in private music-making. The initial ban on theatrical production was relaxed for events of a purely musical nature, so England's first opera, Davenant's *The Siege of Rhodes*, was performed in 1656. The music for this opera, by Matthew Locke and others, has unfortunately not survived, but after the Restoration Locke wrote a large number of verse anthems for the church. These included the use of a recitative style which he had introduced in the opera, and which accorded with the tastes that Charles II had developed during his exile in France. Among the new generation of young composers the name of Henry Purcell (1659-1695) stands out as one of the geniuses of the age. He succeeded Locke as composer-in-ordinary for the violins in 1677, and in 1682 became organist of the Chapel Royal. *Dido and Aeneas*, performed in 1689, was his only true opera, his other stage works being masques or semi-operas. The many songs found in these and in other publications show a wonderful diversity of style and invention, from the simple strophic settings like *Fairest Isle* to the florid mad songs (*From rosy bowers*) and extravagant cantatas like *Begin the Song.*

Another important figure of the time was John Blow (1649-1708), whose reputation would today stand much higher but for the overwhelming presence of Purcell. His short opera *Venus and Adonis* pre-dates Purcell's *Dido* by about five years, and his vocal music is probably his greatest achievement.

Although English songs and theatre music continued being written as the new century progressed, the great musical phenomenon of this period was the success of Italian opera, and Handel (1685-1759) was at the forefront of the fashion. For twenty-five years from his settling in London in 1712 he wrote and promoted Italianate operas which were performed by the finest Italian singers of the day for enormous fees. But towards the end of this time he found that the demand for his operas was falling off, and he took to writing oratorios instead. The cream of London society still remained faithful to this foreign entertainment, but the middle classes were looking for something more accessible, preferably something in English. This need was met in two ways, both of which had a profound effect on the future of English song.

One platform for English music was the Pleasure Garden, the first of which was founded at Marylebone in 1659, closely followed by the most famous of them all, Vauxhall, which started in 1661 and lasted almost two hundred years. Hundreds of others were created during this long period, some of them surviving only a few years, some well into the later part of the nineteenth century. Sadler's Wells (1684-c.1880), Ranelagh (1742-1803) and Cremorne (1836-1878) were three more significant ones. The public was admitted for a small fee and could enjoy promenading, eating and drinking and listening to concerts of music provided by the resident orchestras. Naturally it was not only English music that was heard here, and instrumental music especially was provided by some of the leading German, French and Italian composers. As for songs – and songs were always a major feature of the concerts – they were for the most part in English. Thomas Arne (1710-1778) was director of music at Vauxhall Gardens from 1745. He wrote much incidental music for the stage, and his *Artaxerxes* (1762) was the only successful English opera in the Italian style until the nineteenth century. But it is probably for his songs that he is best known, and he published twenty-two volumes of his collected songs in thirty years: his *Rule, Britannia* must be as familiar to us today as the National Anthem. The style of most Pleasure Garden songs remained generally simple, melodic and ballad-like, and they were taken up with great enthusiasm by the public, hence the number of collections published by Arne and others.

The other platform for English music which appealed to the middle classes was the ballad opera. The star of Italian opera in London had burned very brightly for Handel in the early part of the century, but in 1728 the time had come for a new kind of venture, and John Gay's *The Beggar's Opera* started the fashion for ballad operas. These were effectively spoken plays where dialogue and songs alternated, and where the texts of the songs were set to familiar or traditional melodies. Ballads have a history which stretches back into medieval times, and they usually tell a story related to some subject of universal human interest, whether it be love, war, death, the supernatural, legend or supposed historical fact. But the form of words was chosen to fit the form of the tune, and families of well-known tunes had evolved through centuries from certain common ancestors. From the sixteenth century onwards itinerant ballad sellers issued an enormous number of broadside ballads, printed word-sheets of all kinds of verses, which the purchaser was expected to be able to furnish with a popular tune. This was the provenance of the ballad opera, and from the time of *The Beggar's Opera* there was perceived to be a polarisation in public taste between those who favoured foreign imports, with their flamboyant style and sometimes surgically-aided sounds, and those who preferred honest, workmanlike entertainment where the listeners could sing the tunes because they knew them already. But the vogue for true ballad operas only lasted for about thirty years, and it was succeeded by something similar, a form of dialogue opera using spoken text and tunes that were specially written for the piece.

From about the beginning of the nineteenth century the English operas became vehicles for sentimental ballads, often written specifically with an eye for sales of sheet music. Sir Henry Bishop (1786-1855) was active as director of Vauxhall Gardens, of Covent Garden and Drury Lane, and was one of the original members of the Philharmonic Society. His work for the stage consisted of adaptations and incorporations of other composers' material, and original material of his own. He published hundreds of glees and songs from these shows, one of which, *Home, Sweet Home*, became so popular after its first appearance in 1816 that he wrote most of an 1823 show around it and repeated it for another show in 1829 which he imaginatively entitled *Home, Sweet Home*. William Balfe (1808-1870) was another highly successful writer of English dialogue operas, choosing for his 'arias' a good, singable, ballad-style melody which would ensure profitable sheet-music sales. Publishers saw an opportunity for plugging their products, and in 1866 there started a long series of Royalty Ballad concerts, in which several singers would perform songs from that publisher's catalogue. Professional singers received a fee or royalty for every occasion they performed a publisher's song, and it is clear that they sang many pieces without particular regard to their quality. Royalty ballad concerts continued well into the twentieth century, the latest I know of being Cramer's 143rd concert at the Wigmore Hall in January 1938.

The back covers of songs published in the late nineteenth and early twentieth centuries give us an entertaining glimpse of this royalty ballad world. The songs were usually available in three keys, sometimes four, and alongside each one was often printed a singer's name, presumably the one who was paid a royalty for his or her endorsement. Many of these singers were doubtless well known in their day but have since fallen into obscurity, but there were others whose names should be familiar to a modern reader with a passing knowledge of musical history: Nellie Melba, Clara Butt, John McCormack, Plunket Greene and Gervase Elwes. The list of composers is fascinating as well, since it includes not only those who specialised in the sentimental style of ballad or parlour song (Stephen Adams, Wilfrid Sanderson, Amy Woodforde-Finden and Hermann Löhr, for example) but also those who are now more associated with the concert hall (Elgar, Vaughan Williams, Quilter and Ireland). An accusation which has been levelled at English song composers of the period in question is that they were tainted with this commercial side of the music business and demeaned their art by selling out to the demands of popular taste. My reply would be that the performer or listener should form his or her own opinion on the merits of each song without being too concerned about what the established pundits might say.

A third platform for English music, but one which was not specifically intended for the entertainment of the middle class, or indeed any class at all, was the Church. The cathedrals and Oxbridge colleges have for centuries nurtured a form of music-making which was only briefly interrupted in the seventeenth century by the Commonwealth. These institutions have during that time been major training grounds for English musicians, educating boys at special schools and providing employment for composers, organists and teachers. It must be admitted that pay and conditions were often atrocious, and standards were for long periods rather low, especially during the first half of the nineteenth century. But many of the best native musicians held church posts: Purcell (*qv*), Blow (*qv*), Greene (1696-1755), Boyce (1711-1779), Attwood (1765-1838) and S S Wesley (1810-1876) among others. All of these were involved in the writing of songs as well as church pieces, though Wesley's songs were of a religious nature. Wesley's father, Samuel (1766-1837), wrote more than fifty songs, and though he never held a salaried position of any sort, he was the foremost organist of his day and an important writer of music for the Anglican liturgy. Samuel Wesley had his attention drawn to the young George Pinto (1785-1806), whom he considered to be a genius, and who, in the space of only three years, wrote a sufficient quantity of music to show that this judgment was not far off the mark. The few songs that he wrote give a tantalising idea of what he might have achieved in that field had he lived longer.

The standard of musical education in England was a burning issue for a very long time, as it still is today. As early as 1729 Daniel Defoe had proposed that an academy should be set up to train British performers and reduce the great numbers of foreigners who played in London's orchestras, but nothing was done. In 1774 Charles Burney put forward ideas for a music school similar to those he had seen in Italy, but again, nothing came of it. At last, in 1822, the Royal Academy of Music was founded, not as a college for students of eighteen and over, as now, but as a residential school for quite small children. One of the first pupils was William Sterndale Bennett (1816-1875), who enrolled in 1826. He performed his first piano concerto in 1832 to great acclaim, giving a command performance to the king. Mendelssohn was so impressed that he insisted Bennett come to Germany as his guest, and his visits there over the next few years proved to be a huge professional success, including accolades from the great Robert Schumann himself. His early years saw more piano concertos, symphonies and overtures, but after he started teaching in 1838 a decline set in. Pressure of work, lack of encouragement and recognition, and a rather 'fundamentalist' view about the highest standards of composition and style all served to choke off his creative abilities. His songs have a distinctly Mendelssohnian flavour, unlike any others being written in England at the time, but rather than being forerunners of an established English *Lieder* tradition they give us a hint, as do the songs of Pinto, of what might have been but never was.

Lack of a decent system of musical education was not the only problem facing English composers. The national psyche was an even greater obstacle to the development of music. Peter Pirie in his book *The English Musical Renaissance* (Gollancz, 1979) wrote: 'Napoleon was defeated by a nation of shopkeepers, and England was a shop; a brisk, philistine emporium with a stinking factory in the back premises'. Graft on to this commercial and industrial powerhouse an ethic of charitable condescension to the masses, a high moral tone and a repression of all sensual elements, with the artist portrayed as a dangerous and libidinous reprobate, and a picture of the Victorian era emerges. A man at the forefront of establishing a revival in English musical standards at this time was C H H Parry (1848-1918). He had to work within the confines of Victorian sensibilities, which he naturally shared with the music-loving middle-class public, but it is significant that he admired Wagner's music and betrayed its influence in his own compositions. He joined the staff of the Royal College of Music at its inauguration in 1883, and became its director in 1894. In 1900 he also took the professorship at Oxford, and through his music, his educational work and his scholarship he made a decisive contribution to raising the profile of English music. His many songs show a real appreciation of text and prosody, great care in conception and execution, and a fine melodic gift.

Perhaps even more influential than Parry was C V Stanford (1852-1924), whose position as professor of composition at the Royal College of Music from 1883, and as professor of music at Cambridge from 1887, meant that most of the following generation of English composers studied under him at some time. It would be wrong, though, to describe him only as the teacher of such famous pupils as Ireland, Butterworth and Vaughan Williams. As a composer in his own right he made important contributions to church music, choral music, song and, unusually for his time and place, opera. His whole musical perspective was coloured by the knowledge and experience he had gained from travelling and studying abroad, and, naturally enough, by his Irish upbringing. His songs number more than one hundred and fifty, and they display a wider range of style and mood than those of Parry, with more of the humorous and earthy in them.

The English composer who created the greatest impact at the end of the nineteenth century was Elgar (1857-1934), a man from outside the middle class of his composing contemporaries. His father was a piano-tuner and kept a music shop in Worcester, lacking the means to send his son to study in London or abroad. His musical knowledge was largely gained through listening and playing. The early years were a struggle for technique, self-esteem and recognition, in which he played the violin, taught music and composed. His innate genius was given form by hearing and studying the European music of the time, and the works which resulted place him among the great masters of his age. Many of Elgar's songs, apart from the wonderful *Sea Pictures* of 1899, are often dismissed as lightweight creations in a popular style ill-befitting a serious composer. Performers need the courage to disagree with such grand statements if they feel like it, and if necessary reject the musicological snobbery involved; Quilter (1877-1953) is another whose reputation is compromised by the very attractiveness and accessibility of his songs. Elgar's music has a distinctive, English voice, and yet it does not hark back to an English Golden Age in the conscious manner of some his younger contemporaries.

An element so far missing in this short history is any mention of folk-song. Broadside ballads used tunes whose origins very often lay in an unknown past, united with new words to suit the publishers' needs. They were an urban phenomenon and a product of technology. Folk-songs were rural creations, again rooted in a distant past, and always handed down by word of mouth; they were apparently untainted by modern processes. Their harmonic framework was usually modal or pentatonic, untouched by the ideas of Beethoven or Wagner, and outside the strictures of dry academicism. Vaughan Williams (1872-1958), Holst (1874-1934), Butterworth (1885-1916) and Grainger (1882-1961) embraced the folk-song as a means of solving the thorny problem of creating a new music that did not merely imitate the developments happening on the continent. Others, notably Somervell (1863-1937), Bridge (1879-1941), Ireland (1879-1962) and Gurney (1890-1937), kept away from the folk-song revival, while Delius (1862-1934) used folk melodies as an embellishment, not an inherent part of the harmonic structure.

One of the most important poetic events in the story of English song at this time was the publication in 1896 of A E Housman's *A Shropshire Lad*. Here was a set of poems, ideal as song lyrics, which described rural scenes of love, betrayal, youth and death, in a quintessentially English landscape. The connections with the nostalgic, pre-industrial world of the folk-song made these poems irresistible to a great number of composers, even those who, like Somervell and Gurney, avoided the folk revival. Vaughan Williams's *On Wenlock Edge* is justly famous, as are the two sets by Butterworth. The Great

War gave a new and terrible significance to many of the poems, and the settings by Ireland, Gurney and Moeran (1894-1950) transmit a darker colour. Heard in retrospect, Butterworth's songs, written before the war, possess a strange, prophetic tone as if foreshadowing his own death. The economy of means which he uses enables the poetry to speak with marvellous clarity.

Another way whereby composers sought to find a different voice was in the use of deliberately archaic musical idioms. The work of Arnold Dolmetsch (1858-1940) in rediscovering and recreating Renaissance and Baroque music practices was part of a general reassessment of music's past. The most celebrated song composer to have written in this way was Warlock (1894-1930), who not only chose many texts from the fifteenth and sixteenth centuries, but often set them with Tudor cadences, modal figures, false relations and *tierces de Picardie*. Finzi (1901-1956) also used some of these elements, particularly the false relation, but his music did not have the density and chromaticism of Warlock. One of his greatest achievements was to reinvent the recitative, returning to the text to establish the true rhythm and melody of the song. His settings of Hardy's poems are only rivalled by those of Britten (1913-1976), with his *Winter Words*.

Benjamin Britten created many enduring masterpieces of vocal music; songs with piano, songs with instrumental or orchestral accompaniment, choral works and, most important of all, his operas. He and Tippett (1905-1998) established Great Britain as a centre for new opera, and their successors include Maxwell Davies, Birtwistle, Turnage, Finnissy, Knussen and Weir. There is a good deal of interest and activity in the field of opera, and although it is so expensive to produce, there are many people and organisations prepared to support it. One of the major patrons of new music, the BBC, has commissioned hosts of works for broadcast, especially for voice and instrumental ensemble. Unfortunately, financial cut-backs and policy decisions have resulted in a drastic curtailment of this patronage. Composers continue to produce a bewilderingly diverse array of works for voice, but the opportunities for performing these songs have become progressively rarer. There was once a thriving market for songs for amateurs to sing around the ubiquitous parlour piano, but where are the singers and where are the pianos? For those who wish to sing, the piano has been replaced by the karaoke machine, and the amateurs are belting out their Abba or Sinatra or Lloyd Webber with just as much enjoyment and just as little finesse as their great-grandparents did when they sang *Little grey home in the west* or *Now sleeps the crimson petal*. The more discerning still have choral societies to join, but there are fewer of those than there used to be, and if they have an interest in the art-song repertoire they are attracted to the concert hall and CD player where the professionals do it all for them. The most depressing factor of all is the inability of the education authorities to understand how making music stimulates the mind, improves children's ability to concentrate and learn, and increases social awareness. Schools have been forced to adopt a curriculum which squeezes music out because of a lack of time and resources, and children are not being given the benefits which music can bring.

If the picture seems at present to be one of increasing gloom and songlessness, my feeling is that this downturn will not last. I am certain that educational policy will change yet again, and some bright spark will rediscover that music is an important activity after all. Indeed, the karaoke machine, the choral society or the crowd singing football songs are all telling us that human beings have an unquenchable desire to sing. Most people sing in the car or around the house from time to time, and when they do, it is usually a sign that they are feeling well and relaxed. This private singing acts as a kind of therapy, a release of tension and anxiety, and although the context is different, singing with a group or a crowd can have even more powerful effects. Because it is such a deep-seated human urge, singing will always be a part of our lives, and somewhere in all this vocal activity there will be a place for formal or serious solo song. Song writers will always be on hand to help us give voice to our expressive needs, and I believe that the future has wonderful things in store for us. Maybe in a world of increasing noise, people will wish for unaccompanied songs, or maybe all the verbal overload we suffer from will give us a taste for wordless vocalising. Improvisation may be one of the ways of the future, offering a flexible guide for the singer to follow. Many people are already using their voices in a deliberately therapeutic way, toning or chanting separately or together, synthesising elements from around the world, and I expect this will be another thread in the tapestry of the future. However it may turn out, let's enjoy all the richness we have now.

8 – The Poets

It is often found that a composer has a particular affinity with a certain poet. For example, Finzi set by far the largest number of Thomas Hardy's poems – seventy-seven if one includes all the fragments – more than all the other English song composers of this century put together. Bantock set more Browning than anyone else; Armstrong Gibbs more de la Mare. There are many possible reasons for this, most of them doubtless deeply psychological, but it is beyond the scope of this book or this writer to do more than draw attention to it as a fact. There are also poets whose works have inspired many composers to try setting them to music, and there are certain poems which have provoked many songs, some of which will be found in the *Songlines* section. There are no prizes for guessing that the poet with the greatest number of composers putting their music to his words is Shakespeare, while not far behind are Tennyson, Shelley, Blake and Housman. In this chapter I have made a list of some of the most 'popular' poets (from the composer's point of view), with a short biography of each.

The poets I have chosen, in order of birth date, are as follows:

> Shakespeare, William. 1564-1616.
> Dekker, Thomas. c 1570-1632.
> Jonson, Ben. 1572-1637.
> Fletcher, John. 1579-1625.
> Herrick, Robert. 1591-1674.
> Blake, William. 1757-1827.
> Burns, Robert. 1759-1796.
> Scott, Sir Walter. 1771-1832.
> Moore, Thomas. 1779-1852.
> Shelley, Percy Bysshe. 1792-1822.
> Keats, John. 1795-1821.
> Tennyson, Alfred, Lord. 1809-1892.
> Browning, Robert. 1812-1889.
> Whitman, Walt. 1819-1892.

Rossetti, Christina. 1830-1894.
Hardy, Thomas. 1840-1928.
Bridges, Robert. 1844-1930.
Stevenson, Robert Louis. 1850-1894.
Mcleod, Fiona. [William Sharp] 1855-1905.
Housman, Alfred Edward. 1859-1936.
Kipling, Rudyard. 1865-1936.
Yeats, William Butler. 1865-1939.
de la Mare, Walter. 1873-1956.
Masefield, John. 1878-1967.

Shakespeare, William (1564-1616) was quite simply the most important literary figure in the history of the English language, whose influence is still felt in the words and expressions we use in our day-to-day conversation. Not only are modern English-speakers aware of some of the great speeches from the plays: 'To be or not to be'; 'Once more unto the breach'; 'I come to bury Caesar'; and so on and so forth, but we use idioms such as 'poor but honest', 'salad days', 'murder most foul', 'method in his madness' and hundreds more. Many of the words we speak were either invented by him or first recorded by him. Indeed, such is the posthumous fame of the man that there are societies devoted to proving that he could not possibly have written all of this but that some other genius must have done so. Marlowe, Bacon and the Earl of Oxford all have their devotees in this respect, but I am content to assume that the man baptised William Shakespeare did all that is reported of him.

Surprisingly little is known of the life of someone whose name was celebrated even in his own lifetime. He was born in Stratford in 1564 and married Ann Hathaway at the age of eighteen, by whom he had two daughters and a son. By the time he was thirty he was in London, having written several plays including *Richard III* and *The Taming of the Shrew*. In 1599 he and other shareholders of The Lord Chamberlain's Men dismantled The Theatre in Shoreditch whose landlord was trying to get them out, and rebuilt it in Southwark as The Globe. In 1603 the Chamberlain's men were made members of the royal household and renamed the King's Men. The ten years or so from 1598 onwards saw the writing of his greatest works, including comedies and the great tragedies. The Globe was destroyed by fire in 1613, and he probably lived in Stratford from then until his death in 1616. He was well known not only as a playwright but also as a poet, especially on account of the sonnets, published in 1609. My researches so far find that only nine of the sonnets have been set to music, of which Parry set seven. Only two of Parry's, in my opinion, are at all successful: *O never say that I was false of heart* and *No longer mourn for me*. It is not the sonnets, however, which have provided the large number of song-texts but the lyrics from the plays.

We should not be surprised that it is the lyrics which have caught the composer's eye, since they were designed for singing in the first place. This distinguishes them from many of the later poems dealt with in this book, which were intended either for silent reading or for spoken recitation. The four songs most often set are *O mistress mine, It was a lover and his lass, Come away, come away, death* and *Blow, blow thou winter wind*. Two of these are from *Twelfth Night* and two from *As You Like It*, both mature comedies from Shakespeare's time at The Globe.

Dekker, Thomas (c 1570-1632). Far less is known of him even than of Shakespeare, and apart from his huge output of plays and masques (over fifty in all) and his pamphlets, his personal life is only touched on by references in the diary of Philip Henslowe, for whose group he wrote most of the plays. He seems to have had persistent problems with money which led to his imprisonment for several years. The songs from the plays most frequently set were *Golden Slumbers, Sweet Content* and *The merry month of May*.

Jonson, Ben (1572-1637). A colourful character with an obviously pugnacious streak, he is first described as an actor in 1597 when he was imprisoned for performing in a play called *The Isle of Dogs*. Before this he had probably worked as a bricklayer and a soldier, and was already married. He killed another actor in a duel and was scathing in his opinions of other actors generally. He was charged with popery and treason in 1598, having become a Catholic in that year, but managed to get out of that with forfeiture of property and a brand on his thumb. An early play of his, *Every Man in his Humour*, performed in 1598, had

Shakespeare (*qv*) in the cast. In 1604 he wrote *The King's Entertainment* with Thomas Dekker (*qv*). Notwithstanding his difficulties with authority he was given a royal pension and made the first Poet Laureate in 1619, and he remained for the rest of his life the lion of the English theatre. His poems are considered to be the forerunners of those of the later Cavalier poets, among them Herrick (*qv*), Lovelace and Suckling, all three of whom produced lyrics which composers later made into songs.

Fletcher, John (1579-1625) was a dramatist whose name is most often linked with Francis Beaumont, with whom he wrote a great number of plays, especially after they had together taken over as chief playwrights for the King's Men when the company moved to Blackfriars. He is thought to have collaborated with Shakespeare (*qv*) on the writing of *Henry VIII* and *The Two Noble Kinsmen*, and his most celebrated solo piece was *The Faithful Shepherdess*. The tragi-comedies *Philaster* and *The Maid's Tragedy*, amongst others, influenced the work of the later Restoration dramatists. Of the dozen or more poems which composers have used, the one most often set was *Orpheus with his Lute*, and Arthur Sullivan's song must have put off generations of children, forced to sing it in unison, from ever having anything to do with music again.

Herrick, Robert (1591-1674) was apprenticed to a goldsmith at the age of sixteen, and only went up to Cambridge at twenty-two. He took Holy Orders and enjoyed for some time the delights of London society, so that it was at first a shock to him when he was appointed to a parish in deepest Devon in 1629. He soon settled in to a peaceful existence there but lost the living during the time of the Commonwealth because of his Royalist sympathies. After the Restoration he returned and spent the rest of his life there. Herrick was one of the Cavalier Poets who were influenced by the work of Ben Jonson (*qv*) and whose friend he became. His pastoral lyrics are generally happy and contented in tone, and even the melancholy ones show an enjoyment and appreciation of life and beauty. His one published volume of verse, *Hesperides*, contained 1200 poems, many of which lend themselves to song-writing: *Gather ye rosebuds while ye may* became one of the most famous and popular song lyrics of the seventeenth century. Later composers set a large number of different Herrick poems, of which *To Daffodils* seems to have most appealed to song writers. Quilter's *To Julia*, a set of six poems, deserves special mention.

Blake, William (1757-1827) has achieved lasting fame as both a painter and a poet, with his poem *Jerusalem* in its setting by Parry almost reaching the status of an English national anthem. He was first of all an engraver, whose independence of mind and spirit led him to create and publish works of an extraordinary visionary quality which combined his poetic and visual skills in a unique and challenging way. All his work is mystical in tone, with a personal mythology which he developed over time to convey his own direct experience of God and creation. Blake's dislike of authority, especially of the church, provoked his arrest at one point for sedition (a plot to overthrow the government), and his friendship with the radical Thomas Paine cannot have helped his cause. His self-published books were only made in fairly small numbers, which meant that his reputation during his own lifetime was based on rumour and hearsay, which portrayed him as a strange, eccentric character. Not until after his death did his importance as a poet become recognised, showing, as he did, the necessity for the artist not simply to portray the mythology of the past but to absorb it and recreate it in a new and personal way. Two of the most interesting Blake settings are Vaughan Williams's *Ten Blake Songs* for high voice and oboe, and Britten's *Songs and Proverbs of William Blake* for medium voice and piano. Otherwise more than forty poems have been set to music by a variety of composers.

Burns, Robert (1759-1796), to a Scotsman, is unquestionably that nation's greatest poet, but his wider popularity today suffers, from the perspective of non-Scottish eyes and ears, from being written in Scottish dialect. I know that people around the world sing *Auld Lang Syne* at the new year, but I wonder how many of them know what it actually means. What is an auld lang syne, and can we find one south of the border? Schumann set several of his poems in translation, and to illustrate the difficulties in understanding the text if you are not a Scot, first read this (from *The Highland Widow*):

And there I had three score o' yowes,
Och-on, och-on, och-rie!
Skipping on yon bonnie knowes –
And casting woo' to me.

Now read the equivalent verse of Schumann's song (*Die Hochländer-Witwe*):

Und sechzig Schafe hatt' ich dort;
o weh, o weh, o weh!
die wärmten mich mit weichem Vlies
bei Frost und Winterschnee.

Apart from the fact that this is a paraphrase and not a word-for-word translation, a German reader can understand immediately what the poem means, whereas I need to translate Burns's original into standard English to discover that 'yowes' are ewes, 'bonnie knowes' are beautiful hills and 'woo'' is wool. Burns's poem is in fact more immediately accessible to a German than to an Englishman, and there are probably plenty of Scots who would raise a cheer to that!

Burns's humble rural upbringing, first as a farm-worker then a flax-dresser, without any formal education, gave him a reputation, after the publication of his early works, as a kind of native genius. However, any financial benefit he may have gained from public acclaim was soon wiped out by his attachment to the good life, and he found that he had to become an excise man to support his wife and four children. His democratic opinions led him to sympathise with the French Revolution, which caused some distrust in influential circles. He died in poverty at the age of thirty-seven. Although there are a considerable number of song-settings, it is to be regretted that so many English composers may have felt unable to explore the possibilities of his poetry, since it was mostly written in traditional song form, either adapting an existing verse or writing new words to old tunes. Perhaps the enormous popularity which these songs achieved after Burns's death may have contributed to later composers leaving his work alone.

Scott, Sir Walter (1771-1832) studied law at Edinburgh University and was Called to the Bar in 1792. He read widely in fantastical works such as Germanic fairy-tales, Gothic novels, ballads, French romances and the German Romantic poets. He published a collection of traditional and modern ballads entitled *Minstrelsy of the Scottish Border* in 1802. It was with his later extended poems like *The Lady of the Lake*, *The Lay of the Last Minstrel* and *Marmion* that he established his reputation as one of Britain's leading poets, but when Byron rose to prominence with *Childe Harold* he felt overshadowed by the younger man and took to novel-writing instead. In this his reputation grew even greater, and he worked at an astonishing rate: there are thirty-two of the Waverley novels alone. Scott became very successful and wealthy, and bought the mansion of Abbotsford in 1812. In 1813 he refused an offer to be Poet Laureate, which went to Robert Southey in his place, and in 1820 he was created baronet. He was nearly ruined when the publishing firm of Constable and Ballantyne, of which he was a partner, went bust in 1826 leaving debts of well over £100,000. This spurred him on to write at an even more extraordinary rate – novels, histories, biography, editing and criticism – so that his health was eventually broken by it.

The works were hugely influential, both during his life and after, on English Romanticism and taste generally, but tastes alter eventually, and by the time of the 'English Renaissance' in music, the fashion for Scott was fading and has continued to fade, so that there are not many twentieth-century settings of his poems. They were, however, translated into many languages during his lifetime, and German sensibilities in particular were already attuned to the romance of all things Scottish by translations of old Border ballads and MacPherson's *Ossian* forgeries. Scott rode the crest of that wave. I quote the following extract from the *New Grove Dictionary of Music* as an example of why a knowledge of poetry can aid one's understanding of a song:

'Schubert's seven settings of lyrics from *The Lady of the Lake* are outstanding . . . Schubert had read the whole poem with care, and, as his accompaniments show, he knew that Ellen in her cave above Loch Katrine sings her *Ave Maria* to harp accompaniment, and that Norman is hurrying as quickly as possible to answer Roderick Dhu's call to arms. *Normans Gesang* would be more popular if modern audiences knew their Scott as well as Schubert did and appreciated the clash between the calm words and the hurrying piano part.'

Moore, Thomas (1779-1852) studied law at Trinity College, Dublin, and at the Middle Temple in London. He received an official posting to

Bermuda, but when he discovered that the job was a sinecure he went travelling in North America, leaving his deputy in charge. Later the deputy absconded with £6,000 of Admiralty debt which fell to Moore to honour. He escaped to France and Italy for three years, working to repay the debt which was in the end reduced to about £700. He became famous for his traditional style of lyrics and for folk-songs that he set to his own or traditional tunes, singing them himself. His most well-known work was the ten volumes of *Irish Melodies* published between 1808 and 1834, and he developed a reputation as a poet second only to that of Byron, who was a close friend. He was highly popular, charming and successful, benefitting to an extent from the foreign fascination with the Celtic Romanticism of Scott (*qv*) and Burns (*qv*) with whom he became associated in people's minds. Berlioz, Cornelius, Duparc, Mendelssohn and Weber were some of those who set Moore's poetry. Later, his verse was condemned for shallowness and sentimentality and largely fell out of fashion. The most famous lyrics in their day were *The last rose of summer, The harp that once through Tara's halls* and *Believe me, if all those endearing young charms*.

Shelley, Percy Bysshe (1792-1822). Although he came from a family of landed gentry, Shelley championed the cause of liberty and wrote against the bondage imposed by religion and politics. While still a student at Oxford he published a pamphlet called 'The Necessity of Atheism', for which he was sent down. Some months later, aged nineteen, he eloped with the sixteen-year-old Harriet Westbrook, causing a permanent rift with his family. They travelled the country preaching radical politics and befriended the like-minded William Godwin, author of *Political Justice*. The Shelleys' marriage broke up in 1813 after two years, and Percy took up with Godwin's sixteen-year-old daughter Mary. Harriet drowned herself in 1816, at which point Percy and Mary married and lived from 1818 onwards in Italy, taking with them Jane Clairmont, a year younger than Mary, with whom they established a *ménage-à-trois*. Lord Byron was by now a friend, whom they persuaded to come and live nearby in 1821. Shelley was drowned while sailing off Spezia, and when his body was discovered Byron attended its cremation there on the beach.

During ten years of an extraordinarily vivid adult life Shelley achieved lasting fame as a lyric poet, but this has overshadowed his reputation as a writer of a much deeper kind, both in radical democratic politics and philosophical thinking. His drama *Hellas* was written to raise money for the modern Greek independence movement, which combined his passion for democracy with his belief that ancient Greek civilisation represented the summit of human achievement. Shelley's humanism was not of an atheistic kind, despite his student pamphlet, since he firmly believed in a universal spirit pervading all things, but he rejected orthodox religion and any conventions which denied love and freedom.

Stephen Banfield, in *Sensibility and English Song*, writes: 'By the end of the [nineteenth] century, settings of the Romantics had narrowed into a number of colourless, impersonal, stereotyped responses to stock poems, chosen for their lyrical ease, offering no resistance to the composer; any simple, well-made tune with a rippling accompaniment would fit.', and he goes on to say that amongst others 'Shelley suffered most'. It is the responsibility of performers to discover for themselves whether this is indeed the case, and my opinion is that there is value to be found in some of these less imaginative pieces, if only to highlight the greater value to be found in the better works. Some poems were set again and again, notably *Music, when soft voices die, I arise from dreams of thee* and *A widow bird*.

Keats, John (1795-1821). His father managed a large livery stable in London, so he and his three brothers grew up in comfortable circumstances, though both his parents were dead before he left school at fifteen to be apprenticed to an apothecary. He gave up his medical studies in 1816 to concentrate on poetry, and was taken up by Leigh Hunt, who published *On first looking into Chapman's Homer* and introduced him to Shelley and Wordsworth. Keats shared with other English Romantic poets an admiration for the world of the ancient Greeks, and the 1818 poem *Endymion* was the first of several based on Greek subjects. In the year from 1818 to 1819 he wrote many of his best poems, including *The Eve of St Agnes, Ode on a Grecian Urn, Ode to a Nightingale* and *To Autumn*. Tuberculosis, which had already killed one of his brothers, began to take a hold, and morbid thoughts connected with his state of health were compounded by money worries and his unsatisfactory relationship with Fanny Brawne. In 1820 his doctor advised him to find a warmer and drier climate than England provided, and although he refused an invitation to stay with Shelley, he sailed for Italy and died a few months later in early 1821. His work remains much admired and well known, being considered by many to be some of the finest in the English language. There is not a particularly large body of Keats settings, but two of my favourite songs are to his poems: Stanford's *La Belle Dame sans Merci* and Britten's *O soft embalmer of the still midnight* (from the *Serenade* for tenor, horn and strings).

Tennyson, Alfred (1809-1892) was the son of a well-to-do clergyman, and left Cambridge University prematurely when his father died, having already published a volume of poetry. The death of his friend Arthur Hallam in 1833 hit him very hard, and inspired his great work *In Memoriam* which was eventually completed and published in 1850. Having received a terrible review in 1833 for a collection of poems, Tennyson refused to publish anything until 1842, from which time to the end of his life he continued writing prolifically and, though extremely shy and awkward, he became highly successful and much sought-after. He was made Poet Laureate in 1850, and created Baron in 1883. Early in his career he was influenced by the English Romantics, especially Keats (*qv*), but became known for his high moral tone and nationalistic voice. Later writers reacted against the Victorian values that he represented, and accused him of wishy-washy sentimentality, but his reputation has survived, above all in his shorter poems. *The Charge of the Light Brigade* is certainly one of the most famous poems in the language, and of the scores of his poems set to music two of the best are Quilter's *Now sleeps the crimson petal* and Britten's *The splendour falls*, though neither can rival Balfe's *Come into the garden, Maud* and Barnby's *Sweet and low* for sheer popularity.

Browning, Robert (1812-1889) was influenced early on by the writing of Shelley, who served as a role model for a time. For many years he was unsuccessful as a poet and dramatist, even after he had published much of his best work. In 1846 he married Elizabeth Barrett, a much more celebrated poet than he at the time, and went with her to live in Italy until she died in 1861. It was the publication in 1868 of *The Ring and the Book*, an Italian 'whodunnit' in the form of a long dramatic monologue, which at last brought him the success he deserved. He continued writing and publishing a great deal over the next twenty years, being much in demand socially, and even witnessing the founding of the Browning Society in 1881. *Home Thoughts from Abroad* ('O to be in England . . .') is one of those poems out of which people can recite snatches even though they may not know who wrote it, and *The Pied Piper of Hamelin* must surely be recognised by every child in the land. Granville Bantock set twenty-nine of Browning's poems, but of more musical value are *Prospice* by Walford Davies and Stanford, and Somervell's *A Broken Arc*, described by Stephen Banfield as his best song-cycle, containing his best song, *The worst of it.*

Whitman, Walt (1819-1892), an American poet, was born in Long Island and lived much of the time in New York. He had a variety of jobs over the years, starting as a printer, then teacher, journalist, carpenter, government clerk and army hospital nurse during the Civil War. He first made a mark on the literary world with *Leaves of Grass*, which he printed and published himself in 1855, and which Emerson noticed and praised, predicting a bright future for the writer. *Leaves of Grass* continued to grow during Whitman's lifetime in various editions from the original twelve poems of 1855 to nearly three hundred in 1892, but it had earned Whitman a reputation as a writer of vulgar and immoral material. The 1882 edition had to be temporarily withdrawn on threat of legal prosecution. The most celebrated of Whitman settings are for voices and orchestra: Delius' *Sea Drift, Songs of Farewell* and *Idyll,* and Vaughan Williams's *Sea Symphony* and *Toward the Unknown Region.* For voice and piano there are notably Stanford's three *Songs of Faith* and Charles Wood's *Ethiopia Saluting the Colours.*

Rossetti, Christina (1830-1894) was the sister of the Pre-Raphaelite painter and poet Dante Gabriel Rossetti. Her poems are full of beautifully observed naturalistic imagery and a life-affirming quality. Although she never married – her engagement to a painter-friend of her brother was broken off for religious reasons – her love-poetry is deeply felt and articulated. High Anglican religious faith was at the core of her existence, and yet her religious poems retain an outlook coloured by the natural world. Of her hymns, *In the bleak mid-winter* is probably her best-known. Songs have been made from more than thirty of her poems, of which *My heart is like a singing bird* and *When I am dead, my dearest* hold the multiple-settings prize.

Hardy, Thomas (1840-1928) left school at the age of sixteen to train as an architect. His own sense of having missed out on a full classical education and of the need to better himself drove him to pursue a programme of self-education under the informal guidance of Horace Moule. From 1862 until 1867 he was in London working in an architect's practice, and at the same time starting to write poems. Back in Dorset again he continued to write in his spare time, and at last, in 1871, had his first novel published. Thirteen novels later, in 1897, he concentrated his attention instead on poetry, and spent the next thirty years producing hundreds of poems in an astonishing variety of metres and verse forms, becoming in the process the most revered English man of letters. His relationship with Emma, his first wife whom he married in 1875, grew less and less happy, and there has been much speculation about some of the causes for this and for his earlier unsatisfactory relationships with other women. In spite of this deterioration in their marriage, when Emma died in 1912 Hardy embarked on an outpouring of poetry to rival anything which had been written in the English language before, expressing his love and guilt and sense of what might have been.

The range of his poems is really extraordinary, taking in comic and tragic country scenes from his childhood, marvellous descriptions of nature and deeply-felt and personal love poetry. Underlying all the work is his own view of the world, coloured as it was by his loss of religious faith and his feeling of man's powerlessness in the face of a pitiless Fate. Time is a constant element in the writing, often in the thought that something has been missed, some unhappy result which, if some earlier action had been different, might have proved happy after all. The composer most associated with Hardy's poems is Finzi, who seems to have shared some of the same view of life, inasmuch as he completed fifty-one Hardy songs if my calculations are correct. It is difficult to single any out from such a fine body of work, but *Channel Firing, The Phantom* and *To Lizbie Browne* are amongst the very best. Ireland's *Her Song* and Britten's *The Choirmaster's Burial* and *Before Life and After* (both from *Winter Words*) are three more great songs.

Bridges, Robert (1844-1930) practised as a medical doctor until 1881, since when he devoted himself to literature. At Oxford University he was an exact contemporary of Gerald Manley Hopkins, whose work remained unpublished until Bridges took on the task himself in 1918. Bridges had also written and published his own poetry, plays and criticism since the 1870s, but it was in 1912, when his collected poems were published, that he became widely known and read. In 1913 he was made Poet Laureate, and he continued writing for the rest of his life, with the 1929 poem *The Testament of Beauty* gaining immediate success and popularity. He was a founder member of the Society for Pure English, and of particular interest to singers is the fact that he was extremely interested in prosody and the musical setting of poetry. He edited a collection of hymns and wrote texts for Parry's choral pieces *Invocation to Music* and *Songs of Darkness and Light*. His Whitman-esque feeling for language, the music inherent in the words themselves, is in all his work, but nowhere more so than in the poem *A Passer-by*, which was set for baritone, chorus and orchestra by Thomas Armstrong. Gurney used many of Bridges's poems, and his *I praise the tender flower* is one of my personal favourites.

Stevenson, Robert Louis (1850-1894) was a novelist, essayist, poet and unsuccessful playwright. He was born in Edinburgh, where his father was an engineer. After entering university to study engineering he changed to law, studying to become an advocate. Travels in Europe resulted in his first published book, *An Inland Voyage*, in 1878. While in France he met Fanny Osbourne, whom he followed to America and married there. Returning to Scotland in 1880 he vowed to make his living solely as a writer, and after some essays and stories he published *Treasure Island* in 1884 which was an instant success, and remains so to this day. Long John Silver must be one of the most recognised of all fictional characters, as must Dr Jekyll (or Mr Hyde), who appeared two years later, at the same time as *Kidnapped* was published. Stevenson had been very sickly as a child, and all his life he suffered from weak lungs, which made his extensive travelling all the more remarkable. In 1888 he went to America for his health and soon moved on to settle in Samoa, where he lived as a planter and local chieftain. During this final period of his life much of his writing was concerned with exposing the myth of benign colonialism, showing it to be merely commercial imperialism. His fictional writing displays his power of invention and his questing adventurous spirit, with strong portrayal of character. *A Child's Garden of Verses* and *Underwords* are his two collections of poetry from which many composers took examples. Vaughan Williams's nine *Songs of Travel* are probably the most important of these settings, inviting comparison, at least in terms of subject matter, with Schubert's *Die Schöne Müllerin* and *Winterreise*.

Macleod, Fiona (1855-1905) was the pen name of William Sharp, born in Paisley, Scotland, and educated at the Glasgow Academy and at the University. He went to Australia for two years, something quite common today but very rare in the nineteenth century, and returned to work as a clerk in London. He became one of the circle of artists and writers around D G Rossetti, whose biography he wrote in 1882. Sharp continued travelling and writing biographies and stories under his own name until in 1893 he started writing mystical and romantic work as Fiona Macleod. He died in Sicily with his alter ego still a closely guarded secret. The Macleod writings belong to the genre of the Celtic revival that had its origins in the earlier Romantic work of MacPherson, Scott (*qv*), Burns (*qv*) and Moore (*qv*), and which culminated in the poetry of Yeats (*qv*). Composers attracted to Macleod were Bantock, Bax (who embraced all things Celtic) and Fritz Hart, whose fifty-five settings suggest to me someone who did not quite know when to stop. Hart also set forty-nine poems of another Celtic revivalist, George William Russell, better known as Æ. Rutland Boughton used Macleod's *The Immortal Hour* for his opera of that name, first performed in 1914 at the first Glastonbury Festival. In 1921 and 1922 it was given 216 consecutive performances, followed by another 160 in 1923, and yet today it is never heard.

Housman, Alfred Edward (1859-1936) was a brilliant Classics scholar at Oxford and was expected to perform extremely well in his final exams, but instead of the predicted First he only scraped through with a pass. He worked for ten years in the Patent Office while also writing learned classical treatises, before becoming professor of Latin at London University in 1892 and then in 1911 professor of Latin at Cambridge. In 1896 he financed the publication of sixty-three poems entitled *A Shropshire Lad* which has ensured for him an enduring place in the history of English literature. The countryside of Shropshire forms the backdrop to short tales of love, betrayal and country life, of murder and retribution and death, and overall a wistful nostalgia and a bitter sense of irony. One theory has it that the bitterness and darkness which pervade the collection stem from his disappointment at failing to do well at Oxford and from his forbidden and unrequited love for a fellow (male) student there. Whatever the truth may be, the combination of classical verse form and English ballad with descriptions of a world remote from the normal experience of modern life proved irresistible to composers. Somervell's cycle of 1904 was probably the first of a deluge of songs written both before the Great War and afterwards during the 1920s. The war itself provided the poems with an additional poignancy, since so many of them describe young soldiers going away to fight, never to return. Both Butterworth sets are remarkable, the Somervell cycle and Vaughan Williams's *On Wenlock Edge* are beautiful to hear and sing, and the Ireland and Moeran settings are very powerful.

Kipling, Rudyard (1865-1936) was born in Bombay, India, where he lived until the age of six. After his education in England he returned to India in 1882 and worked as a journalist before again going back to England in 1889. His *Barrack-Room Ballads* were published in 1892, the year of his marriage to an American, Caroline Balestier. After four years in America, where *The Jungle Book* was written, he came back to England to settle. In 1907 he received the greatest accolade of all: the Nobel Prize for Literature. He wrote much that has stood the test of time: of his novels, *Kim* especially; of his stories, the *Just So Stories*; and of his poems, *If* remains at the top of many people's lists of all-time favourites. His reputation was clouded by his support in the late 1890s for an imperialist doctrine that obscured his real sympathy for the people of India and for the common soldier, which he had so clearly shown in the *Barrack-Room Ballads*. Percy Grainger is the composer who is most associated with Kipling's poems.

Yeats, William Butler (1865-1939) was the son of a celebrated Irish painter, and himself studied painting for three years. He was born in Dublin but soon afterwards the family moved to London, where he grew up, moved back to Dublin in 1881, where he attended the Metropolitan School of Art, before moving back again to London in 1887. He was a founder member of the Pre-Raphaelite Rhymers' Club, and in Dublin founded the Abbey Theatre, for which he wrote several plays. In 1889 he met the Irish patriot and actress Maud Gonne, who features in much of his love-poetry. He first met Madame Blavatsky in 1887, and through her he embraced Theosophy, which he subsequently tempered with a mixture of Hermeticism and Spiritualism. In 1917 he married a spiritualist medium who collaborated with him on *A Vision* which further developed his esoteric and symbolic philosophy. He won the Nobel Prize for literature in 1923, a fitting accolade for one of the greatest poets of the century.

Yeats was the leading figure in the Irish Renaissance, which formed with art and his occult studies the bedrock of his writing. His early poetry takes a romantic view of Irishness, best summed up in his own phrase, 'The Celtic Twilight'. *The Wanderings of Oisin, The Lake Isle of Innisfree* and *The Wind among the Reeds* come from this early period, and it was from these that composers mostly chose their song lyrics rather than the tremendous later works like *The Tower* or *The Winding Stair* which showed Yeats' mature mastery. Yeats claimed that he was tone-deaf, and his ideas about declamation were mostly at odds with the requirements of musical settings. He employed someone who was not a musician to inspect any song-settings before they were published, and who passed or rejected them according to some unfathomable and capricious logic. Warlock certainly suffered from this treatment, as did many others, and it is likely that there would have been many more Yeats songs if this censorship had not been operating. There are several settings of *The fiddler of Dooney* and *Down by the salley gardens*, but Warlock's *The Curlew*, made up of four poems in its final form, is the masterpiece amongst the Yeats songs.

de la Mare, Walter (1873-1956) was a novelist, short-story writer and poet, and one of a loosely-defined group of early twentieth-century poets called the Georgians, so-called because of a series of five anthologies published between 1912 and 1922 entitled *Georgian Poetry*. Among the other poets featured in the first volume were Rupert Brooke, John Masefield and D H Lawrence. He is particularly known for his *Songs of Childhood* (1902), *The Listeners* (1912) and *Peacock Pie* (1913). Until 1908 he was writing in an amateur capacity, making his living working for an oil company, but such was the esteem in which his work was held that he received two of the highest British honours: the Order of Merit and the Companion of Honour. The composer Herbert Howells knew him well, and wrote of de la Mare's understanding and appreciation of music and of the process of song-writing. His knowledge of music was developed at an early age at St Paul's Cathedral Choir School, where he was a chorister. His poems attracted a bewildering number of composers; it is astonishing to learn that *Silver*, from *Peacock Pie*, has been set by more than twenty composers. His friend Armstrong Gibbs, who set about forty of de la Mare's poems, achieved his best result with his version of *Silver*, while the best known of all the songs is probably Howells's *King David*.

Masefield, John (1878-1967) was, like de la Mare (*qv*), one of the poets featured in the first collection of *Georgian Poetry* in 1912. At the age of thirteen he left the King's School, Warwick, to go to sea on the *Conway,* but cut short his seafaring career by jumping ship in New York while still only seventeen. During the next few years he held a variety of jobs, bartending and journalism among them, before returning to England, where in 1900 he met Yeats (*qv*), who became a close friend. In 1902 he published his *Salt Water Poems and Ballads*, the work for which he is probably best known. *The Everlasting Mercy* of 1911 was his first extended narrative poem, and this was succeeded by more poetry, verse dramas and action-packed novels. His knowledge and love of the sea were used to good effect in his naval histories – *Gallipoli* (1916) and *The Nine Days' Wonder* (1941) describing the operation at Dunkirk. In 1930 he was made Poet Laureate. The most famous of the settings of his poems must be Ireland's *Sea Fever*, but the poet himself did not approve of it, considering that the rather steady tempo went against the restless and urgent quality of the text. Ireland seems to have developed a love-hate relationship with the song over the years, acknowledging that he thought it possibly his best song, but suffering nonetheless in a way that so many artists must have done when people associate them with just one well-known work; we are told that *Bolero* affected Ravel in a similar way.

Song-writers, naturally, didn't stop with the poetry of Masefield, and all the foremost English poets since then have had some settings made. Auden, Betjeman, Larkin, Hughes, Causley, Kathleen Raine and numerous others have had their work set to music, but composers of this century have still turned to the literature of the past for much of their inspiration, increasing yet further the number of settings of poets from this chapter's list. There is of necessity a time-lag between the publication of poems and the appearance of a quantity of songs derived from them, and in another fifty years from the writing of this book there will presumably be quite an extension to this catalogue. My purpose is to reflect what already exists rather than to try and predict what may come in the future.

9 – Songlines

The printed paper that you buy entitled 'Come into the garden, Maud' or 'Erlkönig' is not a piece of music; it is a series of instructions, in a code familiar to musicians, for performing the song of that name. The composer set out those instructions with the intention that the sounds which he or she had in mind should be reproduced by singers and accompanists. The printed notes on the page are not the song. The song only happens at the moment the performers make the sounds, and those sounds are different every time the song is heard. Musicians make a continuous series of choices about all aspects of the piece and create, in the process, a unique work of art. If it were otherwise, the efforts of an untrained novice would stand as the equal of an artist like Ann Murray or Ian Partridge. The performer is a co-creator of the music alongside the composer, and the great performing artists have always understood that. I want to stress the importance of this idea of co-creation because it enables us to escape from the dead hand of the past and proclaim the relevance of what we are doing. Mere reproduction of old forms makes the living musician redundant; we may as well listen to a CD of an acknowledged master and take up chicken farming.

Indeed, my next point concerns the difficulties we have with recordings. If we feel overwhelmed by the past as represented by the great band of dead composers, we also feel intimidated by recordings of dead or living musicians. Fischer-Dieskau has had such an enormous influence on the interpretation of Lieder over the last half century that he is the yardstick by which all other performances are judged. Schumann's *Ich grolle nicht* has optional upper notes on 'Herzen frisst' which are printed in small type; Fischer-Dieskau took the upper option (with great success) and condemned those of us who cannot manage top As like that to a sense of failure, as if that were the only correct and acceptable way to sing the song. Another singer who firmly stamped his own character on the music he sang was Peter Pears, and if we are considering the songs of Benjamin Britten we know that those were the sounds the composer had in mind. Even recordings made only yesterday can carry a great weight of discouragement for the young singer who cannot imagine achieving such mastery and control.

In the earlier chapters of this book I have attempted to give some ideas about how a singer might tackle a new song, particularly with regard to meaning, tempo and phrasing. In order to give further assistance I have chosen some songs as examples of what you may be presented with, and I give a few comments on performing them. I must apologise to those of you who are familiar with the repertoire and who will doubtless be upset that I have omitted so much, but limited space forces difficult choices. First of all, apart from the songs of the earlier composers, Purcell, Arne and the Linleys, I have concentrated on songs with keyboard accompaniment rather than with orchestral backing. Secondly, there are no American composers represented: why? Because I feel that American song should be treated as something separate from English (or, more properly, British) song, and I do not have the experience to be able to talk authoritatively on it. All along I have been treating the subject from a specifically English viewpoint, and it would be wrong to apply my ideas wholesale to a distinct foreign culture, even though it overlaps ours in so many ways. Thirdly, there are many important British song-composers of the past missing, but this does not necessarily signify my ignorance nor my prejudice; it is simply a matter of space. Lastly, I have missed out a large number of today's composers, and again, this doesn't stem entirely from ignorance, since I have performed a wide range of works by contemporary composers, among them Diana Burrell, Michael Finnissy, Alexander Goehr, Nicholas Maw, Nigel Osborne, Jeremy Dale Roberts, John Tavener, Judith Weir and Malcolm Williamson. The fact is that the definitive book on this subject has already been written: Jane Manning's *New Vocal Repertory*, Volumes 1 and 2. Volume 1 contains songs in English by British and American composers, while Volume 2 also includes some other languages. Both books offer hints on the performance of these songs, which are graded according to technical difficulty, and they are full of the wisdom and insight of a deeply thoughtful and articulate musician. I recommend them to any singer who is serious about his or her craft, and I cannot resist quoting from her preface: 'Damning criticism and fulsome praise should be treated with equal suspicion, and it is advisable to acquire the ability to judge one's own work dispassionately.'

The 168 songs I have chosen out of more than five thousand currently available in print or as authorised photocopies are set out in chronological order of composers' birth dates, and, where known, the dates of publication. They cover all voices, both sexes, and a wide historical perspective. I have marked each song as suitable for female voice only (f), male voice only (m) or both (f/m). Opinions will vary about this, and I'm not absolutely sure if I've got it right, since some song texts may be gender-unspecific and yet be set to music in a way which clearly calls for one and not the other. Housman's *A Shropshire Lad* has a generally masculine tone to it, but I see no reason why *Think no more, lad* or *The street sounds to the soldiers' tread* should necessarily be sung only by a man. The old folk-singers from whom Vaughan Williams, Cecil Sharpe and Percy Grainger collected so much material were quite happy to sing songs apparently designed for the opposite sex to sing. Even if women are uncomfortable with the idea of this sort of cross-dressing, they should consider singing songs from collections which are usually thought of as being for male voice but which are really quite suitable for either. Along with the *Shropshire Lad* settings I would suggest the songs of Gerald Finzi in this context.

There are many more songs with a specifically male viewpoint than with a female one, and the biggest factor here must be that the majority of published poets and composers have been male, though the disproportion is now much less than it was. Looking at a cross-section of English songs from the last hundred years or so, I have found that male composers have given about 25% of songs exclusively to men and only 4% to women, whereas female composers have given about 6% to men and 20% to women. My chosen songs are about 25% men only and 12% women only. Each song is marked as being suitable for high, medium or low voice, with the original key underlined where there is a choice. This is not by any means definitive, and I would expect many sopranos to sing mezzo songs and vice versa, basses to sing baritone songs, and so forth. When in doubt, try it out. Michael Pilkington's book, *English Solo Song* (Thames, 1998), is a mine of information about the songs available and where to find them, and it has been my major source for compiling the list of publishers.

Counter-tenors occupy a special place in the song repertoire, since from soon after the time of Purcell the voice became confined to cathedrals and college chapels. It wasn't until this century and the presence of Alfred Deller that the counter-tenor again became a recognised solo voice. Deller's successors have inspired composers to write an astonishing number of songs for the counter-tenor voice, and the American singer Steven Rickards has just completed his doctoral thesis listing the songs available. He tells me that the list is over nine hundred pages long, mainly of songs by British composers, and although as I write this (Christmas 1999) he doesn't have a publisher, I expect it will be obtainable somehow before long. Meanwhile, there should be nothing to prevent counter-tenors from singing songs from the standard repertoire if they wish to do so.

There are times when I appear to be laying down the law about the interpretation of the songs I have chosen, and certainly I feel strongly about the subject. Don't take me too seriously, though, but read my remarks as a collection of hints which you can use or ignore as you wish, keeping at the forefront of your mind the knowledge that your performance is your own unique creation which should spring from your own sensibilities and experience. Be aware, though, that these opinions of mine are based on years of singing these songs or others like them, and that at least they offer a starting point for your own development. My excitement in writing this is not in the idea that some sort of uniform style or 'school' might appear, but in the hope that readers will gain some insight into performing this music, and a love and enthusiasm for it through what I have set down. The most exciting thing for a teacher is to watch a pupil's growth from inexperience to understanding, creativeness and independence. My task will be complete when the reader writes the book that makes this one redundant.

Henry Purcell (1659-1695)

1. Fairest Isle – from King Arthur (Dryden) – 1691

The original key of this song is B flat, but that was at the pitch of the time, not at modern pitch. The note A was not 440 as now in the UK, it was at about 392 cycles per second, ie. a whole tone lower. I'm all for singers using keys that best suit their voices anyway for most songs, and here it seems logical to describe the 'original' key as A flat provided one is using a keyboard accompaniment. The piece in its context has a *ritornello* played by strings, and in those circumstances the song ought to be played in B flat because of the relative positions of the open strings and the specific fingerings required. The word which most aptly describes the singer's approach to this song is simplicity. A gentle tempo of crotchet = 100 keeps the music flowing without sounding hurried. Venus has decided to move from Cyprus and set up home in Britain, making our lasses and lads the most beautiful and most ardent of lovers. The sentiments are understated but nonetheless sincere, and nothing much needs to be done by way of painting words like 'poisons passion' or 'pains you prove' except to use a judicious amount of *rubato* and dynamic shaping. For example, you can bend the tempo in the melismas on 'sweet', 'kind' or 'poisons' with a little *tenuto* on the first quaver, and another on the first crotchet of 'passion'. The first half of verse one is quite quiet, but that of verse two is quieter still. Let the tempo relax at the end of bars four and twelve to allow time for breathing and preparing the answering half of the opening phrase. The third phrase ('Cupid . . .' and 'Ev'ry swain . . .) has new music, and as it rises give it a *crescendo*. The fourth phrase returns to the earlier music and can be *p*, though where the music rises again it can have a *crescendo* and *diminuendo* to the last bar. At the end of the first verse, make a small relaxation of the tempo, hold the note for a full three beats and allow about a bar of silence before coming in on the second verse. At the very end you can make more of a *rallentando*, with a tender final gesture of swelling and dying away on 'love'.

2. Let the dreadful engines of eternal will – from Don Quixote (D' Urfey) – 1694

This tremendous song for bass voice offers wonderful opportunities for all sorts of contrasted vocal effects. *Don Quixote* was a comic burlesque for which all expressions of emotion would have been played up for every ounce of melodrama. This dramatic scena starts off with serious intent, requiring a dark, forbidding tone. The melismas must always be free – indeed, no two groups of four semiquavers should be the same. 'Thunder' begins quite slowly and gets quicker, even doubling the speed by bar four, and then 'rrroar' slows down again. Britten's arrangement has back-dotting on 'crooked', which strikes me as a good idea (an example of back-dotting occurs on 'horrid, horrid' in bar 14). The short notes on 'theirs', 'fa-' and 'dares' are performed shorter still. For three bars (17-19) suppress the volume and the vibrato before making a big *crescendo* on 'within my breast'. Come back to the quieter, more covered tone for 'Despair's', with a *rall.* and *dim.* on 'winds can blow'. The *arioso* which follows proceeds in strict time till the last 'Lucinda's eyes'. When a phrase is repeated, remember to make the repeat different in some way, whether it be louder or softer, smoother or more *staccato*. Always look for the natural rises and falls in dynamics, especially here on 'mounting reach the skies'. The singer is suddenly woken from his reverie when he sees that the mere mention of the girl's name is enough to cause a host of astronomical events. Don't try this passage so fast that you have to gabble, and always follow the rhythm of the words rather than the notes. The slow 3/4 starts fairly freely and quietly for eight bars, but it picks up speed and volume through 'where are now'. The next set of 'where are now's (bar 91) are quieter than before, and the rest of the movement carries on its pastoral way. There is a *ff* outburst on 'I glow', leading into the short, angry 3/4 piece. 'Cool' is timeless and soft for two bars, and 'rail' is only *mf* to keep it in context. 'When a woman' is bitter in tone, and not too fast for clarity of the words (eg, 'scratch' and 'bite'), some of which have been bowdlerised in one of my editions to avoid using the word 'whore'. There is an *allargando* on 'all are witches', and be careful that it sounds like 'witches' and not 'which is'. The slow coda starts with one breath to the end of the first 'good night', make a *crescendo* to the highest 'night', a *diminuendo* and then another smaller *crescendo* to the next highest 'night', and a *diminuendo al niente* to the end.

3. Ye twice ten hundred deities – from The Indian Queen (Dryden) – 1695

The sorcerer Ismeron is conjuring the God of sleep to interpret Queen Zempoalla's dream. The God, incidentally, refuses to comply beyond veiled hints of death and destruction. Imagine the scene with clouds of incense in the semi-darkness and the solemn incantations of the magician. Make a strong *forte* beginning, coming down to *p* for 'Thou God of sleep', then make a *crescendo* through 'tell, tell', back to *f* for two lines. 'Must on her dismal' starts quieter again, building to a strong accent on the second 'dismal'. Be very accurate with the intonation on the discordant notes on 'discord' and on 'arise', where there must be no hint that the B flat might be a wrong note. All this introductory section, accompanied by continuo alone, is fairly free in tempo. The next part, where the violins play, is strictly rhythmical and quite steady. The best tempo is that which allows the semiquaver passages to be comfortable. Use your clearest diction and enjoy the words, letting the voice make ugly sounds at times if you want. 'Pants' can have audible breathing, 'glides' can be extremely *legato* and 'fierce' can have a snarling accent. 'Full of Death' may have a *rallentando*, and 'twisted' and 'round' benefit from bending the tempo. 'From thy sleeping' remains in time, starting *p* and *legato*, and getting a little louder at the end of the phrase. It is usually a good idea to have a simple mathematical relationship between speeds in music of this period, and generally triple-time movements have a quicker pulse than quadruple ones. I suggest that one minim of the quadruple time should equal one whole bar of the triple. Some simple ornaments on the repeated phrases of this gentle lullaby should bring the piece to a satisfactory end. I have two small notes on pronunciation: 'clifts' may just as well be sung as 'cliffs', and 'use', as in 'use to lull thee', should probably rhyme with 'snooze', not 'goose'. In modern English we only have the past tense of this expression, eg, 'we used to travel by stage coach' – and for some inexplicable reason the word in this idiom rhymes with 'roost', not 'boozed'.

4. Sweeter than roses – from Pausanias (Norton) – 1695

A modern scholarly edition of Purcell's work probably assumes that the accompanying instrument will be a harpsichord or an organ, with or without cello continuo (the piano as we know it had not been invented in his time), and the accompaniment will be left as just a figured bass for the keyboard player to realise. This is fine for the purist or for those who have access to these instruments and the skill to create a suitable accompaniment, but for those who wish to programme Purcell's songs in a normal mixed recital it would pose some real problems. Fortunately there are editions published by the Purcell Society, or with realisations by Tippett or Britten, which are specifically conceived for performance by voice and piano. The comments that follow are general remarks which may or may not fit exactly the instructions given in your particular edition. The girl who is singing here has been knocked sideways by her first sexual experience. Admittedly, it is only a kiss, but it is the very first time that these amazing feelings have been awakened, and she is still very much under their spell. The singer needs to enter the mind of this character and feel what she feels. A sensual *legato* is called for, as is a flexible tempo for the recitative sections. Emphasise the second 'cool' a little more than the first, but when it comes to the second 'sweeter than roses' it can be sung more quietly than the opening. Try a *tenuto* on the first beat of 'evening' (second time), and let the melisma on 'warm' grow naturally as it moves downwards. 'Was the dear . . .' builds in intensity as you re-live the experience, falling away again towards the word 'kiss'. Express your shock (quietly) on 'first trembling', then make a *crescendo* to 'freeze' followed by a *dim. e rall*. The unexpected notes and diminished intervals on 'made me freeze' are best served by having no *vibrato* if possible. The piano starts the short *arioso* section ('Then shot like fire') which goes ahead with a tight rhythm, but the singer shouldn't anticipate the new mood on the last 'freeze'. Sing this part quite *staccato* until the final 'fire', with a *rall*. at the end. Now comes the aria, for which the emotional background has already been painted by the preceding recitative, and it almost carries us through to the end in a paean of praise to the power of love. There still has to be light and shade and dynamic contrast, with natural *crescendos* and *diminuendos*, and the second 'What magic' is lower and softer than the first. The one point where recollection breaks in is at 'that dear, dear kiss', and here the aria is interrupted with a *rallentando* and a *tenuto* on the highest note before gathering itself again for the concluding bars.

5. If music be the food of love – Heveningham –
Final (ornate) setting 1695

Non-strophic songs of all periods often divide easily into distinct sections, and with Purcell this is nearly always so. Here we have a floated, timeless opening (the second 'music' a little more than the first) followed by an abrupt change at 'Sing on'. The rhythm takes a hold, helped by the canonic figure in the bass line. Notice how the vocal line varies in response to the words: 'sing' is set to something like a gentle vocal exercise, 'joy' to a more flamboyant figure. Both of these phrases are more *marcato* than the beginning, and they give way to *legato* again on 'for then my list'ning soul you move', where the tempo relaxes and becomes rather wayward once more. The second melisma on 'move' (bar 15) is more than the one in bar 13, rising to the beginning of the 'pleasures' phrase. Purcell's music here suggests that he doesn't have the funfair kind of pleasure in mind, but rather an intimate, bedroom style; a soft and languid approach probably hits the spot. At bar 19 the tempo picks up again for ten bars. Breathe, if you need to, before 'ev'rywhere' each time. The new time signature at bar 30 of the edition I have has 'crotchet = dotted crotchet *presto*', which is not original but an editorial suggestion (quite a good one, in fact). Such straight-forward, simple relationships between tempi generally suit the music of this period, but it would be a mistake to follow the principle too slavishly or to forget that nearly all rhythm has to have a certain flexibility. Let the dynamics happen naturally; the higher 'Pleasures invade' louder than the second, lower phrase; the rising melisma on 'fierce' growing in volume. Avoid breathing, if you can, between 'fierce' and 'the transports'. The second 'though yet the treat' is an echo of the first, allowing a *crescendo* through the *arpeggio* on 'sound'. The last seven bars are back to the timeless recitative style, with a lovely sensual *legato* on 'save'. Stretch the time on 'me' so that you can take an easy unhurried breath before 'in your arms'.

6. *From rosy bowers – from Don Quixote (D'Urfey) – 1695*

Altisidora is pretending to be mad with lovesickness as part of a plot to make Don Quixote unfaithful to his Dulcinea. Treat it as a marvellous opportunity to show off your skills, and without going over the top emphasise all the contrasts. It starts quietly and *legato*, with a sudden change on 'Hither' (shorten the first note of both 'hithers'). Hold up the tempo on the first 'fly', breathe, and then sing the roulades brilliantly with plenty of 'f'. The editor of my Purcell Society edition asks for a *diminuendo* in bar 8 to a *piano* before 'Teach me'; better, I think (and madder!), to keep it quite loud and go for another sudden change on 'teach me'. Lean more on the second 'tender' without breathing in between, and breathe before 'my heart's', giving the second 'my heart's' more tone, perhaps as much as *mf*. Be quiet again on 'Ah' and let it all increase and decrease naturally to the end of the section. 'Or if more influencing' is quite bold but *leggiero*, and you can make a contrast at 'As once on Ida dancing' by singing it quietly and *legato*. 'With an air' can then be less *legato* again, making a *crescendo* up to the first 'goddess', and the second 'With an air' can be softer as the phrase winds down. To maintain the quality of madness, try singing to the end of this section in strict tempo and allow a moment of complete silence before the piano plays the next bar. The voice enters a fraction later still and the speed is much slower. Keep vibrato out of the voice if possible, especially on the very quiet 'cold despair'. Don't anticipate the new mood of 'Bleak winds', breathe after the first 'blow' (taking time over it) and make the next 'in tempests' louder yet. Again, don't anticipate the change, this time at 'My pulse', keeping the whole section fairly quiet. The Orpheus Britannicus edition has a B flat on the second note of 'lump', followed by a B natural on 'ice'; I think that's better than the Purcell Society's two B naturals. In the next part there is an excellent opportunity to display your abilities at ornamentation from 'Say, say, ye Pow'rs' when it returns. From 'No, no . . .' the speed is pretty violent, making the repeated 'mads' almost incomprehensible in the rush, before relaxing a little during 'my heart will warm'. The short arioso on 'Love has no power' establishes a gentler tempo for a while, whereupon the piano shoots off again for 'Wild through the woods' until the *rallentando* at the end.

Thomas Arne (1710-1778)

1. Jenny – Anon – pub. 1752

A tempo of 72 beats per minute is about right for this song. Clarity of diction and characterisation are essential requirements, and imagine you're telling the story with some choice mates over a drink or two. In the first phrase be accurate on the rhythm of the semiquavers, which can easily degenerate into the same as the dotted 'bright as the' or 'happen'd to'. 'When she angry did say' is not sung angrily – that happens on the girl's question. 'Dear Jenny' can be a little quicker than quaver = quaver (which would give crotchet = 108). I suggest crotchet = 126 here, but without the strict rhythm of the opening. The repeats are probably best left out unless you have the confidence to add some ornamentation for a second time around, in which case the 'Dear Jenny' section could be a suitable candidate. Give your impression of love-struck pleading until 'decreed', then be the narrator again for two notes before acting the girl's haughty reply. After a little more of your lovesick tone for 'pressed her still more to obtain' there is a sudden change of tempo (crotchet = 108 seems just right for this), and you can show off your brilliant coloratura. If you are wondering, the allusion to Daphne recalls the legend of her being chased by Phoebus Apollo for lustful purposes, until she is changed by the goddess Diana into a laurel tree. The final section can be exactly quaver = quaver, giving the same speed as the beginning, and you can treat it either in a pseudo-serious manner with the hint of a raised eyebrow, or with a more robust nudge and wink – it probably depends on how many drinks you and your mates have had by now.

2. O come, o come, my dearest – Pritchard – 1736 (pub. 1741)

The Italian term I would use to describe this song is *grazioso*, implying gentle poise rather than passionate ardour. Try a speed of about 84 beats to the minute, and unlike the previous number, sing both repeats. These should be given additional ornamentation to be stylish, but I realise that there isn't a great deal of scope to put in lots of extra notes. A cadenza for the second time at the pauses on 'kisses, oh!' seems like a good idea at the very least. There are two kinds of trill in the piece; the decorative ones which go by quite quickly, and are really only a single shake starting on the lower note ('bring', 'joy', 'attend'); and the harmonic ones, which start with an *appoggiatura* on the upper note ('blooming', 'blend', 'I die'). The tempo can be flexible in places, especially somewhere like 'die, or else' at the end of the singer's penultimate bar. There are several occasions when the sense must be carried through a rest, eg, 'hither bring Thy lips', 'sweets their fragrant' and 'Heal me with kisses'. The second (higher) 'which in a gale of joy' is louder than the first.

3. The fond appeal – Anon – pub. 1745

The *Largo* marking in my score gives a misleading impression, implying that this song is very slow. There is nothing sentimental here, and the emotions being expressed spring from love, not grief. I think a flowing tempo of perhaps crotchet = 76 is called for, and this means that the demisemiquavers (or 32nd notes) are very quick decorative elements, requiring lightness and agility. The third line of each verse ('When each night from you I part' etc.) has a series of short rests, denoting breathless intensity; let the breaths be heard. The ornaments need some explanation, since they are not all the same. Firstly, there are the short *acciaccaturas* which occur on 'Gentle' at the beginning of the song and during the refrain, and on 'from you' in the third line of verse. Secondly, there are semiquaver *appoggiaturas* on 'starting' (line two) and 'the same' (third bar of the refrain). Thirdly, we have quaver *appoggiaturas* on 'part' (line three) and 'true' (second bar of the refrain). Fourthly, there is a crotchet *appoggiatura* on 'true' (sixth bar of the refrain). Fifthly, the trills on 'rends my heart' both times, and at 'with you' at the end, have a quaver *appoggiatura* above the note. Finally, you'll be relieved to read, I would suggest decorative mordents on 'same with you' in bars four and eight of the refrain.

4. The timely admonition – Anon – pub. 1752

The minuet has a stately and polite quality to it, but the girl finds herself melting into passionate submission, though each time she collects herself again. Be clear about this, the subject is frankly and consciously sexual. You begin to get carried away by it all on 'he kissed and I sighed' (verse 2), so make a *tenuto* on the second 'sighed'. By the time of 'his transports' you admit that you've joined in body and soul, and the *tenuto* here can be even more prolonged. Having established a comfortable speed, be careful to get the word-stresses right, eg, 'New pleasure my fancy insensibly took.' With the paired quavers in this passage it is all too easy to stress each syllable. The *appoggiatura* on the second syllable of each verse would, according to the rules of the time, be a crotchet on the upper note followed by a quaver on the resolution. I think you might do this for verse two ('So sweet'), but maybe try it quaver-crotchet on verse one. Don't be bound by a rule you're not happy with if it doesn't feel right; you may be wrong, but it's your performance after all. The final trill starts with an upper-note *appoggiatura*, but the others, being merely decorative, start on the note. Feel free to add ornaments as the song progresses, one obvious one being a crotchet *appoggiatura* from below the note (an A♯) at the end of the second line of the verse on the repeat ('kissed me again' etc.). In the last line of every verse, make a little *crescendo* on the minim ('thought' etc.) for the first time, but it's unnecessary to do the same when the line is repeated, particularly since the underlying harmony carries less tension the second time.

5. *Where the bee sucks – Shakespeare – 1740*

It is usually quite difficult to make an impression with a famous song, and even though this one doesn't present too many technical problems, you have to be extra-good at it. First of all, it needs lightness of touch and almost conversational word-stress. Choice of tempo is crucially important, and although it has a Common time-signature, normally indicating four beats in a bar, there's a feeling of two in a bar; I would go for minim = about 88. Until the melisma on 'fly', sing *leggiero*, not with a full *legato* tone. Give 'merrily' a stress on the first syllable, avoiding any suggestion of 'merrilee'. The last phrase before the repeat, 'After summer merrily', has some intervals which are quite tricky to tune. The repeat of the second section can be really quiet, and whatever your edition may indicate, the song is nowhere as loud as *forte*. Ariel is a spirit of the air, full of mischief, no doubt, but here he's only flitting around the flowers in a light, fairy-like way. The final phrase of all doesn't need to be particularly grand or important, so any *rallentando* is fairly small.

Thomas Linley senior (1733-1795)

When a tender maid – Sheridan – 1775

Try minim = 90 for this song, and never give too much tone. The first time through verse one, keep a strict rhythm until just before the pause on 'pit a pit a pat', but at the repeat (adding some ornaments if you want) make a *rallentando* and pause on 'swoons outright'. The tentative nature of verse one is swept away by the confidence of verse two, especially on 'Then to church well pleased'. At the repeat this time, make even more of an *allargando* for 'contentment prove', and try a slow start to 'and a pit a . . .', with a little *accelerando* and *rallentando* until the pause. Maybe a *diminuendo* to almost nothing would be an amusing effect, followed by a *subito forte* on 'Her heart'.

Thomas Linley junior (1756-1778)

O, bid your faithful Ariel fly – Shakespeare – 1777

There is a balance to be struck between making the tempo too quick for the triplets to be comfortable, and being so slow that the phrases become too long. My choice for this middle ground would be about crotchet = 128. If the phrase 'I'll traverse o'er the silver sand' is still too long, then it is better to breathe after 'traverse' than after 'o'er'. Come what may, don't elide 'traverse' with 'o'er', otherwise we hear 'sore'. The long 'I like mortals never sleep' (for the first time) probably will need a breath after 'mortals'. The second and third versions of that phrase present more of a problem because there isn't sufficient gap after 'mortals'; the answer has to be that you manage it somehow in one breath. Lightness and agility are the key words in this song, and even the *forte* on 'climb the mountains' is no more than a firm *marcato*. The refrain comes three times, so you need to consider ways of varying your approach: ornamentation is your major ally in this, particularly using the triplet figure, but don't forget the possibilities inherent in altering the dynamics. The triplet figure suggests to me that the rhythm in the second bar of the piano is, in the right hand, crotchet tied to a triplet crotchet, then a passing note on a triplet quaver, followed by two crotchets. The left hand has crotchet, triplet crotchet, triplet quaver, then two crotchets, so that the right and left hands coincide. The situation is the same at the voice's entry. 'To the' ('farthest') is made to coincide with accompanying triplets in a similar way, ie, triplet crotchet followed by triplet quaver. This kind of tidying-up cannot be carried through the whole song, since it is clear that there are phrases which are based on triplets and others based on duplets. All the trills start with an upper *appoggiatura*, and my score has a mistake seventeen bars from the *dal segno* bar, where the sharp is missing from the bass A. Ten bars after that, be very careful that the ornamented last syllable of 'merrily' doesn't come out as 'merri<u>lee</u>' with an accent. The final 'merrily' before the *dal segno* calls for a well-turned little cadenza.

George Frederick Pinto (1785-1806)

1. Invocation to Nature – Anon – 1804

I find this a masterly song, simple yet full of invention and expressiveness. The piano introduction can have a free, extemporised quality to it, and the voice takes up this *rubato* for its first phrase as if lost in thought. The singer collects himself gradually and the rhythm has become properly established by bar 15. The *crescendo* builds to about *mf* for the voice, and the following bars in the piano grow to quite a full *forte*. The *fz* marking is a little unnerving until we realise that it is being used to indicate a stress that doesn't have to be very loud, and I think the context of the icy plains and the whispering tides suggests a fairly subdued effect. The discord itself does most of the work, and a little *tenuto* will help. Make a *rallentando* on 'and ev'ry charm renew', and try a turn instead of the marked trill. Don't pick up the tempo again until bar 49 or so, allowing the pensive mood to take hold for a while. Keep the sense through the rest on 'Still let . . . me love', giving plenty of time on 'love' before breathing. The sense carries through two rests in the final phrase.

2. From thee, Eliza, I must go – Burns – 1804

This song begins quite simply, and the *affettuoso* doesn't start taking effect until line three, where a *crescendo* on 'A boundless' leads to a *tenuto* on the first note of 'ocean's' with its remarkable dissonance. Build the intensity during the following *crescendo,* and try a *diminuendo* and *allargando* on 'Between my love and me', with a pause on 'me'. The two 'nevers' are quite free, then pick up the tempo and carry the meaning through 'divide . . . My heart'. Make a real *adagio* in the piano on bars 33 and 34, *a tempo* on the cadential phrase with a *rallentando* into another *a tempo* at the new key of bar 38. Don't sound jaunty on 'Farewell', just warm and expansive. There's a *subito p* on 'A boding voice' and a *rall.* on 'in mine ear'. There is a hesitant quality to the next few bars before the tempo picks up again on 'But the last throb'. The sense of the poem needs to be highlighted a little here, because it is 'That throb, Eliza, is thy part'. The piano hesitates again for bars 69 and 70, and the *a tempo* for the coda has quite a confident feeling, a generous dedication to the beloved.

3. Eloisa to Abelard – Pope – 1806

The right tempo for this song comes from the quaver passages 'Line after line' and 'Led through a sad', which give a rather slower speed for the opening than the first two lines on their own would indicate. 'Ushered with a' has a small *rall.*, with the *a tempo* on the next bar. There is an urgency throughout the following bars, up to 'solitary gloom'. Be careful not to sing 'varietee'. In bar 30 the piano needs to have some clear air between the D major and D minor chords. Make a little *tenuto* on 'Love and Fame', and another on bar 36 for the key-change. Let the sound be warm, but don't be triumphant at this point, because Eloisa is asking to join her griefs to his, not her, joys. The piano can be quite broad in bars 45 and 46, leading to an *mp* on 'Tears still are mine'. The first 'To read and weep' can be *mf* with a *rall.* to the interrupted cadence, while the second is softer and quite a lot slower, with a natural *rall.* The *a tempo* for the coda is somewhat slower than *tempo I*.

Samuel Sebastian Wesley (1810-1876)

1. By the rivers of Babylon – Byron – c 1836

Wesley was first and foremost an organist and composer of church music, but a glance at the list of his few songs shows him setting the great Romantics Byron, Scott and Shelley. This poem is a metrical psalm (By the waters of Babylon we sat down and wept), but because it was written for piano accompaniment it presumably wasn't intended for singing in church. The last two verses of the psalm in the Book of Common Prayer are: 'O daughter of Babylon, wasted with misery: yea, happy shall he be that rewardeth thee, as thou hast served us. Blessed shall he be that taketh thy children: and throweth them against the stones'. For obvious reasons they are usually left out, and although they don't appear in Byron's paraphrase, they do show the terrible feelings lying beneath the surface. Therefore I believe that the repeated 'May this right hand be wither'd for ever' (bar 53) should be a truly passionate outburst. The equivalent passage in the first verse ('oh ye, her desolate daughters') is intense but subdued. At bar 31, where *rit.* is marked, I prefer a *meno mosso*, and the *rit.* and *accel.* in bars 34 and 35 are clearly the wrong way round (see bars 66 and 67). In the second verse the passionate feelings become more overt, and the emotion in 'They demanded a song' (bar 45) is barely suppressed, leading via a *crescendo* in bar 52 to the big phrase 'May this right hand'. The succession of suspensions in bars 56 and 57 tell us to keep the full sound going through to 'harp'. The following 'our high harp' is *subito p* and slower. Delay the editor's *crescendo* until the next bar, when it is accompanied by an *accelerando*. There is a *rallentando* on 'wither'd for' (bar 62) into a *meno mosso* which is slower than the one at bar 31. The final section is all quite quiet, and don't be put off by the disconcerting Victorian quality of 'Oh Salem! Its sound should be free'. After all, William IV was still on the throne at this time, and these harmonies had not yet become clichés. Make a *rall.* on the last 'tones be blended' into a *molto meno mosso* for 'with the voice the spoiler by me'.

2. Collect for the third Sunday in Advent – Bellamy – 1851

This is a high priest's incantation in the mould of Sarastro or Elijah, requiring great nobility and authority. It is *legato* throughout except perhaps for the repeated 'may then be found to be' (bars 46-48) which is louder and rather *marcato*. Breathe after 'ministers' (bar 12) but not after 'assuming', and breathe after 'be' (bar 37). 'May then be found to be' has a *rallentando* into the pause, and on balance I think it better to breathe after it than to go over without a breath because that way one avoids breaking the musical phrase after 'people'. Take plenty of time after the pause and come in quietly on 'an acceptable'. The accent on the beginning of this word may strike us as a bit odd, but do as the music asks in preference to forcing it on to the second syllable instead. Good luck with the final unbroken 'Amen'.

William Sterndale Bennett (1816-1875)

1. Gentle Zephyr – Anon – 1842

This and the following two numbers are part of Bennett's Opus 23. The dynamics of this song hardly rise above *mp* except possibly in the singer's last phrase. I think that *leggiero* refers to the vocal part, while the piano is quiet and *legato* throughout. The voice has a *subito p* on 'from whose heart' (bar 15) which should also be in the piano part. The equivalent moment in verse two, 'tell her not' (bar 33), can be heightened by a *tenuto* on 'But'. The repeat of 'but from whose heart' (bar 20) starts more quietly but has a stronger *crescendo*. The same place in verse two, 'but tell her not' (bar 38), starts louder and grows even more, perhaps to as much as *mf* in bar 40. If you're not careful,

'Limpid rill', a phrase not often used in daily conversation, could be heard as something fatuous like 'limpy drill'; listeners will accept all sorts of nonsense because it's poetry and must have some abstruse meaning.

2. To Chloë in sickness – Burns – 1842

Andante, applied to the voice part alone, would suggest a tempo moving along at about 76. Apply this speed to the piano part and the triplet figure becomes too frenetic. *Espressivo* gives a more expansive indication than *andante* on its own, leading to a metronome marking of 66 or so. Now the passing chromaticisms in the piano have more time to make an impact. The *acciaccaturas* come just before the beat to which they are attached. The opening verse can be rather understated, concentrating on a quiet *legato* with only minimal *crescendos* and *diminuendos*. Verse two has more intensity, using more dynamic contrast and setting aside the extreme *legato* of verse one, but it remains at the same tempo. Verse three can be quicker and louder with even more emotion showing. Exaggerate the comma in 'Can, can' with an additional impetus on the second 'can' (this is another place where we want to avoid inappropriate misinterpretations). Don't make too much *diminuendo* on 'Oh, in pity hear me', nor on 'Take aught else of mine'. A *rallentando* on bar 64 leads to three bars of *meno mosso*, with *tempo I* on the coda at bar 68. Try a *mfp* type of stress on 'But' in the last phrase.

3. The Past – Shelley – 1842

This is another song marked *andante espressivo*, but here the piano figure is twice as fast. A compromise between the needs of the voice and the piano would be about 58 beats to the minute. The first verse is again *legato*, underplaying the emotional content. Make the repeated 'which were the joys that fell' less than before. Turn up the emotional temperature in verse two, but I'm not sure that a quicker tempo is needed – the animation comes through the tone and quality of attack. The *ad libitum* marking in bar 44 suggests an *allargando* expressing a real fear of what form the ghosts' revenge may take. 'Memories' can then be *pp*, not sweet but fearful. The repeated 'with ghastly whispers is louder, but 'tell' has a *diminuendo* into 'joy'. Make a *crescendo* and *animando* from bar 64 until bar 69, where a *dim.* and *rall.* set in before the *tempo I* coda.

C Hubert H Parry (1848-1918)

1. My true love hath my heart – Sidney – 1881 (pub. 1885)

Rubato is an essential element of Parry's songs, and players and singers should dare to bend the tempo quite freely. There are many indications here for slowing down (*poco sostenuto*, *rit.*, *poco rit.* and *allargando*) and generally *a tempo* is marked immediately afterwards. There are two places where *a tempo* ought to be inserted, and they are in bar 9 and bar 14; but these and all the other *a tempo* points should entail a gradual easing back to speed rather than anything abrupt. The sweeping left hand figure in bar 6, for instance, gives an opportunity to create a natural *accelerando*, as does that in bar 9. The dynamics are carefully marked, although I think that the phrase 'I cherish his, because in me it bides' needs to have a *crescendo* all the way to 'me' with its stressed discord.

2. No longer mourn for me – Shakespeare – 1874 (pub. 1885)

There is a good deal of agitated feeling in this song, and the surging phrases in the piano help to drive the whole thing along. Remember that 'mourn' is not meant to sound the same as 'morn', and in the next bar give an accent on 'dead'. Breathe before 'Then (or Than) you shall hear' and again before 'that I am fled'. There is a natural *rall.* in bar 16 and an *accel.* in the following bar to *a tempo* on 'Nay'. 'For I love' is *dolce* and slower, and before the *tempo primo* there is a small *rall.* The next vocal entry is slower again, and the rest of the song never really returns to *tempo I*. Try a floated *pp* on 'Do not so much'. Even at the change of key into the major at bar 56 the mood doesn't alter much except perhaps to increase the sense of resignation. The piano under 'mock' in bar 60 has *forte* marked – make that *mf* instead. There is another *rall.* on bar 65, and this and many other lesser changes of tempo are all part of the *rubato* necessary to bring the music alive.

3. To Lucasta, on going to the wars – Lovelace – 1895

By his own admission the poet is a soldier first and a lover second, so there is no trace of weakness here. The broad *legato* beginning and the gentler *dolce* bars are followed by an emphatic 'To war and arms I fly'. The *animato* in bar 16 is both more urgent and more *marcato*, and this lasts for the whole verse. Make sure you give full value to the vowel and final consonants of 'field' and 'shield'. The quiet 'Yet this inconstancy' is still virile and soldierly, but I find the accents on 'I could not love' rather misleading. After all, *sostenuto* is also marked, implying something nearer to *legato*, and I would sing it strongly but underplay the accents. The *allargando* continues through the bar of 'much' and on to the *a tempo* in bar 43. Make a glottal stop on 'honour' to emphasise the word a little, and be careful to come off the last note 'more' before the first chord of bar 44 to avoid an unnecessary harmonic clash.

4. To Althea, from prison – Lovelace – 1895

This is a splendidly defiant poem, setting at nought the trials of imprisonment when compared with the joy of love; one of the key feelings is confidence. This is another broad *legato* beginning, with an unforced ebb and flow of *rubato*. Don't breathe until 'gates', and not again until 'hair'. Keep the *crescendo* going through 'eye' and don't make too much of an *allargando* on 'The gods . . .' because you will need to have a bigger one at the end of the song. The *p* 'When thirsty grief' is less *legato*, and the same goes for 'Fishes . . .'. The *crescendo* continues on 'liberty', as if that word is enough to start the poet off on his defiant mood again. We're back to *legato* again for the *meno mosso* 'Stone walls', and in order to avoid snatching at the quaver at the end of 'hermitage' to suck in enough breath, take plenty of time. It's much better to hold up the rhythm for a moment than to make the listener uncomfortable with gasps or involuntary accents. The *allargando* on 'Angels' can be given lots of space, and the tone needs to be fed to the very end of 'liberty'. The piano is then *a tempo* for a couple of bars and is *forte crescendo* to the final note.

5. *Why so pale and wan? – Suckling – 1895*

This goes at a fairly breakneck speed, say crotchet = 170, and I have to admit that there is not much call for *rubato*. Clarity of text is of prime importance, so there needs to be a certain *marcato* throughout. If the first verse is generally *mf*, then the second verse ('Why so dull and mute') can be a little less, with a *crescendo* through 'do't' and quite a firm 'Prythee, why so mute', though I'm not sure that an *allargando* is necessary here. The *animato* is quite a bit faster still, and there can even be a further *accelerando* in bar 40 to a *presto* ending.

6. *Bright Star – Keats – 1896*

The poem may have fourteen lines, but it forms only one sentence. This calls for great concentration on the part of the singer, who must aim to convey the thread of meaning through the subsidiary clauses. I strongly recommend reading it several times so as to see where the sense is leading. To paraphrase, the poem says: 'Bright star, I wish I were as constant as you are, not alone like you, watching the sea or gazing on the snow, but constant indeed to my love, living or dying at her breast.' My attempt isn't very inspiring, I know, but it gives an idea of the poem's basic structure. Notice that 'And watching . . .' has as its object '. . . The moving waters', and somehow you have to connect the two. The time signature indicates two beats in a bar, but *Andante sostenuto* refers more to the accompaniment than the voice part. I think that a suitable metronome mark would be a rather slow 45 beats a minute, and this means that a phrase like 'Not in lone splendour' can be unhurried. Let the first two pages be generally quite quiet, allowing for a good *crescendo* up to *forte* for 'ablution'. The way the song is printed makes the word 'priestlike' (or 'priest-like') unclear. After half a bar of *allargando*, keep a slightly relaxed tempo until *Tempo I* is marked at 'No'. After the next *allargando* and *a tempo*, pick up the speed for a bar with the urgency of the syncopation before once again holding back on the *meno mosso*. Parry's changes of tempo give a framework within which the musicians should feel free to use an expressive *rubato*, not every nuance of which can be marked. The bar of 'swoon' at the end is *lento*; keep this slower tempo for the last four bars.

7. And yet I love her till I die – Anon – 1903

There is an ecstatic quality about this poem which is beautifully captured by the musical setting. We are back in the realms of *molto rubato*, especially in the piano part, which has rhetorical gestures in every bar. For example, the B minor chord on the second beat of bar 13 calls for a *tenuto* to underline the heightened emotion, and this effect can be increased for bar 29 and yet again for bar 44 to build the intensity almost beyond bearing. In a similar way, the amount of slowing down for the *lento* passages on 'till I die' can be increased each time. In the first two verses the voice is mostly quite soft, whereas the third verse starts with a full tone and gets louder. There are accents on 'But change she earth'; 'Yet will I love her' is then the climax of the piece, followed by a floated *pp* 'love' and an even quieter 'till I die' at the end.

8. Love is a bable – Anon – 1903

The rhythmic impulse is crucial to the success of this song. There is one passage of expansive *rubato*, and that is the piano's jovial symphonic interlude between bars 55 and 62. At the very beginning the piano has a joky little ambiguity: the accent on the second quaver sets us thinking that the piece has two beats in a bar, with the first chord as an upbeat. There are more syncopations to relish, eg. bar 19, bar 23 and bar 24. The most interesting ones are in bars 45/46 and bars 50/51; here the singer can imagine a hemiola over the two bars as if they were one bar in 3/4 time, giving '<u>canker</u><u>worm</u> <u>of</u> the <u>mind</u>' and '(-) And <u>such</u> a <u>sly</u> <u>thief</u>'. On 'Tis like' (bar 17) hold 'like' with a *forte crescendo* and cut it off without any moderation, then breathe immediately and hold the breath until you come in on the *p* 'I cannot tell what' precisely in tempo. In this way it seems to the listener as though you are searching for the idea of what love really is like but you just cannot find the right words to express yourself. Make a similar effect on 'It is', although this time there is no pause on the rest before 'and yet it is not'. Connect 'desire' with 'It is' by making a *crescendo*. In bar 69, the singer stays *piano* on 'moe', so the piano plays *mf crescendo*. On the long 'hang' I suggest *forte crescendo* rather than plain *ff*, and it only remains to say that diction is vitally important.

9. Sleep – Sturgis – 1907

The song's opening is very calm, quiet and *legato*. From 'Cometh, as one who dreameth' (bar 19) a note of agitation creeps in, moving the tempo along as the *crescendo* builds; but then the tranquil mood reasserts itself until the end. The first phrase of five bars needs to be in one breath if possible, which at 40 beats to the minute is quite a tall order even though the tempo is always flexible. I breathe in the second phrase after 'Sleep', but the ideal would be to go through to 'me'. In the next section the triplets against the duplets can sound stilted and uneven unless you concentrate on a seamless *legato*, thinking in terms of whole beats and bars instead of individual notes. The volume reaches *mf* on 'sands', and here you must nourish the tone and keep it supported notwithstanding the natural *dim.* towards the end. 'Sleep' (bar 31) has a small *crescendo* and *diminuendo*, as has 'man-kind'. Give a tiny *pp* on 'With lullaby', and don't start 'To kiss' at *mf* but let it grow to that dynamic by the top of the phrase. 'Feet' is marked *p*, but that seems to me a rather artificial wrench to the music, and I think that an easy *diminuendo* here is preferable. Breathe after 'feet' and have the courage to hold 'Sleep' for the full thirteen beats at an even *ppp*; thirteen beats is only twenty seconds at this speed, so go for it.

10. Nightfall in winter – Mitchell – 1904 (pub. 1907)

At no point is there any dynamic marking louder than *piano*, though I think there is a certain amount of justification for allowing it to reach *mp* once or twice, particularly on the low notes. The poem needs to be heard and understood, but don't be too 'wordy'. The tranquillity of the evening mustn't be disturbed by over-emphasised and explosive consonants. In Baroque usage it is generally agreed that a dotted rhythm set against a triple rhythm (eg, the left hand of bar 12 against the right hand) is rationalised to become a triple rhythm as well. Indeed, some pianists would now play Schubert's *Wasserflut* in this manner. By Parry's time I'm sure that he would have expected to hear the dotted notes and the triplets clearly differentiated. Delay the first beat of bar 19 to show the new musical idea, and notice that in bar 23 the piano is *p crescendo* while the voice is *pp*. Make a little break between 'day' and 'down' in bar 26, but breathe after 'down'. Try doing bars 30 to 33 in one breath, make a big *allargando* and *diminuendo* in bar 40, and in bar 50 sing 'The' with a *dim.* and 'night is come' all *pp*.

11. From a City Window – Mitchell – 1909

We are presented with a metronome mark but, unusually, no Italian tempo marking. On the third page *Lento* appears, but on the second line it appears again, which seems a little strange, not to say redundant. Given the mood of the opening and the restless quality of the piano part, we might describe it as something like *andante con moto agitato*. The first *lento* section, with its Hugo Wolf first two bars, goes at about 60 beats per minute, and then we are faced with what to do at the second *lento*. If you look ahead for a moment, you will see that on the second line of the fourth page the piano has the same figure as at the beginning, and it seems to make sense to have this at the opening speed of 80 beats per minute. And yet there is no new marking to show a change of tempo here, so this leads me to believe that the *lento* in the middle of the third page should really be *tempo I*. I have not been able to check this out with the original manuscript, but it can often be the case that mistakes can creep in (or omissions can creep out), and you should be prepared to alter things if you feel you have no alternative. Your alterations may turn out to be wrong, but if you make them with conviction you can often carry them through. Having said that, 'And in my breast again' is back to the opening tempo. I think that it's probably a little slower at first, with an *accelerando* over a bar or two. Let the speed come and go from the *poco agitato* as marked, and in the last phrase breathe after 'tide'; to clarify the meaning, the poet could have written 'the hurrying feet, like a great tide, ebb and flow'.

Charles Villiers Stanford (1852-1924)

---

1. La Belle Dame Sans Merci – Keats – 1876 (pub. 1887)

First of all I ought to point out that there is more than one version of the text of this poem, and this is not the one normally found in anthologies. The poem and its setting are in the tradition of Romantic ballads like Schubert's *Erlkönig,* Loewe's *Herr Oluf* or Schumann's *Waldesgespräch.* When a story is being told, as here, it is important that the narrator keeps quite cool and lets the music set the scene. When the knight begins to speak the singer becomes involved and much more expressive. Since he is 'so haggard and so woe begone' he needs an expressionless start, with occasional bursts of feeling. 'Her eyes were wild' need only be *mf* because there's a long way to go. Bear in mind the anguish which he feels, and use that idea to colour the voice. The F major 'And there I shut' has a tenderness of recollection, but the reverie is shattered by the *ff* 'Ah woe betide'. Let the piano delay its *crescendo* here for two beats to make the outburst more extreme. The *allegro* on 'I saw pale kings' is quite steady and emphatic, a little slower than the previous *più mosso.* 'I saw their starv'd lips' is still *mf,* 'with horrid' *mp,* and the quality of the *p* on 'And I awoke' takes its colour from the disorientation of waking again from the nightmare. For the final verse the voice has as little timbre as possible.

2. Golden Slumbers – Dekker – 1882 (pub. 1884)

Apart from the right hand F coming in on the second beat, there is nothing in the first two bars to tell the listener whether this is in 6/8 or 3/4 time, and since Stanford has put *legatissimo* on the score it might be an idea for the pianist to aim for the 3/4 rhythm to avoid any bumpiness in the line. Bar 8 has a syncopation (3/4 against 6/8) as also does bar 21, but keep it bump-free. Take a little time into bar 7 as well as bars 11, 20 and 24. Otherwise sing it simply and affectionately.

3. Prospice – Browning – 1884

This poem was written just after the death of Browning's wife, and the title is a three-syllable Latin word meaning 'look forward'. I take *Allegro con fuoco* here to indicate about 120 beats to the minute, which is not too ridiculously fast for the piano. The first four bars needn't be precisely in tempo, and to establish the question-mark make a *diminuendo* followed by a *crescendo* on 'death'. It's unfortunate that the next line is so close to sounding like 'frog', especially if you are having trouble with phlegm. I have quite a number of suggestions for modifying the dynamic markings, either because they are not clear enough or because they could do with being changed. On 'nearing the place' (bars 19 to 22) make a *dim.* in parallel with the piano but only down to *mp*. 'The power of the night' and 'the press of the storm' are *mp, cresc.* and *dim.* after a little accent. 'The post of the foe' is then *mp cresc.* to *ff* on 'Arch'. Bars 36 to 39 are *sempre ff*. 'For the journey is done' is *mp, cresc.* and *dim.*, 'and the summit attained' is *mp cresc.* all the way to the accented 'fall'. 'Though the battle's to fight' is *mf cresc.* to an accent on 'fight' and then a *dim.*, and a subsequent *crescendo* to 'gained', and it is *sempre f* until the *dim.* at bar 70. 'And bade me' is *mp* but strong, and 'the whole of it' is on a *crescendo*. Bar 88 onwards is *sempre mf* until the *dim.* Breathe only at bars 113 and 119, and where *con passione* is marked at bar 135 give it full *legato e portamento* in Grand Opera style. 'Again' at bar 142 is surely better with a *diminuendo*, and bar 149 is *molto rall.*

4. Crossing the bar – Tennyson – 1890 (pub. 1893)

A tempo of about 50 beats to the minute seems right, at least for the first twelve bars. It can move on a bit from here before returning again to tempo for bar 18. A similar *accel.* and *rall.* works for bars 26 to 30, bars 44 to 49, and bars 57 to 60. Whenever the opening crotchet/minim rhythm appears it needs to be solemn and priestly, and nowhere more so than in the last ten bars of the song. Perhaps the notes in bars 65 and 66 can be weighty and detached, followed by *molto legato* on bar 67. The piano in bar 50 is more than *p*, but obviously the voice cannot sustain a *crescendo* through bars 51 to 59 going from *mf* to *f*. To solve this problem, each phrase starts *mf* then has a *crescendo*. If you don't lose intensity and concentration it will seem as though there has been one long *crescendo* all the way. Try the held 'face' in bars 59/60 as *mf* with a *crescendo*.

5. Songs of the Sea – Newbolt – 1904

This set is marked with 'optional male chorus and orchestra', though it is also very effective with piano (with or without chorus).

5.1. Drake's Drum. There's a terrible temptation to go for the Long John Silver impressions when it comes to 'Captain, art thou sleeping there below?', with optional 'oh, aarr!' thrown in. However, the first edition of the song tells us that the poem 'contained indications of West Country dialect, which for musical reasons are here eliminated' – so Standard English it is. The declamation is mostly quite *marcato* except where Stanford has placed long phrase marks ('And dreaming all the time of Plymouth Hoe') which are *legato*. The one unmarked *legato* passage is at the change of key ('Drake he's in his hammock . . .') which lasts until 'there below'. Don't get too loud too soon around figure 4, because we need a good strong *forte* even on 'long ago' at the end.

5.2. Outward bound. Don't be too slow in this song; the *andante* refers to the voice part, which must have shape and direction, and it is all *molto legato*. Elide the t and d of 'Fast dawns' and 'last dawn', maintain a *crescendo* through 'what shall comfort then' and breathe at that point. If you are clever you can come in on 'The lonely' with the energy of the preceding note, and it won't sound detached. If 'Gray wakes' is *pp*, 'To misty deeps' can be warmer, with a *crescendo* on 'the channel sweeps'. Breathe after 'birth-home' and after 'exile'.

5.3. Devon, O Devon, in wind and rain. The rhythm is implacably strict except for the occasions where *rit., rall.* or *accel.* are marked. Running away with the tempo is a fault to beware of here. There's no need to shout even if an orchestra is accompanying; if they can't play quietly enough, get another band! 'Fetter and Faith' is *mf* to allow for a decent *crescendo*. From 'Drake at the last' it is *p* until 'Pride of the West' at figure 9, although a small *crescendo* is a good idea on 'slept'. Start 'Call to the storm' *mp* with a steep *crescendo* to *sforzando* on 'drive'. Make the whole verse beginning 'Valour of England' *legato* and all quiet. Don't give away your loudest notes until 'lightning' and somewhere on 'wind', and be careful to sing a B natural when it comes during the final *molto rall.*

5.4. Homeward bound. The vocal line has to flow, and yet the running quavers in the piano must sound calm and unhurried. A metronome mark of dotted minim = 40 would be just right, but it does mean that the singer has to create a beautiful *cantabile* line so as to avoid degenerating into six beats in a bar. The first phrase really goes from 'After long . . .' to 'the great ship glides', and the three subsidiary phrases have to be joined across the rests. There is another enormous phrase from 'Northward she glides' to 'dawns at last', and yet another from 'The phantom skyline' to 'sunny mist aglow'. Such long phrases at such a speed as this require great concentration. Many of the notes at the ends of phrases can be held slightly longer than indicated, provided that they fit with the following chords; some don't fit, and these must be cut off promptly (eg, 'last' at figure 14, 'gleam' four bars after figure 15, and 'home' at figure 16). The second 'faint on the verge' (between figures 13 and 14) is softer than the first, and in the last line, if a breath is needed after 'mortal', make a big pause on '-tal' and take lots of time to breathe slowly and quietly; trying to sneak a quick breath at this moment would disturb the tranquillity of the ending.

5.5. *The Old Superb.* Once again we have a song with an unwavering pulse, and although it has a Common Time signature implying four beats in a bar, the quavers in the piano part are joined in groups of four, suggesting two minim beats in a bar. On the whole I would go for the four-beat option since this underlines the solid manly qualities of the sailors, and the speed would be crotchet = 180; this way we can avoid gabbling. For the wordy quaver passages the singer doesn't need a great deal of tone, which might obstruct the detail of the text, but can sing out more in the other parts, viz, 'all our hearts' (figure 17) and 'The Old Superb' five bars later. Notice that 'So Westward ho!' at figure 18 has *forte* for the voice and *piano* for the accompaniment, whereas at figure 23 it is *forte* for both. Tailor your dynamics to take this into account, but be aware also that for the first two choruses a huge sound is unnecessary. The *portamento* at figure 23 can be extended to include the interval between 'twas' and 'Westward', and I would make a big *allargando* at the same time, with an *a tempo* on 'West-'. The *rallentando* at the end goes all the way to the *Presto*, so there is all the time you want for breathing (probably after the last 'lagging'), and 'the' can be any length you want.

6. A soft day – Letts – 1913 (pub. 1914)

Winifred Letts was an Irish poet who wrote in the Irish brogue at times (see the next song), but here she was writing in ordinary English, which should normally be sung in standard RP. The second of the short piano figures at the beginning can be a little more than the first, while the same place in the second verse is played the other way round as an echo. I favour eliding 'soft' and 'day', but breaking fractionally between 'thank' and 'God'. If you do this, please do not add a voiced syllable to sing 'thank – ah – God'. The rest of the first verse has a natural rise and fall of dynamics according to the musical phrasing, but within a *mp/mf* framework. The second 'A soft day' is *mp*, and it is followed by *p* for 'the hills wear a shroud' and the ensuing bars until the *crescendo* to *mf* on 'the rain'. Don't breathe after 'sweet', and make a *diminuendo* from 'rain' into 'drips'. Hold the attention across from 'drips' to 'from', and the piano's final phrase needn't enter strictly in tempo, as an expansive summation of the whole song.

7. The bold unbiddable child – Letts – 1913 (pub. 1914)

Here's a poem written in dialect, and it demands to be sung with an Irish accent. I can't describe in detail how that is to be done, but there are certain obvious things to do: sound all the r's (unrolled) even where they would not appear in RP; make a short 'a' in 'after', and change 'gutter' to something like 'gotter', but with a softer 't' than normal; 'child' becomes 'choild'; change the '-ing' endings to '-in'. Above all, don't be too serious. The general dynamic of the first two verses is *mf*, but of the third it is *p*. *Crescendo* on 'horns when he sees me, will Mick', and just enjoy yourself.

Frederick Delius (1862-1934)

---

1. The nightingale – Henley – 1910 (pub. 1915)

It seems strange to me that this poem is called 'The nightingale' when it is the blackbird's song which joins the lovers' hearts and lips. Never mind the title, it is a beautiful and romantic idea, and if you read the poem without the music you will notice how easily it flows. Delius, though, has chosen to highlight the separate elements – the nightingale's lyre, the lark's clarion call, the boxwood flute, the mad weather and the intense listening – making a distinct musical point for each. As a result, the song can sound disjointed if you're not careful, but it well repays the effort of getting it right. Your choice of tempo needs to take account of the triplet semiquavers in the accompaniment, and something like 90 beats to the minute works. Make the first vocal phrase *legato* to contrast with the rather *marcato* lark's call. The blackbird is *legato* again, and there is a *subito piano* and a slight delay on 'box-'. Give a big (but not angry) *crescendo* on 'But I love' and don't anticipate it at all at the end of 'flute'. Get softer on 'all' and hold the tempo back on 'For his' ready for the *animando* coming up. You will often find that when you are asked to speed up, a good musical effect comes from starting off slightly slower. Similarly, when presented with a *crescendo*, start a little softer, giving yourself more space to produce a *crescendo* which really counts. The breath after 'life' doesn't have much time available; take time, and I'm sure your pianist will accommodate you. 'Weather', because of the way it is written, will have a natural *diminuendo*, preparing for the quieter 'We two'. Don't slow down on 'weather' but let 'We two' take a new, slower tempo. There can, however, be a *diminuendo* and a *rallentando* on 'have', with a hushed and almost timeless quality on 'listened'. The *still slower* marking is probably slightly slower than the opening. 'Till he sang' is marked *forte*, but let it grow out of the quiet 'listened' into a warm *cantabile*.

2. *I-Brasíl – MacLeod – 1913 (pub. 1915)*

There is a fluid chromaticism in this song, so although it starts quite clearly in G minor, it wanders deliciously with the wind into strange realms before settling on D minor, then G minor again for the second verse, returning once more to D minor and, finally, D major. The wind from the west seems to tell of the mythical golden land beyond the sea, troubling the listener with longing thoughts. Your voice needs to convey the heaviness of this yearning, so always sing a true *legato*. The dotted rhythms are never sharp and snappy but languid and sorrowful.

The piano in the first verse has *mf* marked under 'last stars', but the voice continues *piano* until the *crescendo* on 'tree'. *Forte* is full-sounding but not too powerful. Enjoy the weird chords under 'Come away', and try the second 'come away' a little louder. In the second verse there is nothing marked to prepare for the *forte* on 'last stars'; make a suitable *crescendo* on 'where the'. The quiet chord before the first 'far away' needs extra time to allow for the movement of the hands, and, more importantly for the singer, so does the chord under the final '-way'; give this time by closing on to the 'w' on the lower note, holding it as long as necessary, and moving cleanly to the upper note on '-ay'. Please try and avoid a scoop upwards!

3. To daffodils – Herrick – 1915 (pub. 1919)

Delius marks *becoming gradually quicker* on 'We die as your hours do', but I think you should look for a certain freedom in the tempo right from the beginning. The piano introduction is rather dreamy and hushed, so the singer's opening *mf* seems a little too much to me; try *mp* instead. Bars 4 and 6 can have some *rubato*, and the piano needs to spread the chord early under 'haste' so as not to delay the singer's flow. Take time on the barline after 'noon', breathe before the second 'stay' and get a little quicker (and louder) through 'the hasting day', only returning to *tempo 1* on 'evensong'. 'And having prayed' is still *forte*, with a *dim.* through 'prayed together' to *mp* on 'we will' and a further *dim.* to *piano* on '-long'. There has to be a *crescendo* through 'We have' to join the piano on its *mf*, then you can speed up through 'As quick a growth' and slow down again through 'decay, As you'. Now comes Delius's marked *accelerando*, and since you have already moved the tempo around here and there, this time it should be more pronounced. Three bars of *accelerando* is probably enough, otherwise you'll need to apply emergency brakes on the *poco rit.* bar. 'Ne'er to be found' is still *forte*, and you need to tailor your *diminuendo* to coincide with what the piano does.

4. Twilight fancies – Bjørnson – 1889-90 (pub. 1892)

There are many songs where the music serves to highlight some aspects of the poem without getting to its heart. This one captures the very essence of the words with perfectly-judged musical illustration. We hear the strange distant call of the horn, whose troubled harmonies echo the girl's emotional turmoil. The harmony briefly clears for 'fetter my fancy that freely would soar' before once again becoming clouded and distressed. Now there is no horn call to be heard, and this time it is the lack of it which troubles her. The horn returns for the third verse, and as she cries out: 'What is it I long for' the harmony searches for a home key, seeming to find it in F♯ minor, only to settle at last on B minor. The *ad lib* for the piano at the beginning doesn't extend to the vocal line, which should have a measured rhythm. Leave room with your *mp* to reduce further to *piano* on 'Oh, cease' and on the repeated 'when the sun goes down'. Leave room similarly with the *mf* of 'bitterly sighed' to allow for a *forte* that isn't too shrill. Breathe before 'God help me', giving quite a heavy stress on 'help'.

5. *Young Venevil – Bjørnson – 1889-90 (pub. 1892)*

There is no hint at the beginning of this song of the poor girl's betrayal, and even when the birds first tell her to take care we're not really aware of anything very serious. The speedy little four-bar introduction doesn't have to be connected with the voice's entry in terms of tempo; Venevil is happily skipping along, not trying to catch a train. Make a small *crescendo* on 'fire', then try the second 'to her lover' a bit quieter. The marking is *leggiero*, but I think that 'Good day, good day' can be *marcato* for one bar. The way Delius has set the poem, 'Take care' isn't full of foreboding but still amused. Prepare the breath early for 'Take' so that it doesn't sound like a syncopated hiccup, and don't try making two sounds on 'k-c'; stop the voice early on 'Ta-' and then release on the c of 'care' in much the same way as an Italian would say 'ecco'. *A tempo* refers back to the voice's opening speed, and here's Venevil back in skipping mode. 'He took it' is a rough *marcato*, 'Farewell, my sweet' a cruel *legato*, and 'my sweet, farewell' a mocking *piano*. This time the birds' 'Midsummer day's for laughter and play' is no longer sweet and amused, but a continuous replay of the betrayer's mocking tone. They seem to be laughing at her now, not with her.

Arthur Somervell (1863-1937)

A Shropshire Lad – ten poems by A E Housman – 1904

1. Loveliest of Trees

The first essential for this song is a good *legato* – it needs to be really 'sung' even though it never becomes *forte*. Each phrase has to have a shape to it, with as late a climax as possible. The opening, for example, is a four-bar phrase with its major stress on '-long' and almost as much on 'bough'. Don't be tempted by the *p* marking to sound at all weak, but instead let it be generally warmer than that. Since this is a strophic song it's a good plan to vary the dynamics between the verses, and I would make verse two fuller in tone and verse three even less than the beginning. Somervell doesn't draw attention to the darker qualities of the poem, so a softer final verse reduces the surface happiness and brings out something of the sense of loss. This darker side becomes more apparent when he uses the same melody in the very affecting 'Into my Heart an Air that kills' later in the cycle.

2. When I was one-and-twenty

The light-hearted beginning contains no hint of the longing and pain at the end, so make it jaunty and *marcato*. 'But I was one-and-twenty' is all *mf* and at a slower tempo without any further slowing down (*ritenuto* means 'held back'). Hold your concentration over the pause and come in *a tempo* and *subito p* on 'No use'. The second verse starts off in jaunty vein, but at the *poco meno mosso* the pain begins to tell, with F sharp minor, E minor and D major in place of the brighter F sharp major, E major and D sharp major. The two *crescendi* are surges of sound rather than accumulations of volume, and there is a *diminuendo* over 'two-and-twenty', making the last phrase quiet. *Molto rall.* after both *poco meno mosso* and *rit.* asks for plenty of time, allowing lots of room for the consonants of the final 'true'.

3. There pass the careless people

The pain of the previous song has here turned to anger and self-loathing. Bear this in mind at the *pp* beginning so that the outburst on 'His folly' is not entirely unexpected. It has to get louder from this point, so don't attack too hard but keep something in reserve. 'Day' still has a *crescendo* through it, though it has to be cut a bit short for a proper breath to be taken. Even with a decent breath here, another will be necessary either after 'woman' or after 'soul'. Give a weighted accent to 'heart' (still *ff* if possible), to 'soul' (*f*, maybe) and to '-way' (*mf*, decreasing to *p*).

4. In summer-time on Bredon

In contrast with the song before this, we have no inkling at the beginning of the tragedy that has befallen. Play it straight for love and joy, with a sung *legato* reaching to the end of each phrase. At the C minor *meno mosso* cut out most of the vocal timbre and vibrato to give a bleak, defeated sound, but don't sing *pp* until it is marked. Be careful that the mourners don't get a warmer tone. Now, when C major reappears, let the voice show your true feelings of grief and despair.

5. The street sounds to the soldiers' tread

The martial rhythm dictates the speed, and in this case I would put *Allegro non troppo* at the top, expecting a marching tempo of 120 beats to the minute. If the voice is *p* at the start it won't be heard on the low B flat; nonetheless, the bulk of the first verse is fairly quiet. The original poem has 'And out we troop to see' where my copy has '. . . come to see'. Notice the quiet *staccato* accompaniment in verse two, which means that the voice doesn't have to be too loud yet. Where *ff* is marked, give accents on 'living' and 'dry' to help keep the impetus going. For practical reasons the long notes on 'Soldier, I wish you well' cannot be uniformly *ff* throughout. Use accent, *diminuendo* and *crescendo* to make them more voice-friendly. The tempo remains unchanged right to the end.

6. On the idle hill of summer

Non troppo Andante is an unusual tempo marking, and the key to the right speed is found in the piano postlude, where *maestoso* might fit the bill. The marching pace of the previous song has here become the trudge of weary men making their way to certain death. Snatches of the accompaniment to *Loveliest of Trees* appear, recalling the innocent beauty of springtime and youth. Now that beauty is being driven to the grave. The first two verses have well-shaped *cantabile* phrases, but for verse three the voice should be bleak and unexpressive. The listeners are by now perfectly well aware of what the poem is saying, and the full-voiced final verse can simply be presented as a triumphal procession. The postlude carries this through to the very last note without any *diminuendo*.

7. White in the moon the long road lies

For *molto sostenuto*, read *molto legato* and very slow – crotchet = c.36-40. The tempo can move on a bit for verse three ('The world is round') in parallel with a fuller sound. The *crescendi* don't accumulate volume but give a sense of forward movement and purpose, never reaching much more than *mf*. Express the pain of separation in that steep *crescendo* on 'far, far must it remove', and then return to the desolate *pp* on 'White in the moon', keeping it virtually expressionless until the word 'love' with its sweet B major chord. There is a misprint at the top of the last page, where under 'hies' the piano should have an A sharp in the right hand. In addition, the bass of the final chord is wrong in my copy, and ought (according to the manuscript) to be a B, a fifth lower than the printed F sharp.

8. Think no more, lad

Rather than bursting a blood vessel to achieve a *fortissimo* throughout the first verse, concentrate instead on making a harsh, unyielding tone to express the bitterness and sarcasm of the poetry. 'Oh, 'tis jesting' is an ungainly dance of mock jollity, ending on an ugly upward *portamento* on 'ever'. Take time out to breathe after 'Think no more' at the *molto rit*. There are few singers who can make a really effective noise on a bottom G in the context of a *fortissimo* passage, so don't feel embarrassed by opting for the upper note on 'sky'. Pianist, keep *sempre a tempo* and loud to the bitter end.

9. *Into my heart an air that kills*

By referring back to the melody of *Loveliest of Trees,* Somervell magnifies the significance of the earlier song, making it stand for vanished youth and the forsaken home. Let the monotone beginning be *molto legato* and very clean, with no scooping and slipping out of tune, letting it all be quite deadpan. Warm the tone at the *molto espressione,* but keep it soft, doing most of the expressive work in the way you deal with individual words through *rubato, crescendo, diminuendo,* attack, delay and so on. My personal opinion is that this should be the last song of the cycle, giving it an appropriately bleak ending in the same way as *Der Leiermann* ends Schubert's *Winterreise.* However, that is not what Somervell and/or his publishers wanted.

10. *The lads in their hundreds*

For me, in some ways, this is a disappointing song, because it doesn't seem to express what I think the poem is about. 'The lads that will die in their glory and never be old' are those young men who marched off to war and didn't return, and the poignancy that I find in those words is perfectly summed up in Butterworth's setting. The triumph which Somervell makes of this sits uneasily with modern sensibilities, coloured as they are by a century of appalling horror and bloodshed. Somervell's view is that of an earlier era when to die gloriously for one's country was the noblest thing one could possibly do. This is therefore an example of what I described at the beginning of the chapter on meaning, where the reader's understanding of a poem may be at variance with that of the composer, and yet for the purposes of the song the composer's interpretation must hold sway. I do not detect any irony or sarcasm in this setting, so you should sing it as a celebration of the glorious sacrifice of the soldier in war, coupled, of course, with sorrow at the loss of so much young life. There are more misprints in my score of this song, an expensive authorised photocopy from the publisher, and considering the price I think an attempt should be made to correct simple errors: 'in <u>for</u> the fair'; 'The lads for the <u>girls</u>' (plural); 'And then one could talk <u>with</u> them friendly'; 'But now you may stare as you like <u>and</u> there's nothing to scan'; 'The mintage of <u>man</u>'.

Charles Wood (1866-1926)

Ethiopia saluting the colours – Whitman – 1898

The accompaniment for the first two verses maintains a firm unwavering tempo until *quasi ad lib*, and the left hand is *staccato* throughout. The singer should keep the same strict pulse, but he doesn't have to be *staccato*. If you speak the poem you will find little of that inexorable rhythm; it is a descriptive device which the composer has added. At *quasi ad lib* try a white, 'unsung' tone, and let the words linger or move on as seems natural. Don't force yourself to sing out of tempo if it doesn't feel right. At *meno mosso* there is no need for wayward rhythm, just keep a steady slower pulse. I suppose *Tempo I* is *p*, and the voice can come in *mp* or so. Don't make too much of the *cresc* and *dim*, and incidentally, 'courtesies' is an old-fashiones spelling of 'curtseys', and 'guidons' (pronounced 'guide-ons') are flags or pennants. Gradually the marching soldiers recede into the distance, and although the last verse is *poco meno mosso*, the pace remains steady to the end.

Granville Bantock (1868-1946)

---

1. A Feast of Lanterns – Yuan Mei – 1917

The key to performing this song lies in mood and tempo. In the opening four bars the pianist will naturally dwell a little on the octave Ds in the bass, picking up the speed for the ensuing phrase. Don't overplay this effect here because later on there are several *animandos*, and those are the places where the phrases should really show a dramatic surge in tempo. For example, before the reprise of 'In spring for sheer delight' we have *poco animando e molto rubato*: in other words a big *accelerando* through about 1¾ bars (that's the *poco animando* bit), followed by a delayed A ♯ on the new bar (that's the *rubato* bit) which is played with quite some force (that's the *energico* bit). This ebbing and flowing of the tempo continues until 'delight', which is *animando*, calling for a continuous and increased acceleration through 3½ bars. I suggest slowing down quite markedly at *rall poco* (ignoring the *poco*), giving room for another two bars of acceleration. As a welcome contrast to the rather hectic movement so far, I would make a lot of the *allargando* for two bars and then go for four bars of acceleration right through to the finish, with no *rit* at all. Having dealt with the various tempo requirements of this song, I now return to the beginning, where the marking *animato con brio* ('with vigour') can be interpreted as one of mood and not of tempo. Similarly, *con anima* on page 16 describes the feeling the singer has to convey, and it literally means 'with soul', but notice that the first phrase is *mf* and the identical second phrase is *forte*; don't confuse emoting with singing loudly. Bear in mind also that the word 'delight' occurs three times, and a song of delight is never likely to be too heavy or too loud.

2. Adrift – Li Po – 1919

This song has a lush Edwardian harmonic style, and unless one is careful it could degenerate into sentimentality. The quality of the poem and the sincerity of the singer will prevent this, but it is essential that the performers understand the importance of *rubato* here, because without it the song will not come alive. The larger changes of tempo are written in, but the stylish stuff comes in between. For example, in the bar of 'again', leading to 'And dream', there is quite a *rallentando* preparing for the *poco animando*. Let the speed pick up but then relax it at the *espressivo* figure on 'past'. Move on again on 'their fadeless fire' and relax on 'cast'. Raise the tempo a bit more at *più moto* and relax it a fraction on 'song'; move ahead again on 'behind' and then make more of a pull-up on 'bars'. Move on at 'but these', move on even more on the first 'and walk'd' and don't let the tempo fall back until the *poco allargando*, where some expansiveness should begin, but it shouldn't reach the slower *Tempo I* until 'In vain we cleave'. I've attempted here to show the structure of two pages of *rubato*, but I'm aware that it doesn't really happen in this prescriptive fashion. The subtle ebb and flow of tempo has to spring from the performers' feeling for the music. *Animando* means 'animating', while *Affrettando*, which comes a little later, means 'hurrying'. This tells me that there is more intensity of emotion on 'When man's desire', but even though the vocal part is littered with *più f*, *sf*, *cresc* and *f*, don't go over the top. The voice will naturally reach a healthy peak on 'gale' without any struggle, and note that the accompaniment has *p* with a *crescendo* under 'and let the gale'. The next bar could do with a *diminuendo* on 'waters', and I believe that the D quaver on the third beat is wrong: it should be a tied C. This has the benefit of allowing a slight shortening of the syllable to get in a good breath for the next phrase. It's also my opinion that there should be a dynamic marking of *mp* here at 'and let the waters', letting the long notes on 'bear' soar effortlessly. Finally, in the last bar of the piece the pianist holds the left hand while releasing the right hand and pedal, then re-applies the pedal, releases the left hand and plays the final chord with crossed hands.

3. Song to the Seals – Boulton – 1930

This is one of the six *Songs of the Western Isles,* and presumably the refrain (Hoiran, oiran etc) has Gaelic origins. Part of its distinctive flavour comes from the use of the pentatonic scale. There are two points where the composer moves outside this scale, and the first is at 'For the seals with a splash dive into the deep' where he adds an A flat. The mysterious quality of the scene has been momentarily disturbed by the seals' movement, but then the mood returns with 'And the world goes on again', and it is pentatonic once more. The other point is in the G flat verse where 'The (maid)' is on an F. If you look at the rest of the song you will see that the expected note is a D flat – equivalent to a B flat in the outer two verses. I know that it probably doesn't make much difference, but I wonder whether it should in fact be a D flat here. Be that as it may, the song is mostly quite quiet, but I think it calls for a well-sung *legato*, and even the *pp* refrains are *cantabile.* A breath after 'belief' in the first verse seems fairly obvious, and at the equivalent place in verse two a breath after 'bough' seems right. The problem is after the word 'hillside'; does the comma have to be shown by a break of some sort? The music wants to carry on over the barline, and I think that decides the issue. Sing through it but avoid the meaningless 'hillside birds' by giving more value to the consonants 'd' and 'b', which will do enough to create a tiny separation, keeping the sheep on their hillside and the birds on their bough. The pronunciation of the refrain struck me as a problem area, so I asked the pianist Iain Burnside's mother, Anna, for advice. She is a teacher of Gaelic, and she admits to having sung this song to the seals herself with some success. There are two places where the sound differs from normal English pronunciation: the 'H' of 'Hoiran' is so lightly aspirated that it is effectively inaudible, and the long word is 'ee-la-loy-ran'. Any other versions are probably Irish or some Scots dialect.

Ralph Vaughan Williams (1872-1958)

1. Songs of Travel – Robert Louis Stevenson

Numbers one to eight of this set were first performed in 1904, but three of them (Nos 1, 3 and 8) were published in 1905, four (Nos 2, 4, 5 and 6) were published in 1907, No 7 was published in 1902, and No 9 did not appear until 1960. In spite of this confused chronology, the songs were conceived as a song-cycle and fit together well in the published order; the last song uses thematic material from the earlier songs to wrap up the set.

1.1. The Vagabond. The singer needs a warm, robust tone for this song, even when it is *p*; this is a tough, hardy character. The opening fanfares in the piano are like distant precursors of the vocal melody which, when it enters, can be almost *mf*. The *forte* has to leave room for the *ff* phrase in verse four. Let the *diminuendo* on 'me' and at other similar places be a controlled, positive matter, not a removal of vocal energy and timbre. Keep the intensity there as you get softer. 'Let the blow' is quieter than the beginning, say *mp*, with a big *crescendo* only where marked. The slur over the two syllables of 'below' implies a *portamento*, probably best done on the 'l'. *Animando* means 'getting more animated', and to be practical you should do it in stages. Start off a little quicker, then speed up again on 'White as meal', then again on the rising piano quavers before 'Not to autumn'. Make the tiniest *rall.* On the last two quavers before *tempo 1.* The phrase-marks above the vocal line imply *legato*, and when they are missing, the voice is *poco marcato.* The *pp* last verse is still in character, and be sure to keep quiet until the huge *crescendo.* The *portamento* is on the vowel of 'me', which reaches the upper note before the attack on 'All'. Be careful to make a positive *diminuendo*, and let the piano trudge off into the distance in tempo.

1.2. Let Beauty Awake. The reader can find some comments I made about this song in the chapter on phrasing, and I only want to add some remarks about dynamics here. In the first verse, the *forte* marking for the voice calls for a rich, generous tone with no hint of aggression; keep it *cantabile.* The second verse is all more subdued, but it should not be weak in any way, bearing in mind the character of the first song of the set. 'Let her wake to the kiss' can be a little softer, befitting the tenderness of the moment, and at the same time following the general rule that a repeated phrase should be different from its preceding pattern.

1.3. The Roadside Fire. Sing the first four bars in one breath, even though there are two phrase-marks involved, and do the same with the next four bars. Make the opening a little less *legato* and a little less loud than 'I will make a palace', and I think the *scherzando* marking calls for a rather conversational approach. Be careful not to emphasise the second syllables of 'brooches', 'kitchen' and similarly placed words. The *mf crescendo* mustn't grow too loud, and it is one phrase from 'Of green . . .' to '. . . at sea'. Notice that 'In rainfall' is marked *pp*, while 'green days', at the same place in verse one, is marked *p.* Let the *rallentando* at the end of verse two take you smoothly into the *meno mosso* of verse three, which is more *cantabile* – more sung. The *largamente* probably applies only to the triplet of 'no one'. 'That only I' is a little subdued, preparing for the *diminuendo* to 'admire'. The piano comes down to *pp* here, but the voice should not go below *p*, always maintaining the underlying strength of the narrator's character. 'That only you' has a *largamente* marking, followed by *tranquillo*, and the tempo can remain a fraction slower than the *meno mosso* for the rest of the song.

1.4. Youth and Love. There are four tempi in this song, each progressively quicker than the one before. The relation between them needs to be carefully considered, to avoid the first being too slow or the last being too fast. *Andante sostenuto* applies mainly to the vocal part; if the accompanying figure is over-indulgent the singing line can become impossibly slow. Crotchet = 60 is probably about right, and the *espressivo, tempo rubato* needs to move around that basic pulse. Use the rhythmic ebb and flow to highlight the direction of the melody. The singer should breathe after 'youth', but must connect musically and textually with the following phrase. 'And on either hand' has an unexpected harmonic shift on 'hand', so make a small *allargando* before that note, delaying the barline slightly, almost as if you hardly dare make a sound on it. Another such moment occurs in the *pp misterioso* bar. The pianist should be aware throughout of the need to differentiate between the slurred groups of notes and those which are partially detached. Delay before 'Call him', starting marginally under tempo and accelerating. None of this first section is louder than *mf*. *Poco animando* is the next tempo marking, and crotchet = 72 is appropriate for this. The piano is very *legato* here, and *risoluto* suggests a slightly slower speed, while *affrettando* means 'hurrying', taking us into the *più mosso* at crotchet = 90. Let the tempo relax naturally in the bar before the next *più mosso* on 'sings but a boyish stave', and by now the crotchet should be about 100. The *rall* into *tempo 1* is quite considerable, but the right-hand figure should stay light and boyish all the same. Pace the *diminuendo* in voice and piano so as not to become too quiet too soon.

1.5. In Dreams. The first two lines of music in this song have a claustrophobic feeling to them, with diminished intervals and chords depicting the poet's troubled state of mind. Strange chromaticisms and awkward intervals take over, further underlining his anguish. In the last page, Vaughan Williams combines standard, rather hackneyed Edwardian harmonies with the earlier chromaticism to increase the sense of pain and longing. Make something of the little surges at the beginning of each verse, and don't be too loud on the *poco f* on 'no more'. The next 'no more' is a little quicker and more intense, yet still only *mf*. The *f* on 'grace' is very brief, with an even *dim* to the *p* on 'enshrines' two beats later. Don't breathe here, but wait until after 'enshrines'. *Poco animando* signifies an acceleration for three bars, and the whole of 'face and' should stay *forte*. *Smorzando* means 'fading away', though how this differs from *diminuendo* I'm not sure. Since it drops to *pp* on 'and then forgot', the preceding phrase must be a little more. 'Ah me' is a warm *forte* which lasts until the natural fade on 'smile', but notice that it is *a tempo*, not *poco animato* as in the first verse. Connect in your mind over the two beats' rest between 'smile' and 'forgets'. *Morendo* means 'dying', and is virtually the same as *smorzando*, though the *colla voce* in the piano part indicates that the voice should slow down somewhat. The piano postlude is a seven-bar *rallentando*.

1.6. The Infinite Shining Heavens. The even tread of minims in the piano part seems to portray the remote and impersonal stars, and they can be deliberately unexpressive. There should be an implacable tempo except at those two moments where the poet introduces intense personal feeling at 'dearer to me' and later at the end of the song. As to the correct tempo, that is best found by trying out a comfortable recitation speed through the triplets on 'infinite' at the beginning and 'night after night' towards the end. In the phrase 'dumb and shining and dead', finish the word 'and' with a careful d, and be daring enough to have a moment of silence before the much softer 'dead'. It's amazing how expressive silence can be. The two *forte* markings need to be moderated rather to suit the overall style of the song, and I wish you luck on the final *diminuendo*!

1.7. Whither must I wander. One of the keys to performing this song successfully is to find a natural rhythm for the text. For example, there is a phrase-mark over the first vocal bar, followed by another over the next bar, and the two sections of text are separated by a comma. Let the final quaver of 'me' die away almost to nothing before moving on to 'whither' without a breath. The following two bars are under a single phrase-mark, but again there is a comma which can be indicated by a small glottal stop on 'I'. This seems to me a better approach than singing through the phrase with a driven *legato*. The long *legato* phrase comes in the next line: 'Cold blows . . .', where *mf* probably provides enough of a climax. Keep a rich tone on 'my roof is in the dust' even if it is *p*. *Fortissimo* on 'spoken' strikes me as overdoing it, and anyway the loudest point of the song is at 'house with open door' in verse three. Take time to breathe after 'roof-tree'; the tempo is fairly flexible in this song, and a gasping gulp of air at this moment would be even more disturbing than usual. 'You come again no more' is clearly intended to have a *rallentando*. For verse two, treat the comma after 'my dear' as you did in verse one. The sense of the line 'Lone let it stand now the friends are all departed' could have been clarified by putting a comma after 'stand', so sing it as if there were one. Verse three is *pp* until 'Fair the day', but be sure to keep the timbre in the voice – after all, this is not a pretty song, but one full of deep feeling. Don't overdo the emotion at the end, letting the audience in to your pain rather than hitting them with it.

1.8. Bright is the Ring of Words. This is a confident poem, telling of the triumph of art over death. When you sing about the singer and poet being dead and buried, don't let feelings of regret and sorrow enter your performance; the songs live on, and that's the whole point. The opening is generous and loud, certainly, but never bombastic. 'Words' is an octave lower than 'Bright', and that should act as the measure of how loud the first phrase can be, avoiding an involuntary *diminuendo* to the weaker bottom note. 'Still they are carolled' remains quite warm, allowing room for the later *p* and *pp*. 'Carried' needs a full tone, and the second syllable must have time to resonate before breathing. The whole of the remainder of the song is *pp* or less, but that is no excuse for a weedy sound. The tone on 'embers' needs nourishing, even on the weaker second syllable; give the crotchet its full value. Enjoy the 'l' on 'lovers' and 'lingers', and each 'm' in 'remembers'.

1.9. I have trod the upward and the downward slope. The tempo of the first bar is not related to that of the first song, but the rhythm is similarly solid, as it should be again from the next *a tempo*. My score has *quasi rit* for the singer, which must be a misprint for *quasi recit*.

143

Don't be tempted into singing the semiquavers too fast just because they look fast; take as much time as you like. There is a natural relaxation of tempo on 'bid farewell to hope'. The piano then leads the ebb and flow for the rest of the song. We must hear that the final word is indeed 'door', and it may be helpful to make a small *crescendo* into it because the piano is doing so at the same time. The *rall.* four bars from the end applies mainly to that bar and half of the penultimate bar.

2. *The New Ghost – Shove – 1925*

The strange name Fredegond Shove belonged to Vaughan Williams's niece, and her poem describes the ecstatic union of a soul with God when this earthly life is done. It is essential that the singer should perform this song sincerely, and it seems to me that if you cannot allow yourself to believe in what a song has to say it is better to leave that song alone. This applies not only to religious or mystical poems but to any text at all. If you are completely non-plussed, for example, by the feelings of the 'character' that you are portraying, be it a jilted lover, a crushed flower or an ecstatic ghost, then look for something else. In this piece there is only one place where the volume is more than *mp*, and that is the *f largamente* at 'the greatness of their love'. Within this generally quiet dynamic there are opportunities for finding different colours. The half-sung opening is followed by a little more tone on 'his spirit showed'. There is more involvement on 'and seeing him', but it remains quiet. From 'And the Lord came on' don't try too hard to paint the scene; let the words do the work quite simply. 'The spirit trembled', while still quiet, prepares for the climax. 'To a far distant land' is the only point where the voice is marked *pp*. There are two places where the superscript says that the voice and piano don't have to be together. In fact, they don't have to be apart either, unless you are comfortable with that freedom, in which case you just let it happen; if you aren't comfortable, don't try and force them apart. At both these moments I suggest that the singer keeps a fairly constant tempo while the piano moves around it with a flexible *rubato*.

Gustav Holst (1874-1934)

Vedic Hymns (1st group) – from the Rig Veda – 1907-8 (pub. 1920)

The first of these three songs is a revised version of one from *Six Songs for Baritone*, published in 1903. My feeling is that it is ideal for a mezzo-soprano (shades of *Savitri*, perhaps).

1. Ushas (Dawn)

Ushas, the Dawn, is a goddess, and you are one of her worshippers. The beauty of the scene you are painting is compounded by the awe you feel at her appearance. Be very still and centred from the beginning, keeping a regular, even tempo. 'Arise! For the night hath fled!' is all a warm *mf,* followed by a *subito p.* 'Welcome her' is also *p,* with only a slight *crescendo* where marked. Do not begin any *crescendo* in the *poco animato* section until the *stringendo.* Picture the glory of that moment when the sun first appears above the horizon, and communicate that on the high note. Return to the centred stillness of the opening, and try the last phrase breathing only after 'Bow down', but making a comma after 'thee' without a breath.

2. Varuna (Sky)

After the piano introduction depicting the great vault of heaven, the voice enters as in prayer. Usually such prayers, even improvised ones, are quite low-key, so don't be too expressive or wordy in the quiet passages. At the *crescendo* each time you can raise the emotional temperature, only to let it fall again to a calm *p.* The third climax is marked differently for the voice, and the text doesn't have such intensity; don't be too loud. 'He doth appear' is no longer part of the prayer, but an awestruck whisper. 'I am delivered' is still *pp* but calm and *legato.*

3. Maruts (Stormclouds)

These are no ordinary clouds, and this is no English rain. The monsoon, which I have never seen, must be a tremendous experience, and the clouds that bring it might easily take on god-like qualities. The rhythm of the riders is inexorable, as is the building of tension to the end. There is no *diminuendo* anywhere in the song, so each *crescendo* starts again *p*; don't drop the excitement of your delivery. In the last verse the long *crescendo* needs to be taken in stages, reducing the start of each new phrase slightly from the previous phrase and growing anew. You may wish to wait on the first beat of the bar of 'Throughout the' to let the piano chord disperse a little. If so, I suggest an *allargando* before the *presto,* otherwise it should be strictly in the preceding tempo.

Roger Quilter (1877-1953)

1. Now sleeps the crimson petal – Tennyson – 1904

Notice first that there is a difference between the introductions to the two verses of this song; they both have *crescendos* from about *mf* to about *f*, but whereas the first is *espressivo*, the second is marked *con passione*, which we can assume to mean more expressive still. By putting the accompaniment down the octave, Quilter increased the effect of richness and sonority. The voice, however, goes the other way, having *pp tranquillo* the second time instead of just *p*, so give it more tone the first time. It may be difficult to make these little distinctions tell, but it is from such small things that a song can come to life and unimaginative repetition is avoided. Be aware of the *tempo rubato* instruction and give, for example, a moment to complete the word 'petal' before moving on. 'The porph'ry font' can move forward through an implied *crescendo* and then 'firefly wakens' can be *tenuto* and expansively *forte*. 'Waken thou with me' doesn't have too much *dim.*, allowing the piano to grow again from a firm base. The second verse needs a beautifully delicate *pianissimo*, *legato* and, above all, loving sound. There is no need for a break at the commas in 'dearest, thou, and'; they can be implied by using *tenuto* judiciously. Quilter made many small revisions to this song, and his original version of the *pp ad lib.* bar has 'Slip into my' on four semiquavers. My opinion is that this is better than his later 'Into my' on three triplet quavers. 'And be lost' has a small *crescendo*, 'be lost' a little more, and 'in me' has a *diminuendo* back to almost nothing.

2. Love's Philosophy – Shelley – 1905

Hold your emotional horses at the start – there's a while to go before you reach *f appassionato* and *ff*. I think we can assume that the longed-for kiss will indeed be given and received, so you can cast aside anxiety and doubt about the outcome. Let there be an inner joy at the beginning without getting too loud. Breathe after 'law divine' but carry the sense through the rest. Maintain the *forte* until the second 'not I'. The *piano* second verse is still joyful, only this time it has a more intimate quality, even at 'disdained its brother'. Where *agitato* is marked, give the words more energy, especially the consonants, and up the tempo by a fraction. There is now a long *crescendo* to 'thou' (*f appassionato*) and the piano continues to press the tempo on a little up to the voice's 'if', which can take a slight *tenuto*. I know that *ff* represents pretty well the maximum the voice is capable of, but the real climax of that high note is the final held quaver at the beginning of the *rall.* bar. If you need to, breathe before 'kiss' without taking too much time out. Hold 'me' for the indicated time, but for no longer than that – it clashes with the beginning of the piano's *con fuoco* postlude.

3. Three Shakespeare Songs – 1905

These three songs are all from the plays; the first two from *Twelfth Night*, the third from *As You Like It*. As an example of how fashions in performance change, the metronome markings for all of them are slower than we would now expect to hear. I do not think it is just a personal foible of mine to prefer quicker tempi, because I believe it runs through all types of music these days. Listen to old recordings of Klemperer or Richter conducting, or of Elena Gerhardt singing Lieder, for instance, and speeds are almost always slower. Doubtless it will be 'all change' again during the twenty-first century, but in the meantime I can only say what seems right to me now.

3.1. Come away, Death. The marking *poco andante* seems better served by a speed of 76 or so; 63 feels more like *lento*. An essential ingredient of this song is *rubato*, and one method of finding out how and where the tempo alters is to play it as a piano piece, with full expressive licence. The first two bars make no rhetorical point since they act as a sort of vamp-till-ready, so there is no need to vary the speed. The falling minims in the left hand, coupled with the right hand syncopations, call for some acceleration, followed by a slowing on the last two left-hand falling crotchets. The sl- of 'slain' can be stressed, as can the triplet on 'fair'. There are more opportunities for *rubato* to vitalise the rise and fall of the phrases. Don't breathe between 'true' and 'Did'. Notice that the second verse starts quieter and quicker than the first, but the tempo is still flexible. 'Corse' can be modernised to 'corpse', a good thing if it serves to help the listener's understanding. The loudest notes are not aggressive but *cantabile*. Breathe after 'where' if you have to (not ideal), and keep a warm tone on the next line. The three 'weeps' need even more flexibility of tempo than the rest, and don't fade away to nothing on 'there' but feed the tone a little.

3.2. O Mistress Mine. My preference is for a marginally quicker metronome mark: 85, say. Each verse is effectively one long phrase, and the brisker tempo helps the singer make the long arch. This is a happy song with a good deal of swagger in it, and the pianist can set the scene by playing the opening with a sense of bravado. Try a *tenuto* on the first beat with an *accelerando* into tempo before the *poco rit.* in bar three. The singer then joins the pianist as if he's been singing along silently throughout. Keep the tempo going until the *poco rit.* at the end of verse one. Verse two begins *p*, in contrast with the opening *mf.* Stay quiet until the *cresc.* is marked, then make a generous (but charming!) climax on 'kiss' with a little *tenuto* on the first beat. The subsequent *dim.* is very gradual, and the vocal coda is gently amused and enticing.

3.3. Blow, blow, thou Winter Wind. This poem is about the bitter subject of the thoughtless negligence of discarded friendship, and yet it is presented in a carefree, detached manner. It's an old story and that's the way of the world, it seems to say, and the singer never becomes entirely swallowed up by the feelings being expressed. I prefer a metronome mark of 80 for the beginning, and 100 at the *poco più allegro* to differentiate the tempi, which should be always strict except where indicated. Make 'wind' rhyme with 'unkind' and give full value to the word 'rude'. In the *poco più allegro* sections the *largamente* can be stretched quite a lot, but the passage running into Tempo 1 has no pull-up at all, going directly from one speed to the other. Between 'sharp' and 'As', be sure to make a proper rest, but carry the sense of the phrase through the silence. At the end of each verse *poco ... dim ... e ... rit.* is printed. I interpret this as meaning: start the *poco rit.* at the same time as the *poco dim.* The closing piano bars remain in tempo to the end.

4. Drink to me only with thine eyes – Ben Jonson – 1921

I cannot think of any song (this is, of course, an arrangement) which requires to be sung more smoothly than this one. The singer stretches out the sound between the notes through the vowels and voiced consonants: 'me-only-oo-ith-ine-eyes-and-I(portamento)-oo-ill-pledge-oo-ith-mine.' Yes, it does look odd like that, but I hope you get the idea. It is only when the word 'kiss' appears that there has to be a hiatus, and we can use this to our advantage as a way of placing the word in inverted commas. Sometimes the note can be approached from beneath with a little *portamento*, eg, 'Doth <u>ask</u>' or 'di-<u>vine</u>', which may sound a bit schmaltzy to some people, but I like it. At the end of the piano introduction the *ritenuto* must run seamlessly into the beginning of the vocal line as if only one person is playing and singing, and the same goes for the introduction to verse two. Try to find a difference between *mp amoroso e legato* (verse one) and *p dolce* (verse two). At 'It could not withered be' the piano's *espressivo* bar has quite a big *allargando*, with *meno mosso* perhaps on 'thou thereon'. The commas at the end can be a pitfall unless you're careful; go over 'grows, and' without a break and try a little glottal stop on 'I' ('smells, I swear') just to separate the words a fraction. Breathe after 'swear' and again after 'itself' provided there is lots of expressive *rit.* and the problem is solved, but don't forget in all this not to let the note die on 'thee'.

Frank Bridge (1879-1941)

Probably Bridge's most famous song is *Go not, happy day*, which must have put off a large number of singers from trying the rest of his work.

It's not that the song is a bad one; indeed, it is a beautifully balanced composition. The problem, in my opinion, is the frightful poem which, notwithstanding the adult notion of waiting for a maiden to yield (is it only a kiss, or is she expected to go further than that?), manages to combine sentimentality and childishness to a remarkable degree. Sing it by all means if it doesn't offend you, but do try these splendid songs as well.

1. E'en as a lovely flower – Heine, tr. Kroecker – 1903 (pub. 1905)

The *tempo moderato* of this song must keep moving, otherwise the poor singer hasn't a chance with these long phrases. The breathing in the first verse takes care of itself, and in the second there's an obvious breath after 'folded' in spite of the sense continuing through. The next section should ideally go from 'Praying' to the end of 'thee' without a breath, but I have to put one in after 'Praying'. Then, if the extra length is required on 'fair', I would breathe after 'lovely' and 'pure'. In the singer's first phrase the tempo is quite free as well as being slower than the opening, and with a real *legato* there can even be a *portamento* between 'fair' and 'so' (but don't overdo it!). There is a natural rise and fall from *piano*, and 'may keep' might reach as much as *mf*: if so, let it be fractionally less than the *mf* of 'fair'. The return of the opening line is marked *dolcissimo* this time, and I think this means a more delicate and less overtly expressive treatment. Don't give it the *portamento* here but breathe before 'so pure' instead.

2. Blow, blow thou winter wind – Shakespeare – 1903 (pub. 1916)

There is tremendous energy in the piano's opening bars which carries through in tempo to the pause in the fourth bar. The temptation at this point is for the performers to agree a formula for the length of the pause, like adding one beat before moving off again; try to avoid this if possible, letting the hiatus happen organically and holding the note for an unspecified time. Three *legato* bars are followed by two less loud *marcato* ones. The dynamics are *f* and *mf crescendo* and a probable *ff* at the end, which doesn't give much room for differentiation. 'Thou art not so unkind' is low in the voice, so it cannot come down too far, but 'because thou art not seen' can perhaps start at *mp* to allow for the *crescendo* over the next three bars. Notice that 'Although thy breath be rude' is marked *poco rit.*, whereas 'As friend remember'd not' has *poco rall*. I take this to mean that there is more of a pull-up the second time, therefore not much of one in the first verse. There is a breath after 'seen', not after 'keen'. Don't let the tempo relax on 'Heigh ho', but be aware that in both verses this should be rather genial, in contrast to the angry opening. The *diminuendo* at the end of 'most' (first verse) seems a little odd to me, and I would prefer to make the climax on '<u>jolly</u>'. The final 'jolly' is even louder, so hold something in reserve. Exaggerate the consonants at the beginning of 'Freeze', and to be sure of 'bitter' being understood (not 'beater'), it may be necessary to pause on the '-tt-' as you would in German. In this verse the breath comes after 'warp', not after 'sharp'. In my edition there is a *crescendo* from 'friendship' to 'folly' in the second verse but not in the first. Since the dynamics are otherwise the same, I would retake 'most loving' the second time with another *mf* and then another *crescendo*. 'This life is most' can do with an *allargando*, and the *a tempo* comes on 'jolly'. The piano has only a slight *rit.* into the last chord to accommodate the bottom notes.

3. Fair Daffodils – Herrick – 1905 (revised and pub. 1919)

The restless (though smooth) accompaniment should be balanced by a generally calm, *legato* vocal line. The piano and the voice occasionally have different dynamic markings, and these need to be observed quite accurately. There is a good number of changes of speed, some indicated and some not. The third bar for the piano asks for a little relaxation of tempo, and the *rit.* on 'rising sun' is very slight, less, in fact, than the one on 'together'. 'Stay, stay' moves on a bit, culminating in the *rit.* on 'together'. 'We will go with you' is *meno mosso* and fairly free, with an *a tempo* on '-long'. 'As you, or anything' is still in tempo until 'dry away' (marked 'tranquillo') which should be *poco meno mosso* with an *a tempo* on 'Or, as the pearl'. Give more time on 'morning's dew' than on 'pray'd together', and let 'Ne'er to be found' also be slower than 'we will go with you', with a breath before 'again'. 'Again' is marked *con moto, leggiero* in the piano, which probably signifies something a little quicker than the original speed, and it gives the singer a better chance to achieve the long held note on 'again', including the extra four-and-a-half beats.

4. Come to me in my dreams – Arnold – 1906 (revised and pub. 1918)

The piano's five-bar introduction needs to have some *rubato* before settling to the rocking tempo of the song proper. The *pp* and *tenuto* in the singer's first bar should be less extreme than when they appear again at the recapitulation. The *crescendo* to 'pay' mustn't have too much passion – that's reserved for later in the song; make it full and *legato* with that small stress on 'hope' and another on 'longing' (which can be accomplished by lengthening the 'l'). Take time over 'longing – of' In the bar before *più mosso* the piano remains quite expansive, not anticipating the change of speed. Feel the increase in tension but don't get too loud, keeping it *mf* (in spite of the piano's *p*) and making a *diminuendo* to *p* on 'rest as me'. The *p crescendo* on 'as thou never cam'st in sooth' reaches only *mf*, with a *subito f* on 'Come now'. The bar of 'truth' is exactly in tempo throughout, giving a sudden silence at the end. Feel the love and tenderness as you sing the next quiet passage, quieter still on 'My love . . .'. Remember to be quieter on 'Come to me' this second time, and don't make too much of an *allargando* when it comes so that you don't have to breathe until 'of'. The voice needs to have a good timbre on 'day' even if it is *piano* because the song hasn't yet wound down to its *pp* conclusion.

5. My pent-up tears – Arnold – 1906 (pub. 1982)

With its melancholy key of G flat and its harmonic tensions suggesting hopeless yearning, I would certainly be looking for plenty of *rubato*, and this is an opportunity to give some hints on how that might be done. Pick up the tempo on 'My pent-up tears' and drop it again on 'oppress my brain', doing the same in the next two bars. After holding 'Ah' for a moment, move the tempo forward again through 'weep and tell my pain', letting the piano relax again during the bar of 'pain'. The following two bars ('And on thy shoulder') are rather free, and then the piano starts picking up the tempo once more. I suggest an *accelerando* a bar earlier than *poco animato* is marked. This more passionate section is generally in strict tempo except for a comma after 'mine' which is necessary for breathing. 'Immunity from my control' is all still loud, with the *diminuendo* only really coming on '-trol'. The piano's *diminuendo* for a bar-and-a-half comes down to *mp*, and the voice comes in (after a pause) that much quieter, singing three bars quite freely. The *rubato* returns for the last page in a similar fashion to the beginning. 'Dead' doesn't need an accent, rather a stroked kind of stress (*mf dim.*), and the piano should probably make a *diminuendo* with the singer on 'smart'. Give a bleak, white tone on the final phrase, just placing the word 'joy'.

6. *Love went a-riding – Mary Coleridge – 1914 (pub. 1916)*

There are not many songs which, in my opinion, have to be in a particular key, but I think this is one of them. The first published key was E, and the more usual G flat version did not appear until two years later; for me, it just has to be G flat. The range is surprisingly small – just an octave plus a tone – but the voice must be able to dominate without strain when necessary; it's not a 'belter'. It seems clear to me also that this is a song for a woman to sing, not because Mary Coleridge was female, simply that the vocal line has to soar through and above the accompaniment. I think that a dramatic soprano or a mezzo soprano would be ideal. The singer starts the song with a good *legato* which, with a few exceptions, should be the general style. The piano at the end of the first vocal phrase has a *dim.* to *mf* and a *tenuto* before starting again with renewed energy on the next bar. The singer's second phrase grows more than the first, and the piano should follow suit, coming away a little for 'Pegasus' to let the voice through. The *marcato* 'Pegasus . . . he rode' has to *crescendo* to the front of the low note (with a generous rolled r), and then the piano takes over – don't attempt to fight it. In some circumstances it might be an idea to hold 'rode' into the bar of the new key to give the listeners a chance to hear the end of the word, but I expect they will have worked out the meaning anyway since it is implied in the title, so clear the note before the barline instead. It is now back to a full *legato* until 'Stay here' and let the *p dolce* retain something of the strength of the rest of the piece. Breathe before the second 'Stay here' but go on then without another breath. Take time to breathe after 'But love said', breathe again after 'No' and the first 'ride' but then go through. The recapitulation is much like the beginning, and the final 'he rode' has an *allargando* and *a tempo*. Give a good front to the note on 'rode' then come away, biding your time for a *crescendo* through the *ad lib.* part of the long note if you can.

7. What shall I your true love tell? – Francis Thompson – 1919

There is one bar of *lento* followed by *moderato* with *ad libs* and *a tempos* and so on, and *Tempo Imo* for the last six bars. The song is therefore *moderato* with variations, even though there are places like bar four which have the same material as is used in the opening *lento* bar. Clearly the *moderato* moves rather quicker, and *ad lib.* denotes a certain freedom from strict rhythm. The girl is at death's door but still sings with passionate expressiveness, and it is the questioner whose tone is hesitant. Her first reply has a *diminuendo* on 'our side the grave' to a warm *mp* for 'Maid may not believe'. 'That's so sad' is *p* with quite a big *crescendo/diminuendo* and without vibrato if possible to emphasise the clash of notes. The next question is *ad lib.* again followed by a warm-toned answer, finding a weaker sound for 'Now my eyes are blind'. The third question (*poco più mosso*) is in tempo and more involved, though I think that 'postulant' should not yet be quite as loud as 'Tell him love . . .' will be. *Tempo Imo* is the original *lento*, calling for a sustained *legato* line. Make a *tenuto* on the piano's last note under 'life', and when it comes to the word 'death' let it be clear without being accented.

John Ireland (1879-1962)

1. Sea Fever – John Masefield – 1913 (pub. 1915)

There are no dynamic markings for the voice part in this song, and the obvious thing is to follow what the piano is given. The mood of the poem is very strong and masculine, so the softest sounds should never be at all weak. The opening is a warm *mp*, rising to *mf* on 'the wheel's kick'. The pause bar can be *p*, with a small up-and-down on 'breaking'. In verse two, don't breathe after 'tide', which means breathing after 'again' if necessary, and after 'a clear call'. The last verse, unlike the first two, is *non legato,* building up to a *marcato forte* on 'whetted knife'. 'All I ask' is then *legato* and *f* before the long *diminuendo* to the end.

2. The Trellis – Aldous Huxley – 1920

The langorous sensuality of this poem is beautifully captured by the music, reminiscent of the style of Debussy's songs. The voice is always *legato,* the consonants not crisp but languid, never disturbing the flow of sound except once; delay the k of 'kisses', keeping it *pp* all the same, and relish the moment of memory. The pianist should also make flowing lines, even at the *ff* climax; the accents must imply joyful release, not anger. In the first phrase I think you should not breathe between 'joys' and 'From', so breathe gently after 'trellis' and again after 'malice' if necessary. On a phrase like 'And we lie rosily bowered' try to avoid any involuntary swelling of sound at the end of 'lie'. We often hear this kind of thing when a singer is trying hard to make a smooth line, whereas in reality it upsets the flow. There's a long phrase in the second verse which goes all the way to 'Drawn out' without a breath. 'Sounds our light laughter' is very quiet indeed, and the singer needs to hold the attention through the intervening bars until 'With whispered words'. Make a very slight *crescendo* up to 'caresses'. Place 'birds' with a tiny delay, but with no accent.

3. The Encounter – A E Housman – 1921

There is a harsh quality to this song with its hard-edged marching bass, its astringent harmonies and its unrelenting rhythm. The accompaniment is either *f* or *mf* until the very end, and though the voice has no separate dynamic markings it seems clear that it should stay in the *f/mf* range throughout. Don't indulge in any sweetness of tone at all, even where you come down to *mf*. 'See' in bar 8 can have a *crescendo* to prepare for the highest note, 'red', which is something more than *forte*. 'He turns' at *mf* is quite quiet by comparison. The second verse starts with a strong *mf* and what I would describe as *marcato/legato*, in which the beginning of each note has a small impulse (usually denoted by a short line above it) but the rest of the note is held without fading. The quavers of the dotted rhythm on 'man, from sky to' and 'leagues apart' need this treatment so that they aren't swallowed. Make 'world's ends' *staccato* and give an accent on 'no'. Verse three is *mf* again with a *crescendo* almost to *ff* on 'dead or living, drunk or dry'. Sing the last phrase from 'But dead' in one breath, keeping it pretty well *ff* to the end. As the piano gets quieter the tough *marcato* and the taut tempo continue to the last note.

4. Three Songs – Thomas Hardy – 1925

4.1. Summer Schemes. I'm not sure why there is a time signature of four crotchets in a bar when the metronome marking is minim = 66, and the ligatures on the left-hand quavers show two beats in a bar. The correct time signature would be two minims. The published key of A flat gives an odd vocal range; the F on 'trace' shouldn't really be as loud as a baritone would sing it, while the bottom Cs make it low for a tenor. A mezzo-soprano is probably ideal. The alternative key of G makes the song more baritone-friendly. Since this is a Hardy poem there is a dark side implied by the words 'but who shall say what may not chance before that day', but this setting plays that element down, concentrating rather on the light-hearted qualities. Breathe but carry the sense over between 'fifers' and 'to these hills', and between 'leafage' and 'where they prime'. When the birds are giving us their quavers, minims and so on, remember that they are small creatures which will fly away if you sing too loudly at them. Be sure to make plenty of the n in 'ferns' so that we don't mistake it for 'furs'. During the five bars from 'We'll go' and also from 'We shall', a decision needs to be made about the tempo. Letting it slow down emphasises the darker side of the poem and the feeling that something bad may happen to stop the wished-for event, whereas keeping it going during those bars makes us sense an eagerness to meet whatever the future will bring. I favour keeping a strict tempo for the first occasion apart from placing 'that day' and moving straight back into the *perpetuum mobile* in the piano. The second time is down a semitone and therefore more subdued, and the piano doesn't return immediately to the left-hand quavers. For these reasons I would make a *rall* and a *dim* on 'another moon will bring', communicating some anxiety about what may come. If *Her Song* is to follow, with its bleak retrospection, then this would certainly be an appropriate way to finish *Summer Schemes.*

4.2. Her Song. Some copies wrongly print minim = 60, whereas that should be the crotchet speed. There are no dynamic marks in the voice until verse three, so the singer must be guided by those in the piano part. Hardy used language in a very individual way, and unfamiliar words or constructions can pose problems for singers. The strangest line in this poem is the last of all: 'And time untouched me with a trace of soul-smart or despair'. The listener, who may never have read or heard the poem, needs all the help he can get to decipher the meaning here, and clarity of diction is most important. The crucial word is 'soul-smart', and 'soul' must be given the full value of its diphthong and its l; this is what I would term relishing the text. Another interesting line is: 'I thought not what might shape before . . .'. In speech the final phonemes of the second to the sixth words are all modified, giving something like: 'I though' no' wha' migh' sha' before . . .', which has a peculiar *staccato* effect. I am going to shy away from giving a ruling on this one, trusting to the taste and good sense of the singer. I will say, though, that putting in every final consonant is likely to sound precious, and I will also say that a way of avoiding the uncomfortable *staccato* is to bend the rhythm a little and approximate the flow of speech. The poem is full of feeling from the very first, hardly hinted at in verse one, becoming more apparent in verse two (with the marvellous 'cup-eyed care and doubt'), and coming to a climax of grief in verse three. Be in touch with that pain and despair from the beginning, and even though it is not expressed, it should colour your intention.

4.3. Weathers. The tempo of this song is quite steady and relaxed, 'with lilt' as Ireland writes. Keep it simple, and don't 'sing' too much except on the occasional long note; there is not a lot of hidden significance in the poem. Words like 'chestnut' and 'sprig-muslin drest' are not *legato*; that can be saved for a phrase such as 'dream of the south and west'. Carry the sense through the rests after this and connect with 'And so do I'. There are some difficult Hardy-esque words: 'And hill-hid tides throb, throe on throe', and I challenge any singer to get that across to a listener who has never heard the words before. Give it your best shot anyway. Don't start the *dim* after 'meadow rivulets' too early, and give a beautiful, unfussy *legato* on the repeated notes (G in my edition). The markings in the piano part (dots, lines and slurs) are all carefully placed, and the player must differentiate quite scrupulously between the various forms of the dotted figure.

Arnold Bax (1883-1953)

1. Cradle song – Colum – 1922

Sing this all quite simply. Connect across the rests at 'Tread softly, softly, o men coming in' and 'Where Mary will fold him with mantle of blue'. The accompaniment of this song has a constant rocking rhythm in the left hand, but in the right the *cantabile* melody has a wayward *rubato*. For instance, the semiquavers after 'O men coming in' and the quintuplets after 'with mantle of blue' hold back at first, then gather speed as the notes fall, rejoining the left hand exactly at the next barline. On the phrase 'and the cold of the floor' there is a *crescendo* to *forte*, which I think needs to be taken with a pinch of salt; after all, you don't want to waken the baby. As an example of the simplicity needed, sing the phrase 'O men from the fields, soft, softly come through' with an unaffected *legato*, allowing only a little extra stress on the 'softly' to point the repetition.

2. In the morning – Housman – 1926

Stephen Banfield, in *Sensibility and English Song*, calls the intense harmonic treatment in this song 'overbearing for Housman's poem'. I believe it is only so if the playing is laboured and pedantic. If, instead, the pianist can let the chromaticisms glide by in an understated *legato*, the complex harmonies provide a beautiful basis for the birdsong melismas. These melismas are inherently more musically expressive than the vocal line, and whereas they call for *rubato*, the voice part does not. Indeed, at 'and silver morning on the haycock as they lay', the steady pulse of the voice can be interwoven with a flexible tempo in the piano melody. The only rhythmic break for the voice is at the comma on 'looked away'. In the piano part before the voice's second phrase, place the *dim* a beat or so earlier than marked, and sing through 'by the light of day' without delaying 'day'; the expressive delay, if you want one, is better one bar later at the suspension. At the bottom of the page make it a *subito p*. Until the last line of the poem we can believe that this is a song of two happy and sexy young lovers, and even then the music continues on its sensual way. But 'And they looked away' suggests an undercurrent of dissatisfaction, and the music finally reinforces this darker feeling in the last four bars. The *poco più f*, though disturbing the lovers' peace, isn't at all harsh, and certainly isn't *marcato*.

Ernest Farrar (1885-1918)

Brittany – Lucas – 1914

This was written for soprano in the key of G, but it works very well in E flat. Indeed, the way the melody keeps dipping down to B flat (D originally) makes it feel more like a mezzo song or even, dare I say it, a baritone one. The vocal line has unusually large intervals, making the true stress of the words sometimes difficult to achieve. Take care that it's not 'In Brittany the churches', for example. The style of the accompaniment suggests slowly swinging bells, so it's almost one very slow beat in a bar. *Poco mosso* is only a touch quicker than the basic tempo, but at the end, after a slight *rall* on 'for love of Him', the *poco allargando* represents a substantial amount of slowing down. Sing 'The Lord who loveth all' with tenderness and, above all, belief; remember that the poem is describing people with a strong religious faith, and even though you may not share that faith you must sing as if you do.

George Butterworth (1885-1916)

Six Songs from A Shropshire Lad – A E Housman – 1909-11

1. Loveliest of Trees

Notice the *sempre rubato* marking at the beginning; there are hardly two bars together which remain at a constant speed. Let the tempo hang quite freely for the first five notes in the piano, then begin to tumble down, gathering pace until just before the voice entry, which again hangs almost timelessly. The quavers in the piano at bar five signal an *accelerando* into tempo for about two bars before slowing down at the *poco rit.* 'And stands about', unaccompanied, should be thought of as recitative, and the piano's repeated opening phrase once again hangs timelessly. At 'Wearing white' the tempo picks up gradually along with the *crescendo*, allowing the four bars from '-tide' to be at last in some sort of strict rhythm. The speed slackens off for the next two bars, preparing for another vocal recitative. The *crescendo* from 'springs a score' is accompanied by a small *accelerando*. The third verse is in a regular rhythm again for about five bars, and I suppose crotchet = 90 is somewhere near the mark. It is not clear from the score how long the *largamente* on 'woodlands' lasts, but I think it should be for about two bars. 'Snow' is sung over a *crescendo* in the piano, but let it get softer nonetheless. Remember that the singer is only twenty years old, so a young, fresh tone should be your aim. Never let the *forte* get too loud, and be aware that the two main *crescendos* are quite long, and need careful placing. The pianist can help on 'Eastertide' by holding back somewhat so that the singer never has to force.

2. *When I was one-and-twenty*

The crossed-common time signature means two minims in a bar. *Vivace non troppo,* if it applied to the minim beat, might send us off much too fast. It really applies to the crotchets in the voice part, and a suitable speed is about 100 minims per minute. The tempo is quite strict in the first verse except for a slight *tenuto* on 'free', perhaps. Reduce there to an *mf* in both verses. The *allarg.* on 'plenty' is not a sudden change of tempo but a slowing-down. Make sure we hear and understand the word 'rue'. At *a piacere* comes another slowing-down, but don't lose timbre on ''tis true, 'tis true''; keep the special soft sound for the last two bars.

3. *Look not in my eyes*

A tempo of 144 crotchets per minute seems about right, but it has to be flexible. The last three crotchets of the piano introduction have a slight *rallentando,* for instance, leading into the voice entry. The low Cs on 'fear' and 'clear' may not be heard without feeding them some richer tone. The phrases are all quite long, and whether to breathe before

'Perish' is for the individual to decide; a breath is certainly acceptable. The second verse, introducing the legend of Narcissus, is all very quiet. Reading the poem, one might well make a pause between 'showers' and 'A jonquil'; a moment of silence rather than a *legato* 'showers A' seems indicated.

4. *Think no more, lad*

The sarcastic mood of the poem calls for a hard edge to the voice, without being angry or hectoring. The delivery of the words is always *non legato*. The tempo is dictated by the need to make the text clear, and by the melisma on 'falling'; it cannot be allowed to run away. The quality of the *forte* and *fortissimo* in this song gives a clue to dealing with the *forte* in the others, none of which can be as loud as here.

5. *The lads in their hundreds*

A simple, conversational tone suits this song, with clear, unexaggerated diction. Breathing after the third line of each verse requires time, and this will seem quite normal if the tempo is flexible anyway, and *senza rigore*. Subtle word-painting is needed, but don't become too emotional, particularly on 'die'. It is enough to delay 'die' by a fraction and give it a small accent.

6. *Is my team ploughing?*

This is a masterpiece of simplicity, chillingly accurate in its portrayal. The most obvious point is to differentiate between the two characters – one disembodied, the other vigorous. When the living one gets quieter, be careful that his voice doesn't merge into the tone used for the ghost. This is especially important for the *p* of the last line; maintain some of the richer timbre. Give plenty of prominence to 'dead man's', otherwise the punch line will be lost on the audience.

W Denis Browne (1888-1915)

Epitaph on Salathiel Pavy – Jonson – 1912 (pub. 1927)

In his introductory notes to volume three of *A Century of English Song*, Michael Pilkington writes that he decided to revert to Browne's original key of E minor rather than the published F♯ minor. I entirely agree with him (I would, wouldn't I?) because there seems very little point in taking a tenor up to top A several times in a quiet, undramatic song. Even the final top note stays the gentle side of *forte*. It's a simple tale simply set, and it needs little in the way of vocal embellishment to colour the text. The irony of the song is lost unless you know that the Parcae were the three Fates of Roman mythology, and Jonson's poetic conceit was that because Pavy played old men so well he must have been one himself. Therefore the Fates, in whose hands lay the thread of all men's lives, thought he was ready to die. I bet not one in a thousand of your audience will get that reference without being told it.

Cecil Armstrong Gibbs (1889-1960)

1. The Fields are Full – Shanks – 1920

To choose a tempo for this song you need to consider the marking of *lento*, the triplet quaver accompaniment where it occurs, and above all the length of the vocal phrases. I think something like crotchet = 60 fits the bill. For the first page a really good *legato* is necessary, particularly on the triplet 'upon the air', which mustn't be bumpy. There is a *rallentando* in the piano bar leading into the triplet-accompanied section, and that being so, don't make much of a *rall.* on 'sense can bear'. Ease back into tempo afterwards. The first two lines of the second verse don't require quite the same exaggerated *legato* as before, but at the climax on 'And loved with strength' a full-toned *cantabile* is needed. This is marked *forte*, which means that the *mf* and *più f* earlier in the verse must be chosen accordingly. The last line of all is a floated *legatissimo pp*.

2. Silver – Walter de la Mare – 1920 (pub. 1922)

The time signature of this song is four crotchets in a bar, but the right hand plays two minims nearly all the way through. This makes a slow song seem even slower, and an appropriate metronome marking of about 56 crotchets to the minute sounds wonderfully slow – effectively minim = 28. The most important aspect of this piece is its stillness, and I think the *molto espressivo* marking can be misleading if it entails anything to disturb the peaceful flow of night-time which you want to portray. Keep the consonants underplayed, especially the sibilants, reducing the individual colours of consonant and vowel to mirror the monochrome effect of the moonlight. Let the first two pages have a regular hypnotic pulse for the same reason. The first eight bars for the voice are made up of two four-bar phrases, and yet the composer has given two-bar phrase-marks; so I suggest breathing between 'sees' and 'Silver' as seems to be indicated. Clear the end of 'dog' before the third beat to avoid a clash with the right-hand chord. 'From their shadowy' is *pp*, which means that the opening *p* must not be too soft. 'Cote' sounds like 'coat', even though 'dovecote' ends like 'cot'. The scampering harvest mouse hardly causes a stir, and the *poco agitato* is only a tiny fraction quicker; please don't be too playful and 'amusing' here. Breathe after 'claws' and make a *rallentando* into *a tempo* on 'eye'. 'Gleam' can grow a little from its *p* beginning and then decrease to *pp* ready for the final phrase.

3. Titania – Mordaunt Currie – 1934

This is another peaceful moonlit scene. Be very gentle again with the sibilants (sleeps, still, sails, stirs), and in trying to sing long *legato* lines don't fall into the trap of making pear-shaped notes, each of which swells and falls away. That doesn't make for a true *legato*, even though it feels to the singer that it might. It certainly gets rid of the attack from the front of every syllable but it's not pleasant to listen to. The huntsman when he appears doesn't make enough noise to waken Titania, and his phrase is only marginally *marcato* to give a little descriptive colour. Try to persuade the pianist that no time needs to be taken over 'No ringing echo', but that it can be taken on 'That charmed' to accommodate the change of consonant. There are some places where the barline needs to be delayed, viz. at the key-changes and on the final 'Titania'. Don't breathe in the long phrases if you can help it, but I suggest that you do breathe between 'fills' and 'The shadow', and after 'Stretched at her side' and again after 'horse and hound' but not after 'Oberon'. Tailor all the dynamic range to allow them to sleep on, even at Oberon's *mf*.

4. The Splendour Falls – Tennyson – 1943 (pub. 1944)

Except for the *largamente* and *rall.* sections, the music should move along in the first two verses with plenty of energy. The *forte* opening must not be too loud because of the *ff* which comes later. The only place where the energy dissolves is on the very last 'dying', otherwise there is always a degree of intensity present. The first vocal phrase is in one breath, and 'And the wild' can start at an eager *mp* to give room for a good *crescendo*. The *ff* 'Blow, bugle, blow' is a broad *legato*, but the *largamente* 'blow, bugle' has a more deliberate articulation. The third, *pp* 'dying' picks up the tempo precisely. 'O hark, O hear' is *poco marcato*, with an accurate declamation of the text. Don't let the *dim.* on 'Elfland faintly blowing' drop to a weak sound, and notice how the dynamics are one notch down from the previous verse. The *maestoso* for verse three means slightly slower than *tempo I*.

5. Philomel – Barnfield – 1956

The markings in this song should be scrupulously observed. The commas have to be given extra time because of the speed involved, which makes for some interesting and necessary rehearsal. The piano occasionally has *crescendi* which are not in the voice part (eg, 'made', 'alone' and 'refrain'), and the singer shouldn't be tempted to do the same. The one place where the voice can be *legato* rather than *leggiero* is 'She, poor bird . . . a thorn'. There are some moments which are *marcato*, eg, 'Senseless trees they cannot hear thee'. Sing 'Ruthless beasts' at *mf* to make way for the *più forte* on 'King Pandion'. The *diminuendo* on 'dead' is so quick that the effect is almost of a *subito p* on

'All thy friends'. The two brief pieces of self-pity ('Made me think upon mine own' and 'None alive shall pity me') are not sentimental – don't overdo the emotion. My best guess for the pronunciation of 'Tereu' is 'Tiroo'.

Ivor Gurney (1890-1937)

1. Spring – Thomas Nashe – 1912 (pub. 1920)

A speed of about 96 beats to the minute works well for this song, and the piano generally plays *leggiero*. *Piano* for the opening of the vocal part seems a trifle too quiet, particularly considering the big *crescendo* on 'year's pleasant' up to the *forte* 'King'. There's another *crescendo* to 'dance', and perhaps a *tenuto* on 'maids' is a good idea. Give a little accent on 'sting' and make 'cuckoo' *legato* without *portamento*, to contrast with the *staccato* 'jug-jug' and the slide downwards on 'pu-we' (pronounced 'poo-wee'). It's a *subito forte i on* 'towittawoo'. When the piano reaches the *ff* bar before the second verse it becomes *pesante* with a small *rit.* and then an *a tempo* for the *pp* bar. 'The palm and may' is *legato*, while 'Lambs frisk and play' is *leggiero*. Let the *crescendo* reach only *mf* on 'day'. The piano again becomes rather *pesante* before 'The fields breathe sweet', which comes in *legato*. The comma above the music after 'meet' is meant to avoid the interpretation: 'Young lovers meet old wives'. Take plenty of time and expand the tempo quite considerably for the two bars of *allargando*. 'In every street' is *legato* again and 'cuckoo' this time is *staccato*. 'Pu-we' has a big *crescendo* to prepare for the *ff* outburst on 'towittawoo'. The piano is *fff* under the singer's *pp* 'Spring', so give it loads of 'Spr-', and you only need small *crescendos* and *diminuendos*.

2. Sleep – John Fletcher – 1912 (pub. 1920)

This song is very slow, like a heartbeat that has reached the threshold of sleep. Colour the voice with the feelings of peace and healing. Even the *mf* climax on 'powers' carries the influence of sleep with it. Little *tenuto* moments on 'delight' and 'bereaving' reflect the tensions in the harmony at those moments. The second verse begins like the first, with quite a definite slowing-down on the *colla voce* bar. The long *crescendo* leads to an ambiguous climax; the cry of joy is also a call for release from care and suffering. The second *f* on 'some' is more like *mf,* but it is there to emphasise the poet's expectation that his joys will not last and the cares will return. Breathe after the second 'joys' rather than at the place indicated. The piano then dies away gradually into nothing.

3. Severn Meadows – poem by Gurney – 1917 (pub. 1928)

It is remarkable that Gurney was not only one of the great English song composers of his day, he was also one of the finest poets. Our understanding of this song is greatly enhanced by knowing that he wrote both words and music in a trench in France during the First World War. With this knowledge, the line 'Do not forget me quite', marked *con passione,* becomes unbearably moving. The simple melodic arch of the first verse is repeated in the second but for the inversion of the third line. The singer doesn't need to do much at *con passione;* just enter the heart of the poet at that moment and your intention will communicate the feeling. The last line has a beautiful, calm *legato.*

4. Thou didst delight my eyes – Bridges – 1921 (pub. 1952)

'Short my joy', says the poet, and likens the girl to the sighting of a distant ship which 'for a day has cheered the castaway'. Yet notwithstanding the depth and sincerity of his love, the prevailing mood is one of melancholy, stemming from his inability to win and keep her. Aim for a tempo of about 60 beats to the minute, and let the singer take care that he doesn't swell on each note in sympathy with the off-beat piano accompaniment; a true, seamless *legato* is essential both here and for the rest of the song. Breathe according to Gurney's instructions even if you might normally be tempted to go over 'nor first Nor last nor best' and breathe after 'best' instead. Carry the sense through from 'time' to 'thou shalt'. The phrase 'Makes all ears glad that hear' becomes full-toned but never joyful – the gladness is too much overlaid with heavy-hearted feeling. The same goes for the next phrase with its admonitory 'do not forget', on which there can be an *allargando* followed by *a tempo* on '-get'. 'For what wert thou' can be even softer than *p*, remaining so until the *crescendo*. Notice how 'A sail' is *mf* immediately after the piano's *f*, and there is a difficult *diminuendo* to achieve through 'day' and on to the end. The tempo can relax a little on 'Has cheered the', with *a tempo* on 'castaway'.

5. The Scribe – de la Mare – 1918 (pub. 1938)

This song falls into three sections: the opening four lines, which are a short catalogue of God's creation; the bulk of the poem with triplet accompaniment, telling of the poet's futile attempts to describe what he sees; and the coda. The first section can have a tendency to get stuck, with its short piano interjections, so be sure to keep it flowing. The wayfaring ant is given a *mezzo forte* marking, but nonetheless it is still only an ant, and I think something less than *mf* might be better. The second section has a feeling of movement and teeming life, and it builds through a series of *crescendos* to the appropriately *forte* 'Leviathan'. At 'To write of Earth's wonders' the piano left hand jumps down by two octaves and a tone, which is a good excuse to give a small *tenuto* on 'To' to accommodate the pianist's needs. The marking of *sonore* on 'The dark tarn dry' asks for a rich tone, especially on the low B flat, and the next phrase should still have some richness in it. The words 'Thou, Lord' seem to come out of the blue without connection with the sentence before. In fact, the meaning goes 'And still would remain (my wit to try . . . all words forgotten) Thou, Lord, and I', implying that the final and unfathomable enigma is the relationship of mankind with God.

6. Black Stitchel – Wilfrid Gibson – 1920

The *Allegro* marking seems to me a little misleading. The time signature is four crotchets in a bar, but with the ligatures in the piano part as they are, it feels more like two minims. At a speed of minim = 68 or so, this represents *Andante* instead. The voice always needs a warm tone, even when marked *mp*. 'Mouth' is the climax of the first verse, which may be why 'my love's' is marked *mf* after the earlier *mf crescendo*. Return to the warm *mp* for verse two, and if you like, try a *diminuendo* on 'of my love's' in place of the marked *crescendo*. Try all of that phrase in one breath as well. Verse three, *più animato,* can be *mf*. The piano in the bar after 'North' needs to stay strong, and the subsequent *forte* phrase reaches almost *ff* on 'wrath'. (The OED makes the vowel in 'wrath' the same as that in 'taut', and it therefore rhymes with 'North'. I rhyme 'wrath' with 'moth', but I'm obviously wrong.) Verse four is marked louder than verse one; this allows for a contrast with the *mp* coming up, which could indeed be as soft as *p*.

Arthur Bliss (1891-1975)

The return from Town – Millay – 1940 (pub. 1980)

A great many songs can be sung by men or women, and many others are really only suitable for men to sing. This is one of those which can only be sung by a woman. The two cradle songs in this volume aren't specifically for a woman's voice, and *Reading Scheme* is only limited to women because of the way the composer has set it. With this, however, it is the poem which dictates the sex of the narrator. The simple folky style requires a simple response from the singer, without any coquettishness. After all, the poem is about marital fidelity, not a subject which usually gets much of an airing, infidelity and disaster being more exciting material. The strange harmonies in the two bars before 'As I went over' have to stand as they are, though from the simplicity of what comes before that, you might expect a dominant seventh on the D followed by a G major chord on the minim.

Benjamin Burrows (1891-1966)

Mistress Fell – de la Mare – 1928

There is real passion in this splendid song; a terrible grief which has unhinged the poor woman. Her name is significant – 'Fell' as an adjective is given in my dictionary as fierce or savage, though this quality is mostly suppressed in the poem. The question-and-answer format echoes the style of the old ballads, many of which would tell similar stories of loss and pain. Your questions are quite matter-of-fact, and the 'slow' tempo is about 60 beats per minute. The intensity lies in the answers, though at first hardly at all; even the word 'wild' only needs a hint of stress. At 'stranger' (top of page 25) she engages for the first time with the questioner directly. Breathe after 'such an one' and give a glottal stop on 'I' for emphasis. 'Prythee' is pronounced 'prithee', with the first syllable as in 'this'. The 'fast' sections seem to work well at about 90 beats per minute. At bar 47 the tempo gradually pulls back for four bars, reaching the right speed for the 'slower' section. Although 'I must go' is clearly *forte*, be sure that you don't make the song's climax here; that comes at 'All that he loved' on the last page. 'Touched me his fingers', though quiet, is packed with suppressed emotion, unlike the quiet question which follows. The next part, from 'Magic laid its dreary spell', is generally quiet until 'out of her bower' on page 29. There is a *rall* in bar 71, but an *a tempo*, I think, on 'cry' (bar 72), then another *rall* as marked and another *a tempo* on 'sigh' (bar 74). From 'out of her bower' don't be too loud, but let clarity of diction do the work. In bar 83 and the first beat of bar 84 I'm sure the right hand should be an octave higher. The 'slow' at bar 90 is Mistress Fell speaking, not the questioner, and 'Thus have they told me' is full of bleak pathos. Stress 'Thus' a little, without too much tone, and don't anticipate the new movement. Indeed, let the piano's new tempo awaken you from this passionless moment so that by 'And I come' you are fully involved again. A *poco stringendo* might be a good idea here, and the *rall* lasts for a bar and a half until 'Clasped', which can be somewhat slower and more expansive than the basic 'fast' tempo. After the *rall* in bar 108 I suggest a bar of *accelerando* to *a tempo* on bar 110.

If the phrase is too long for one breath, finish the word 'All' at the end of bar 111, breathe well, and put another 'all' on the F♯ of bar 112. Try a *diminuendo* and then a *crescendo* on 'loved', holding the note right into bar 119. There is then a *dim* over three bars to *pp* on 'whispering', but don't lose the emotional intensity. I think there are two misprints in the piano part: in bar 99 the fifth quaver should be an F natural (cf. bar 45), and in bar 108 the upper D on the third crotchet must be a D natural.

Herbert Howells (1892-1983)

---

1. King David – de la Mare – 1919 (pub. 1923)

Frequently, a good way to form an idea of how to tackle a song is to look at the musical structure, in this case the key-progression. It starts in E flat minor for the first verse before moving to the relative major (G flat) for the second, which modulates into A flat minor. The third verse is in E major, and the fourth verse starts in D, modulating into B major, B minor, G major and E minor, leading us to E major for the last verse. Each verse therefore has a distinctive musical character, and this mirrors the development of the text. The tempo should flow easily, never becoming self-indulgent and pedestrian, and most of the time a good *legato* is needed. At the beginning the singer is just a narrator, uninvolved in King David's emotions; let the music convey them. The change to G flat for verse two heralds the warm, full sound of the hundred harps, sung *dolce,* though. If necessary, breathe after 'David'. There is now a wonderful enharmonic change on 'rose' from A flat to G sharp, introducing the new key for the nightingale. Here again, let the music make the point, and I think that *placido* indicates a return to tempo 1. When D major appears for verse four, that is the time for the singer to become involved in the king's newly-awakened feelings. The phrases are less *legato* than before, suggesting more intensity. 'Tell me' is marked *f*, but the question is addressed to a little bird; don't frighten it away. *Più tranquillo* for the last verse probably means tempo 1 again, and the voice returns to long *legato* phrases. The narrator can betray something of the king's relief and joy at the end. Breathe after 'own' if necessary.

2. Gavotte – Newbolt – 1919 (pub 1927)

'Tempo di gavotte' covers a wide range of possible speeds, from quite quick to moderate and stately. The two constant elements to this dance movement over the centuries are two beats in a bar (two minims here) and four-bar phrases. One of the guiding factors was always the degree of ornamentation required, and the more florid and complicated it was the slower the piece became. In this song the semiquaver piano figures in the second system of page 38, the bottom of page 40 and the second system of page 41 all point to a moderate tempo. Confirmation of this comes in the text: 'Stately measure and stately ending'. The two outer verses are almost identical for the voice, but you will notice that in verse one the phrase-mark is broken between 'creeping' and 'softly', allowing for the implied comma there, whereas the equivalent place in the last verse has no break. I would say that unless a breath is needed I would have no break either time, to avoid any fussiness. Enjoy the charm of the G major verses with their deliberately archaic courtly style, singing them quite simply. The middle verses, set in the minor key, describe the ghostly scene which the music conjures up for the poet, and you can be a little more expressive here. But it seems to me that even at its loudest the voice should never become too present. 'Untender' probably lies in the brilliant part of your range, and the temptation is there to show the listeners what a splendid sound you can make. Risk disappointing them this time and choose a show-off piece for your next song. The rhyming of 'tender' with 'untender' seems a little weak, but it follows the pattern set in the rest of the poem ('sleeping' in verse one, 'straying' in verse two and so on). This particular rhyme emphasises in a rather sexist manner the contrast between the gallant gentlemen and the calculating ladies. If their grace is in fact 'untender' in comparison with the 'tender' courage, then the first syllable 'un-' needs to be stressed. The accompaniment throughout this section hasn't been asked for anything more than *piano*, but at the louder *mf* under 'Suppliant conquest' the singer should be no more than *mf* herself.

171

3. Come sing and dance – from an old carol – 1927

There are many songs which can be sung by men or women, and many more which can be transposed to suit the vocal range of the singer. This song, however, because of the type of melisma on 'Eia' and 'Alleluia', seems to me clearly intended for a soprano to sing, and only in the key of A flat. The 'gentle dance movement' refers not to the voice part but to the swinging compound rhythm of the accompaniment, and it implies a speed of around 84 beats per minute. Since this is a song of joy, the big *ff* on the last page should be unforced and easy. The first 'Eia' is *mf* to allow for an echo effect on the second one. Slow triplets are often a problem (eg, 'heals our fear'), and they can be somewhat bumpy as you negotiate the cross-rhythm; make them *legato* and natural-sounding. The second 'Alleluia' is still *f* until the last syllable. The first 'Alleluia' of verse two stays fairly loud, and the piano had better be *mf* at this point. The *sempre un poco accel* starting on 'Now all mankind' continues for almost five lines of music, which is hardly a practical proposition. Choose certain moments to push ahead – 'Eia', for example, and 'Christ and King'. The *poco allarg.* can become *molto allarg.* on the triplet leading up to the cathartic top A flat. Stay *legato,* start 'Sing Jesus' mf (the piano, too), and make no *rit.* until *colla voce* is marked.

Peter Warlock (1894-1930)

Many of Warlock's songs have a specifically male character, either because they are about drinking or the love of a pretty girl. I have chosen some of that sort (*As ever I saw, There is a lady sweet and kind*, and *Captain Stratton's Fancy*), but the rest are suitable for male or female voice.

1. As ever I saw – Anon – first setting, 1918 (pub. 1919)

The metronome marking gives minim = 92, and yet the time signature is four crotchet beats to a bar. Perhaps Warlock's metronome couldn't manage a speed of 184, but the important thing is that the song should not be sung as if it had two beats to a bar; the danger of thinking in two is that each minim beat would be emphasised and the listener would get a bumpy ride. The rhythmic impetus is smoother than that, and in fact the major stresses are usually on the middle of the bar, viz. 'She is gentle and also wise; of all other she beareth the prize, that ever I saw.' ('all', 'other' and 'ever' also have a sort of subsidiary stress). At this speed the five-bar phrases may as well be in one breath, with punctuation breaks where necessary; indeed, after 'dance' (verse two) and 'say' (last verse) there is no time for a breath anyway. The exceptions are after 'wrought' (verse four), possibly after 'beauty' and of course after 'lady' (verse five). For the first two-and-a-half pages the singer follows the piano's dynamics, but at 'I have seen many' both performers can come down to *mp*, and at 'Yet is there none' they can reduce even further to *p*. Now the *crescendo* before 'Therefore I dare' becomes bolder, but remember to keep something in hand for the final *ff*. There is no obvious place for a breath: 'say' has to go through, and a break after 'may' upsets the musical progression. My advice is to go all the way to the first 'saw' and make a *poco rit.* three beats early, taking time to breathe before the last 'that ever I saw' with an additional *ritenuto*.

2. Lullaby – Dekker – 1919

The marked tempo of 152 beats to the minute is quite fast, and it is interesting to see that *con moto sempre* has been put in as a reminder. One of the results of this is that the song cannot lapse into sentimentality at any time, though it is important to let the tempo flow without being driven. The baby is expected to go to sleep, after all, and if the pace of the song makes the singer sound in any way tense and hurried, the child will definitely stay awake. The singer follows the piano's dynamics except at 'eyes' in the first verse, and 'sleep you' at the same spot in the second verse. Use one breath from 'Sleep, pretty wantons' to 'lullaby', *diminuendo* as marked on the first 'rock', don't breathe, and then lean on the second 'rock' with a very swift *dim.* as if it were a gentle *fp*. At the *pochissimo rit.* at the end of verse two, the singer must lead the bending of the time with something like a *tenuto* on 'Rock' and an *accelerando* on 'a lulla' to an *a tempo* on 'lullaby'. I know that this is not precisely what is written, but there is a slightly stilted quality about it otherwise, and I think my version feels more natural. See how *non rit.* appears twice at the end: I believe he means it.

3. *There is a lady sweet and kind – Ford – first setting, 1918-19 (pub. 1920)*

This song, at least until near the end, has a feeling of sensuous contentment, of quiet confidence. The rhythm is flexible throughout, not only where tempo markings are placed, and it is almost all *legato*. The high notes on 'kind', 'smiles' and 'range' are all floated; nothing is more than *mp* for the first two-and-a-half verses. In the second verse the commas need to be hinted at, and I suggest a little *tenuto* on the second syllable of 'gesture' and on 'wit'. Make a break in the sound (but don't breathe) between 'motion' and 'and', and do the same for 'love her . . . till I die'. For the last verse the singer makes a small *crescendo* on 'change' while the piano makes quite a large one, then comes in *forte* on 'But change..' with an *accel.* and *poco rit.* The *tenuto* on 'sky' really applies to the tied quaver, which can be given plenty of time. 'Yet will I love her' is virtually *a tempo*; 'till I die' is *rit. molto* like the piano.

4. *Captain Stratton's Fancy – Masefield – 1921 (pub. 1922)*

'With great heartiness' says the score, and this implies a good, solid tempo suitable for a good, solid drinking man; crotchet = 120 should do the trick. The words have to be as clear as possible, but over a strictly measured accompaniment the sung notes can be bent a little to give the text the speech-rhythm it needs, and also, if the truth be known, to suggest that some liquid refreshment has already passed down the singer's throat. The dynamic markings are the same for singer and pianist, even in verse three ('Oh some are for the lily . . .') where the instruction to be *mp* throughout is quite unexpected. Since there is no *rall.* given at the end, the song should be *a tempo* to the last note. I do think, though, that *poco meno mosso* on the very last 'Says the old . . .' is a good alternative.

5. Sleep – Fletcher – 1922 (pub. 1923)

What a wonderful song this is: shaped like a lute song with false relations, ambiguous rhythms and other archaic touches, and through it all a weird, wandering harmony that always returns eventually to the home minor key until the *tierce de Picardie* at the end. It's also available with a string quartet. Don't be tempted by the luscious harmonies to perform this song too slowly and lapse into a quaver beat – the pulse is the crotchet or, in the case of the 5/8 bars, a crotchet followed by a dotted crotchet. Warlock's comment at the beginning about phrasing according to the natural accentuation of the words not only takes us across barlines – it also takes us across the lines of the poem. For example, it is 'Come, Sleep,' (breath) 'and with thy sweet deceiving Lock me in delight awhile;' (breath). Similarly, we have 'Let some pleasing dreams beguile All my fancies' (breath) 'that from thence There may steal an influence' (breath). Incidentally, the poem as published had: 'I may feel an influence', the version Gurney used. I prefer Warlock's alteration. The second verse has more intensity in the words, and Warlock has responded with a more complex version of the harmony. The poet gets quite worked up to the heartfelt cry 'O let my joys', but the composer lets it subside a little sooner than would a reader of the poem, I think. The *rit. molto e dim.* bar has a lovely progression of strange, edge-of-sleep harmonies leading to peace at last on the final major chord.

6. Three songs – Belloc – 1927

6.1. Ha'nacker Mill. A metronome mark of about 50 is slow enough for this song, allowing the phrases to flow. For the first verse the singer needs to create a picture of ruin and desolation, for which I suggest taking much of the brightness out of the tone, and singing *legato* without any 'wordy' diction. Breathe after 'blindly', not because you need the air but for the sense of the poem, and for this reason the tempo should be briefly held up. At 'clapper is still', however, the pulse must move on so as to connect with the next phrase. Verse two is louder and more wordy: 'Desolation', 'Ruin' and 'unploughed' need emphasis. Where the *dim.* is marked in the piano part under 'Spirits', remember to start at *forte*. 'Spirits abroad in a windy cloud' is all *mp* without

175

further *diminuendo*, signalling a connection with the next verse. Make a steep *diminuendo* on 'done', taking time to do so, starting 'Wind and thistle' *p*. The *crescendo* in parallel with the piano takes you almost to *mf*, certainly no more. Within the *diminuendo* on the singer's last bar there is room to lean on the second 'Never', having made a small break without breathing. The piano hardly makes any *rallentando* in the final three bars.

6.2.   The Night. 'Soft and chant-like' ought perhaps to have the additional qualification 'without vibrato'. I'm well aware that singing *senza vibrato* is for some singers well-nigh impossible, since it seems to come naturally with the development of the voice. It is certainly easier to cut it out when one is singing *pp*, as here, but the reader may wonder why it might be necessary at all. Not only does it give an ethereal, other-worldly quality to the voice, it enables all the semitone dissonances to be heard with perfect clarity, eg. 'my tired' (bar 8), 'requi-' (bar 15) and '-light' (five bars from the end) amongst others. Another qualification to the opening marking is that it should all be *legato* which doesn't only suit the character of the song, it also helps the dissonances to tell effectively. There is a very clear development of harmonic complexity through the three verses, and this is mirrored by the way the dynamics change from plain *pp* in verse one, *mp, crescendo, diminuendo* to *pp* again in verse two, and *mf sostenuto* back to *pp* for verse three. There is something disturbing about the strange harmonies in the last verse, connected maybe with the line 'and cheat me with your false delight', but this makes the sweet resolution to the major chord on 'Night' all the sweeter.

6.3.   My Own Country. Warlock has not followed the conventional path of picking a time signature and sticking to it, but has preferred to stay with one note for each syllable (in this case a quaver), altering the bar length to suit the rhythm and stress of the poem. The singer should not treat these changes of stress as syncopations but should adjust so smoothly that the listener notices nothing unusual. Be aware also that the song starts with four quaver beats to a bar rather than the more normal two crotchet beats. The poem speaks of a journey and a search not as a matter of longing and homesickness but with a confidence that the way will bring the poet inevitably to the promised land. This may be the land of childhood and memory or it may be the place of life after death ('And then I shall dream, for ever and all'). Whatever or wherever it is, there is a sense of expected fulfilment and joy, particularly at 'In the month of May . . .' which Warlock places in A major before returning to the home key of F. The piano part seems to want a tiny pause before the third beat in the bar of 'ever and all', so the singer can delay 'all' fractionally. 'A good dream and deep' has two pairs of 'd's, and the question is whether to finish one 'd' before starting the next, or to connect the two and leave a silence ('goo – pause – dream'). If the former, don't make it 'good – ah – dream', and if the latter, give it a big silence between the words.

Harry Gill (1897-1987)

In Memoriam – Dixon – ?1919

Ernest Farrar (*qv*) taught Gill and the poet Percy Dixon as well as Gerald Finzi (*qv*) and this song makes a fitting tribute to his memory. Sing *legato* and with a good timbre throughout, taking each phrase in one breath. Don't be too spiky on the dotted rhythms, allowing the semiquavers their full value. 'But sorrow walks with me' is marked *più f*, but that is relative to the *p* and *mp* which have gone before. Make a *diminuendo* on 'along the way he came'. The bells' chimes in the piano part need to be brought out a little from the *pp* texture, and the voice's dynamic for 'on the scented air' should fit with that.

Michael Head (1900-1976)

1. Sweet Chance, that led my steps abroad – W H Davies – 1928

Michael Head's reputation has suffered because he wrote songs that were attractive to sing and to hear, and which attained a wide popularity beyond the confines of the art-song connoisseur. I urge you to make up your own mind. From the piano's opening bars the tempo of this song can be quite flexible. Breathe after 'chance', then allow the phrase to ebb and flow in dynamics and tempo naturally. *Poco accel* suggests more movement than *rubato* would give, but let the speed relax again on the fourth line. The long phrase over the next four lines seems rather static, the melody getting stuck on the same few notes. You can help matters by making a fairly big *crescendo* and *accelerando* at the same time, and do breathe after 'staring'. The coda from 'A rainbow' can be slightly slower, and slower still on the final phrase.

2. *The Estuary – Ruth Pitter – 1945*

The estuary I know best is at Fowey in Cornwall, but that is one with deep clear water and steeply shelving wooded banks, quite closed in. The estuary of this poem is very different; the land around is flat, open and sandy, with a shipping channel somewhere in the middle, gouged out by a powerful current, and the music clearly describes the wide open spaces. For four lines of music the voice part remains very quiet, no dynamic contrasts disturbing the vocal landscape. The words throughout the song are in speech rhythm, with accentuation marks carefully placed on important syllables. The first *crescendo* hardly reaches beyond *mp* before falling back to *pp*. The next, starting on 'like evening', is shown stretching as far as 'through the bay', but it has only reached *p* by 'changes'. For practical purposes it needs to grow more than that and come down again to *p* at that point. Much of the *poco più mosso* effect is achieved by the quicker triplet movement in the piano part. Now, at last, the *crescendo* goes to *mf* and then further still, but bear in mind that the loudest place of all is probably on 'crescent arising'. 'Pallid and thin' is on a *diminuendo,* but don't be tempted to take too much timbre from the voice in painting the words, because there is a long way to go until the *pp*. The *poco ritard.* only lasts for the 'crescent' bar. Return to the faster speed afterwards to allow for the *poco meno mosso* to be about the same as the opening tempo. It is *p* for this final part, not *pp* as at the beginning, and 'river' should start *mp* to give room for the long *diminuendo.*

Gerald Finzi (1901-1956)

1. Let us garlands bring – poems by Shakespeare – 1942

These songs are also available in a version for accompaniment by string orchestra.

1.1. Come away, come away, death. Some discussion of this song appears on pages 63-64. The piano opening has a heavy tread even though it is marked only *mp;* ensure that this is more than the *p* for 'Fly away'. The voice needs some dark timbre throughout to accompany the plodding rhythm and tough harmonies. The low Bs and the C sharp on 'yew' require additional vocal weight to balance them against the higher notes. This is even more necessary for the low notes on 'weep' which are at the climax of the long melisma. Avoid the temptation to make the semiquaver pairs too quick. There is no need to breathe between the 'come aways' and similar places, except after the first 'Not a friend', because that is followed by a long phrase in one breath (unless you have to breathe after 'corpse'). 'To weep there' is best in one breath, I suppose, but I snatch an extra one at the end of the tied F sharp. This allows for plenty of tone and a good *ritard.*; nobody wants to hear a singer struggling at the end of a phrase through a misguided attempt to perform a feat of pulmonary athletics.

1.2. Who is Silvia? The quirky rhythm of the accompaniment needs to be strictly applied except where *rit.* and *allargando* are marked. Don't be serious, even at the climax. It is all *p* until the *crescendo* on 'there', which should keep pace with the longer *crescendo* in the piano. Sing 'She excels . . . dwelling' as one phrase, then breathe before 'To her'. The pianist can take plenty of time in the *ritenuto* bar to leap down all that way, with a really heavy *pesante* dying away to nothing.

1.3. Fear no more the heat o' the sun. 42 beats to the minute is a very slow pulse, but if you get it right it flows beautifully. As with the first song, a dark timbre suits the seriousness of this setting. The singer is not heart-broken but gently expressing his love for the one who has

179

died. Don't lean on every main beat but sing long phrases instead. The *forte* is warm, not aggressive, and there should be a noticeable contrast with the *mf* on 'Thou hast finished'. The solemn final verse lays an enchantment upon the place in a mood of quiet confidence. 'Consummation' is nothing to do with consuming but it is connected with summing; please pronounce it accordingly.

1.4. O mistress mine. There is a delightful interplay between the two parts in the right hand of the piano introduction; perhaps this is the playful dance of the girl and her lover. Certainly there is a teasing, playful quality throughout this song. The vocal part enters in the middle of this piano dialogue, and it must not disturb the piano's flow until 'lovers' meeting'. Although there is a rest between 'stay and hear' and 'your true love's coming', keep your intention clear through that silence, almost as if there were no rest. 'Roaming', 'sweeting', 'hereafter' and 'laughter' all carry the danger of stressing the final syllable; take care to taper the voice away. In 'Every wise man's son', don't release the s (effectively a z) of 'man's' before the s of 'son'. If possible, move seamlessly from one to the other, which means voicing briefly, unvoicing while still hissing, then moving on. Keep the timbre on 'know' and on 'endure' at the end of the second verse. 'What's to come' is marked *f*, but it is less, I think, than the *f* on 'lovers' meeting', which is itself less than 'kiss me, sweet and twenty'. Be really quiet on 'Youth's a stuff . . .' as if you were whispering into her ear at that moment. The *molto rit.* is more here than on the previous occasion.

1.5. It was a lover and his lass. As I wrote in the chapter on tempo, one reason why this speed of minim = c. 72 is right for me is that I can manage the rapid-fire 'ding a ding a ding'; anything faster would tie me up. To suit the dancing rhythm of the poem, 'the only pretty' is never fully *legato.* The vowel of 'birds' is difficult to enunciate properly; give the vowel its full value to avoid 'buds'. Remember to keep the *forte* suitable for a happy song, and to sing a real *p* where marked. In the third verse the word is 'flower', not 'flah', and there is no need to breathe after it. The great outburst of joy on 'crownèd' can be accompanied by a little *allargando,* taking time to breathe after 'prime', then back into tempo for 'In spring'. Start the long note of 'love' quite quietly, make an accent on 'spring' followed by a *diminuendo* and a big *crescendo* to the end. Piano and voice come off together on '-ng'.

2. *Earth and Air and Rain – poems by Thomas Hardy – 1936*

2.1. Summer Schemes. The flexibility in this song is largely indicated by the composer – *poco ritard., a tempo; ritard., poco accel., a tempo* and so on. This acts like written-out *rubato* for those specific moments, allowing the rest of the piece to flow with a fairly strict rhythm. Finzi makes a distinction between *ritardando* – getting slower – and *ritenuto* – slower; the singer should avoid slowing down any further during the *ritenuto* bars. There is an equal partnership between voice and piano, with sometimes one taking the initiative, sometimes the other. The voice can use the piano dynamics as a guide and make plenty of contrasts. If you breathe between 'minims' and 'shakes', try not to clip the end of 'minims', and sing 95% of 'trills' on the vowel and then close on a properly audible '-lls'. The same goes for the last word of the song, 'bring'. 'But who may sing' at the end could do with being a little slower than 'but who shall say' in the first verse, and a little softer too. In these two passages Finzi leaves the more straightforward harmonies he uses elsewhere and brings in aching suspensions and false relations. He clearly shares the typical Hardy view that the future wears a dark aspect.

2.2. When I set out for Lyonesse. This poem has Hardy describing the time years before, when he first went to Cornwall and met the woman who was to become his first wife. With a home key of E minor it is not as triumphant in tone as it could have been, but it is probably best to sing it for its youthful eagerness and let the contrast with the other songs around it tell of any bitterness or regret. The first high E 'hundred' is quite soft, and the next, marked *f* in the piano, is full-toned but not accented, while the final top E on 'magic' is loudest of all but still without accent; the sound of happiness can easily turn to anger with the wrong kind of attack. The name 'Lyonesse' is each time set as triplet quavers, whereas the equivalent figure in the piano is two semiquavers and a quaver. It may seem like a small point, but it makes the word more comfortable to sing with the slightly slacker rhythm. It should be pronounced not as if it were French, but like 'lioness', the animal. There are three held notes which can present problems, and they are the final syllables of each verse. 'Eyes' has a *dim* marked, and '-way' needs to tail off a little as well. Make the *dim* a positive thing, not a removal of energy and intensity along with the volume. 'There' at the end of verse two can have a small *crescendo* and *diminuendo* to keep it from sounding fixed and dead. The *crescendo* from 'All marked' lasts for eight bars and requires careful grading. The '-less' of 'fathomless' needs to be kept alive, as does '-gic' of 'magic'. Feed the tone through 'in my eyes'. The pianist has a carefully controlled *dim* at the end, the start of which can be delayed by half a bar from where marked. Don't make a *rall* even to place the final bass chord.

2.3. Waiting Both. Finzi has expressly avoided any sudden changes of tempo, choosing rather to run smoothly through with *rall.* and *accel.* When the piano has *accel.* in bar six, take care not to seem eager and anxious; that happens at the *affrettando* on the next page. The opening is very calm, impersonal and quiet, both in the piano and subsequently in the voice. The second 'mean to do' can be a little less than the first. The *affrettando* has a very quick *crescendo* to 'all I know'. 'Wait' is perhaps a bit less, and there is a *dim.* on 'Till my change'. The three bars of *accel.* have to be balanced with five bars of *rall.* to take us back to *tempo 1*. Now the left-hand rising chromatic scale rumbles away in the bass, enhancing the strangeness of the encounter between human being and star, but the voice is again very quiet to the end.

2.4. The Phantom. The piano and voice are marvellously interwoven in this piece, and at times the vocal melody is doubled in the piano, while at other times they go their separate ways with imitation and counter-melody. Although the poem speaks of another man in the third person, the experiences here are really Hardy's own. As a result there should be an inner identification with the feelings described. Except where marked, the pulse is quite strict. *Ritenuto* means a slower speed, not gradually slowing down. The opening dotted rhythm is slightly detached, in contrast with the *legato* passage at the *poco meno mosso*. The *a tempo* at 'A phantom of his own figuring' is back to the *meno mosso* of crotchet = 76. *Tempo 1* doesn't reappear until '-rider' on the following page. The *poco affrettando* at 'day, night, As if on the air' involves quite a considerable *accel.* for four bars, followed by eight bars of *ritard.* which should feel rather like pulling on the reins of a horse to slow it down, and here the speed reaches well below 88. 'And though toil-tried, He withers daily' is *legato*, but 'Time touches . . .' is quite detached. Feel the urgency at the *più animato*, and again use the reins to pull back hard on the tempo, especially at the *largamente*. The syncopation at 'And as when first' is difficult to render both accurately and naturally. Incidentally, I find that there is a word problem on 'What his back years bring'. 'Back years' is an unusual pairing of words, and the listener might substitute the nonsensical 'back ears' instead. I'm not sure there's anything to be done about it if one doesn't want to over-emphasise the clarity.

2.5. So I have fared. The footnote to this song talks of the crotchet approximating to the reciting note of Anglican chant. An appropriate response to this is to keep the whole thing chant-like and unemotional, in which case the 'flexibility and freedom of ordinary speech' has already been largely written in to the music by the composer, and too much further bending of the rhythm could spoil the song's effect. I would counsel adhering quite accurately to the note-values on the page. The *A tempo giusto* is a short section of hymn-writing, very *legato*. The final *meno mosso* is very quiet and still understated. The kind of Latin we hear nowadays (if at all) in churches would rhyme 'fecisti' with 'misty'; here the Latin endings must rhyme with 'missed I'.

2.6. Rollicum-Rorum. This goes at breakneck speed to the very end without deviation. The poor pianist is the one who bears the brunt, and on him or her depends whether the song sounds in or out of control. The singer must enjoy the words with a metaphorical smile, never straying into seeming angry. Play with *legato* and *staccato*, and with loud and soft. For example, 'march his men on' can be *legato*, 'London town' *staccato*', but not necessarily every time. The first 'Then Boney' is *sf, p* in the piano, the second is straight *f*, and the third and fourth are *mf*. 'Tollolorum' twice has a *crescendo* to the low B which is asking a lot; start the phrase a little softer, perhaps, and don't breathe before the upper C natural. Breathe before 'And march his men' in the last verse, making a *crescendo* on the long 'town' and then a *subito p* on 'Rollicum'. By the way, England during the early years of the eighteenth century had lived in fear of invasion from France, and Hardy's grandmother, like many of her generation, used the threat of Boney (Napoleon Bonaparte) to make children behave themselves.

2.7. *To Lizbie Browne.* We don't know how long it is since you, the singer, have seen her, but you are still in love with her. The feelings here are of wistfulness, yearning and regret, but there is no bitterness or anger. The footnote to *senza rigore* is very interesting: 'Such suppleness cannot be determined by directions on paper'. It is the singer's role to bring each thought off the page as if it were entirely new and spontaneous, and it is the pianist's more difficult role to respond and support. There are times when a few bars of regular tempo are called for, such as from 'But, Lizbie Browne' at the bottom of the fourth page, but generally it is the speech rhythms that predominate. To understand the flow of the poem it definitely helps to read it and find where stresses come and where the phrases are leading. As an example, the sentence starting 'When, Lizbie Browne' at the top of the third page carries through for five bars, and even holds over the bar's rest to 'My Lizbie Browne'. The similar 'Lost Lizbie Browne' near the end is more significant – it represents the death of his hopes. The only phrase-mark in the voice part is over 'How you could sing . . .' which calls for the *legato* treatment. At the bottom of the third page linger on the L of 'Love'. The loudest moment of the song is probably 'Touched never your lip', and even that is hardly *forte*. 'And who was he?' is quite quiet, notwithstanding the *crescendo* in the piano part, and think of a wry smile on the final answer.

2.8. *The Clock of the Years.* At the top, before the music, is the line 'A spirit passed before my face; the hair of my flesh stood up'. This is a quote from the Bible (Job 4:15), although the story that follows is not the same. In performance I think the line needs to be spoken, with the piano entering immediately afterwards. The poem is one of real horror, worthy of Edgar Allan Poe. There are three characters to consider: the spirit, with a cold, cruel delivery; the narrator in dialogue with the spirit; and the narrator telling the story. The narrator in the dialogue watches as the deeds unfold, and there is an immediacy to his response. The narrator as he relates the horrors is now removed from them, so his overriding feelings are of defeat and despair, even from the beginning. Don't *crescendo* before it is marked at 'first had known'. After 'enough', bring 'let her stay' in a little early, holding the intensity through the rests. 'No stop' has to have a full enough tone to allow for a *diminuendo*. Throughout the next five lines the pulse has to be absolutely inexorable, especially during the held chords at the top of the fourth page. The process of making her younger and younger doesn't stop until she has in effect ceased to exist, even in memory. The accented bass quavers in the piano (G sharp and C sharp) are still a hard *forte*. The pause bar should be stretched out almost beyond what is comfortable, before once again continuing in tempo, this time very *legato*. Connect 'lived in me' with 'but it cannot now'. Give a strong 'd' at the end of 'ordained' and place the piano chord fractionally later so as not to lose the consonant.

2.9. In a Churchyard. I think it worth explaining that the ones who 'ride their diurnal round . . . in peerless ease' are in fact the dead, who go on to say that they are having such a pleasant time underground that they hope the Day of Judgment is delayed indefinitely. The piano bass gives us the creeping roots, and the middle voice triple rhythm on the second page represents the easy jog of existence below. Some of the lines are very long, particularly 'If the living . . . no one would weep', and until this point everything has been fairly soft. Don't break the tempo at all between 'there' and 'no one'. Use a sustained tone on the *largamente* section, controlling the *diminuendo* in parallel with the piano part. Now comes a moment reminiscent of Fauré as the key changes to D major and the narrator has come to terms with what he has heard.

2.10. Proud Songsters. We listen to the extended piano introduction just as the poet listens to the birdsong around him, and when the singer enters, it is in a subsidiary role musing on what he hears. It is only on the last page that singer and piano come together to sum up the wonder of it all. Let 'all Time were theirs' grow naturally with the piano. Don't let the tempo go slack on the bar of 'thrushes, But only'. Keep the ending simple until the tiniest delay on 'rain', preparing for the piano's final *espressivo* phrase.

Elizabeth Poston (1905-1987)

Sweet Suffolk Owl – Vautor – 1925

The piano opening and the whole of the first verse should be simply sung without much nuance or descriptive word-painting; that comes in verse two. I suggest starting a little louder than *piano*, allowing for 'like a lady bright' to be definitely quieter. 'Thou sing'st alone' is louder again, preparing for the *più piano* at 'Too whit, too whoo'. This owl's Suffolk accent makes it hoot rather more than normal with its two 'too's instead of the usual 'Te whit, te whoo'. Let your voice carry some brilliant resonance on 'shrill', make a *diminuendo* on the last two *legato* quavers of the bar, then give a *non legato* impetus to the beginning of the next *scherzando* bar. It is warm and *legato* for 'And sings a dirge', and the *poco rall* leads to quite a free *meno mosso* 'Too whit, too whoo'. Here the piano can move the tempo on again for one four-beat bar, leaving the voice free once more on the downward scale.

Benjamin Britten (1913-1976)

Winter Words – poems by Thomas Hardy – 1953

There are two great contrasts between these and the Hardy settings of Finzi, and they are in Britten's repetition of parts of the text and in his use of melismas. These two elements are so prevalent in his vocal music that they have become mannerisms, satirised by Dudley Moore in *Little Miss Muffet,* his 'Britten folk-song arrangement'. Repeating words as often as he does shows a certain arrogance towards the poet and his work as he moulds them to fit his artistic conception; and yet, that very confidence in his own creative genius is what helped to make him an internationally renowned composer. Some repetitions are clearly for emphasis, as in the first song, for example: 'when no trees, no tall trees grew here', where Hardy writes simply: 'when no tall trees grew here'. Others are less obvious, as in the second song: 'Or whence he came, or whence he came'. The rhythm of Hardy's words, and the astonishing variety of meters and verse forms he used, are very important components of his poetry. The short final line in each verse of this poem is a masterly device, which should in my opinion be allowed to stand as it was written. Many of the melismatic phrases are examples of word-painting: song 1, 'waiting', song 2, 'journeying', song 3, 'prinking', and song 5, 'seraphim', when the music is used as a dancing hymn of praise. Some, though, are unnecessary decorations which draw too much attention to the music and distract from the flow of the text.

1. At Day-Close in November

The opening piano figure pictures a gusty autumn day, a decoration suggested by the pine trees that 'give their black heads a toss'. The impetuousness asked for at the beginning is in this piano figure and the various syncopations in the voice: a small *marcato* on the second note of 'wings', for instance, helps to convey the urgency required. The triple time comes from the 'waltzers waiting', and on this line the first beat of each bar can be exaggerated to evoke the scene. Be careful, though, that the accentuation remains true, with no stress on the second syllable of 'waiting'. The series of *crescendos* from 'Beech leaves' needs to be controlled by starting each phrase slightly quieter than the end of the preceding phrase so that an impression of a gradual *crescendo* can be given, up to the only real *forte* of the song where the piano is *ff*. The opening *forte* should therefore be a little less. The last page, from 'And the children', is all *pp*, but practically speaking there has to be some rise and fall within that marking, with a warming of the tone on the last line.

2. Midnight on the Great Western (or the journeying boy)

The tonality of this song is continually shifting, as if it cannot make up its mind where to settle. It starts in C major and ends in C minor, but the vocal line keeps changing key: G major, A flat minor, F major, etc. This reflects the boy's listlessness and ignorance of his origin or his destination. The 'very slow' opening can be quite free, but the 'deliberate movement' sections should maintain a really strict tempo,

187

describing the rhythmical drumming of the train wheels. Verse three differs from the others, and needs to be treated as a recitative, with the singer daring to take liberties with the rhythm. The first three verses are generally *p*, never louder than *mf*, and this allows for the *forte* climax in verse four not to be over-blown.

3. Wagtail and Baby (a satire)

The pianist should be very accurate in the cross-rhythms; the left hand is in compound time, but the right hand is effectively in simple time with triplet semiquavers. The voice goes its own way, undisturbed by what is going on elsewhere, corresponding to the unruffled bird. There are plenty of opportunities for using different vocal colours: the blaring bull, a *marcato* stallion, a *legato* and sinister slinking mongrel, and a bit of brilliant prinking. In verse four the scene changes with the introduction of the quirky little caricature of the perfect gentleman (remember, it's not gentle<u>man</u>). 'Quick' means something around crotchet = 132, and if you're clever the *molto rall.* can lead you neatly back into the opening tempo, but don't be tempted to start it until it is marked.

4. The Little Old Table

I hope it's not too fanciful to liken the right-hand piano part to the smooth table-top, and the spiky left-hand interjections to the creaking. The central element of this poem, the table's creak, is a very small thing, and the song should therefore be treated as a miniature. The loudest points are where 'warm' is marked, and this is hardly *mf*, notwithstanding that the piano has the odd *sf* creak to play. At the beginning, take care to hold 'creak' for long enough that the word can be understood properly, and not come out as 'crick'. Playing out to the end in strict time seems to fit with the eccentricity of the words and music.

5. The Choirmaster's Burial (or the Tenor Man's story)

This song falls into sections according to Hardy's indicated stanzas. The first, ending on 'seraphim', is reminiscent of a chant, and it should be almost conversational in tone. The melody in the accompaniment is the 'Mount Ephraim' mentioned in the poem. The next short section, marked 'quicker', is at minim = 72 approximately, and this tempo is maintained through the vicar's pompous reply. Don't lose the character of the vicar's voice on the *diminuendo*. The hurried burial follows, still in strict time, with very little voice but plenty of good diction. The entry on 'But' must be precisely placed, not in the spiky mood of the quicker section but in the gentler mood of the next chant-like figure. This time 'Mount Ephraim' is found concealed in the upper notes of the right-hand triplets and quadruplets. The last line rounds the song off quite simply.

6. Proud Songsters (Thrushes, Finches and Nightingales)

The whole style of this setting suggests the teeming hurry of nature as it rushes to achieve everything it needs to in a few short months. It is not an obvious way of interpreting the poem, which reads in a much calmer way, and even has the line: 'As if all time were theirs'. The singer should avoid singing too *legato* except for the first and second lines of verse two, which have a less frenetic feeling. Clearly the final climax has to be loud, but be careful not to let the *crescendo* grow too early. Keep an inflexible tempo right through to the very end.

7. At the Railway Station, Upway
(or the Convict and Boy with the Violin)

If the singer can find a childlike tone for the boy, perhaps avoiding vibrato, then a plain, serious beginning suits this song. The narrator's voice can then be one's normal tone, but still with a straightforward, conversational manner. This is the only song of the set which has just one note to each syllable, implying that it is the least 'song-like' of them all. As the *crescendos* appear and the tempo speeds up a fraction, be sure to retain the quality of the narrator's voice, even on 'glee', so that the new sound for the convict, probably rather harsh, makes a telling contrast. Keep that convict sound going through the *diminuendo*. The piano passage under 'free' ought to stay in the rhythmic style until the last sextuplet, when it can relax into the previous improvised manner.

8. Before Life and After

The strange accompaniment has murky triads grinding along in the left hand, maybe representing the heartlessness of nature before mankind's consciousness awakened. The serene right-hand melody and the voice part, however, depict the 'primal rightness' of the pre-human world. For the first three verses there should be no expressiveness in the song; then, as the dynamics and the tempo build up, the final anguished outburst on 'How long?' Is thrown into relief. In this last verse, marked 'moving forward', urge the tempo on a little for each phrase. But let it relax again each time before moving ahead once more. In the last phrase, lean on the quaver 'how's and drag the time a bit, until the accent on 'long'; The accompaniment carries on serenely to the end.

David Cox (1916-1997)

Fine English Days! – Anon (17th century) – 1956

The poet tells us quite bluntly that there is no such thing as a fine English day – it is a contradiction in terms and a nonsense, as nonsensical, in fact, as pretending that a donkey might be a unicorn, or an ape a marmoset. Tullia was the daughter of one of the early kings of pre-classical Rome, but I can't discover anything about her ape. Leda was ravished by Zeus in the guise of a swan, and I wonder if 'goose' may be a play on words. As for the weather, it's probably a good idea to throw a sop to Providence by allowing it to be pleasant and sunny, just as you are likely to get a decent ride in the coach if you compliment the driver. The tempo marking of 84 beats to the minute strikes me as very pedestrian, and I think something like 100 would be more lively and exciting. The limiting factor (for the singer) is being able to get 'idle, idle' out tidily. The syncopations should be neat and clean, thrown off as if they come as naturally to you as to a jazz musician, and above all, don't let them bulge as if you can't get away from the underlying four-beat bar. This is a crazy song, so be bold and make plenty of distinction between *staccato* ('He tickles this age'), *marcato* ('So, so'), *non legato* ('this world doth pass most merrily') and *legato* ('O sweet delight'). For the same reason give more than the usual contrast between *forte* and *piano*.

Antony Hopkins (b 1921)

A Melancholy Song – Trad – 1950

When you start singing this song the audience will be puzzled that the title and the music seem to be in conflict. The difficulty for the performer lies in reconciling the two. The girl is obviously fed up that the boys ignored her in favour of her sister, but the piano is mocking her feelings and enjoying the joke. There's nothing funny in it for you, but on the other hand you're not overtly sad or cross either, at least until the climax. Try 'young and bashful' as your mood at the beginning, and let it gradually become 'petulant' and then 'cross' ('angry' is too powerful and adult an emotion). Remember that the listeners will be hearing this for the first time, and it's only on the last word that they'll fully appreciate the joke. The next thing is to get the tempo right, and I think that dotted crotchet = 96 hits the mark. That done, keep the rhythm very tight and accurate, and avoid hurrying at all in passages like 'mother sent me for some barm', which can easily run away. Don't make false accents on words like 'tren<u>chers</u>' and '<u>dishes</u>'. The second verse is more animated, with a stepped *crescendo* through stresses on 'broke', 'huff'd' and 'kiss'd'. You can stay cross to the end, in which case there's not much *diminuendo*, and even an accent on 'me', or you can retreat into disappointment, which calls for quite a steep *dim* and a pathetic 'me'. There is a bass clef missing in the piano left hand under 'me'; it's a chord of D major.

Elaine Hugh-Jones (b 1927)

1. Futility – Owen – 1994

The composer has chosen a recitative style for this song, which has the effect of giving precedence to the words. It is set in speech rhythm, and its melodic line follows the natural stresses of the text. It is essential, therefore, to study the poem carefully if you don't know it already, finding where the sense leads and whether rests are structural or for emphasis. For example, the original poem has:

> Are limbs, so dear achieved, are sides
> Full-nerved, still warm, too hard to stir?

The poet is asking one question: 'Are his limbs and his sides too hard to stir?' If you're not careful the song can ask two questions, one being 'Are his limbs so dear achieved?', the other 'Are his sides too hard to stir?'. The Elgarian phrases in the piano will help the singer to maintain the connection from 'Are limbs' to 'too hard to stir', but keeping one vocal colour through the two lines will do even more, and I suggest a rather veiled tone here to contrast with a more robust sound for 'Was it for this'. By following all the meticulously marked dynamics, tempi and pedallings the performers will discover the shape of the song, though I think that the *marcato* in the final line only applies to the first two or three beats.

2. Remember – Christina Rossetti – 1998

The sonnet seems to be a difficult verse-form for composers to set since it calls for through-composition and can end up rather shapeless and rambling. Part of the success of this setting lies in the way the composer leads the listener onwards by building phrase upon phrase in a kind of musical architecture. The sombre introduction suggests that the singer should start with a warm tone, growing naturally as the line rises. *P sub* at the next 'Remember me' retains some of this warmth, and it is at the third *pp* 'Only remember me' that the voice thins right down. At the *poco più mosso* don't get agitated, and even at your most passionate be aware that this is a poem not of grief but of consolation, almost touching triumph and joy at 'Better by far'. 'Than that you should re-' is a string of unaccented syllables which lead to the stressed '-mem-', and you can lose the feeling of three beats in a bar here, thinking of it as one long up-beat. I know that producing an unmodified vowel and a final 'd' on 'sad' is a bit tricky, but it is an important word, and it deserves better than 'sah'.

James Butt (b 1929)

Virtue – Herbert – 1958

I find it fascinating that tonality can be pulled about and stretched to make strange new harmonies which somehow sound 'right'. The first two piano chords contain all the notes of the upward E minor melodic scale, but not in the usual combinations. The ear adjusts within moments and accepts them as the basic harmonic framework from which the composer can move and modulate. It's almost a relief when the opening chords return at 'Only a sweet and virtuous soul'. All the dynamics are carefully marked, and apart from the *poco rall* at the end I think there should be two other changes of tempo. One is in the piano just before 'Only a sweet and virtuous soul', where there are three bars of *diminuendo*, slowing down a little and then picking up the original speed again at the warmer *mp*. The other change, to my taste, is an *allargando* through 'But though the whole world turn to coal' up to the comma, with an *a tempo* for 'Then chiefly lives'.

Betty Roe (b 1930)

Satires of Circumstance – Hardy – pub. 1993

These songs are subtitled *Six duets for mezzo-soprano, baritone and piano*, and nowhere else in this book have I mentioned songs for more than one voice. There is only one phrase in the set where the voices sing together (in unison), otherwise they take turns to relate the stories, narrating or singing dialogue appropriate to the sex of the performer. I see no reason why they cannot be sung by a solo voice, using imagination and subtlety to differentiate the characters. Schubert's *Erlkönig*, for example, has three protagonists and a narrator, and yet it is normally sung solo. Roe's *Satires of Circumstance* were written for a particular purpose, and they may not be especially characteristic of her work; but I want to include them here because they depend essentially on the delivery of the text. The composer herself writes: 'I have kept the singing lines comparatively simple because it is supremely important that the words get across and, where appropriate, are "acted". Nothing should be allowed to get in the way of communicating these vivid moments of truth.' It is not enough simply to enunciate clearly; the singer has to convey the feeling and the meaning behind the words. To achieve this, there are two things the singer can do. Firstly, read the poems several times and enter this hard-hearted world which Hardy has created, acknowledging that this is an aspect of reality even if a cruel and pessimistic one. Secondly, consider using movement to heighten the impact of the words. I don't suggest a full-blown staging, but a few well-chosen gestures, which in the context of a generally static vocal recital can have a very powerful effect.

1. At a Watering Place

The opening page sets the scene quite matter-of-factly, so don't be tempted to 'emote' yet. There is some difficulty in clarifying the words for the listener: 'the man and his friend' are sitting and smoking, and they are also looking at the bay. I would make a tiny hiatus after 'friend' and a new impetus on 'and regard'. Be aware that it is the whitish chalk cliffs over to the left which 'smile sallowly'. Sing a *cantabile* line for the first time on 'A handsome couple among the rest'. Sneering at the couple, the man now sings in a hard-edged tone without warmth or sympathy, except for the narrator's line 'says the man to his friend'. 'Are to marry next week' can be *marcato* and a little slower. Try 'How little he thinks' slower still and then gather pace through 'dozens of days'. 'Stroked her neck' slows down a lot, 'unhooked the links of her sleeve' is faster and *cantabile*, while the *rallentando* on 'to get at her upper arm' emphasises the sensual nature of what he remembers. This passage has been very carefully marked by the composer, but none of this slowing down and speeding up will be convincing unless you can enter the mind of the speaker and understand his thought processes. 'What's the harm' is marked *parlando*, and I would apply the same tone to 'Well, bliss is in ignorance'.

2. Outside the Window

I would prefer a slightly quicker basic tempo than the one marked, say crotchet = 70. This prevents the slower sections from being too static. The narrator enters the spirit of the story by taking on something of the girl's tone of peevishness as she argues with her mother. The mezzo takes over, relaxing the tempo a fraction, only to become *agitato* again through the bar of 'eyes a-glare'. He sings two bars quite freely, carefully tuning 'behold her' and 'soul' against the chords in the accompaniment. Feel his shock at discovering the girl's true nature, followed by a hushed realisation of his lucky escape. Try a big *rallentando* through 'my precious porcelain proves it', with a definite delay before 'delf'. Then comes the first 'sung' phrase of the song: 'His face has reddened', with a clear, dry final two bars. Incidentally, delf is a kind of earthenware from Delft in Holland, and would be considered cheaper and coarser than fine porcelain.

3. In the Restaurant

There is a terrible age-old conflict here between the man who wishes to extricate himself from any responsibility for both the woman and her unborn child, and the woman with her feelings of love and honour and her disgust at the prospect of continuing to share a bed with a husband she no longer loves. The man applies what he sees as unassailable logic to an unfortunate problem, so he should sound reasonable and well-intentioned, with a hint of pomposity at 'I feel an elopement is ill-advised'. Her response is grounded in the heart, with a tone of pleading in her voice. The bleak 'Let us go' is filled with her knowledge of the hardness of her future whatever the man decrees; the dishonour always falls more heavily upon the woman. The final chord, mixing E major and D major, shows their unresolved disagreement.

4. By Her Aunt's Grave

My score mistakenly marks 'quaver = 80', whereas it should read 'dotted crotchet = 80'. Given that speed, the tone should be conversational throughout. This is not lyric poetry of the normal kind, but glimpses of real life set in verse. Read it aloud until you have found the true rhythm and emphasis of the words, and when it comes to recreating the music, don't 'sing' too much. The girl speaks, but she is almost thinking aloud, especially when she says: I must do something about it. With *parlando* on 'Twas to cover', the composer implies that the first two lines of the song should be given a singing tone, but I would suggest that you avoid a beautiful sound and sing it *non-legato*. The man's reply has none of this reflective mood but is rather brash and jovial, parodying the girl's opening music. The girl's simple response becomes reflective again at 'eighty weeks, or near'. He breaks in with his nefarious suggestion, using a full *cantabile* for the only time for 'There's a dance tonight at the Load of Hay' (a pub, I imagine). The mezzo is meant to sing 'She passively nods', and he joins in for the last phrase. The major/minor last chord suggests some ambiguous feelings about what they have just agreed to do.

5. At the Altar-Rail

The groom is so shocked by what's in the telegram that his emotions have been held in check. Notice how the piano twice imitates his music on 'My bride is not coming', insisting on that central fact. Follow the tempo markings very carefully, though some *rubato* can be used to underline the text during the first page. The first long run at a strict tempo is the waltz section from 'Ay, she won me'. He then reads out the telegram in her words, but here the mezzo gives them with a good sung *legato* on 'It's sweet of you, dear, to prepare me a nest'. Then she's off in her true colours, a woman whose morals are looser, and whose age is greater than he had ever suspected. Try *non-legato* from 'But a swift', and *legato* for 'I had eaten'. She's all for the good life but she knows it won't last, and I think her last phrase can have something of regret and longing in it.

6. In the Moonlight

There is nothing in the poem which tells us that the first person to speak is a woman, but by giving the part to the mezzo, the composer has emphasised the prying, gossipy nature of the character. The slowly tolling bell in the accompaniment lays a hypnotic stillness on the scene, allowing the voice to recite the verse with very little nuance of expression. *mf* is possibly too strong for the song's opening, and a warm *mp* might be better. The man retains the strict, slow tempo, I think, even though the piano has forsaken any rhythmical pulse. 'Ah – she was the one' is marked *forte*, but it seems to me that the loudest moment of the song is when the man sings 'whom all the others were ranked above'. Clearly there is enormous pain in the man's reply and, from what we know of Hardy's life, we can imagine that the dead woman may have been his wife, whom he had not sufficiently loved in her lifetime. After all, it was as a result of Hardy's feelings of guilt and remorse that he poured out his great love-poems to his wife Emma after she had died.

Trevor Hold (b 1939)

Song at Night – Nicholson – pub. 1983

This beautiful poem, densely packed with vivid imagery, explores the synaesthetic idea of one of the five senses standing for another. Music's sound can conjure up the vision of a smile, sighs can have a shape and starlight can have a sweet taste. Yet when it comes to articulating the departed loved one's name you cannot do it yourself, calling upon the echo to do it on your behalf. Both words and music are interwoven with Purcell's famous song, making a highly satisfying work of art. The piano part is marked 'with pedal', which clearly applies throughout the song, but it doesn't mean just plonking down the right foot and keeping it there. The sustaining pedal should be used to blur the edges of the notes with judicious application and release, and the minims at the ends of vocal phrases should similarly be allowed to spill over their allotted span. Imagine that as the coda winds down to nothing, you can actually hear the adored name.

Roderick Williams (b 1965)

Reading Scheme – Cope – 1994 (pub. 1998)

It's not often that we have a genuinely amusing song to sing, but here's one with a gem of a poem. We've all come across these books for learning to read – *Janet and John, Roger Red Hat* and so on – so we recognise the style. Part of the humour lies in the juxtaposition of the childish delivery with the difficult adult situation it is describing. Sing generally *non legato* and, naturally, be sure the text is clear. Close early on the 'n' of 'fun', 'run' and 'bun', even when the note is quite long. 'Here is the milkman' (bar 26) is innocent, and only 'call' has a knowing quality to it (*molto legato*). 'Go Peter' is *marcato*, suggesting 'go away' rather than 'go on'. 'Come, milkman, come' is very *legato* and seductive, and then 'the milkman likes Mummy' is innocent and *non legato* again. Shutting out the sun with curtains while the milkman is there is highly suggestive to the adult mind, but keep treating it as a child would. 'I hear a car' is childishly excited, but at 'Daddy looks very cross' you could either preserve the innocent excitement (even through 'Up, milkman') or step out of character as you did with the seductive 'Come, milkman, come', in which case 'Up, milkman' becomes a cry of fear and warning. It's probably enough just to deliver the text childishly, which is what happens anyway for the rest of the song; you're really enjoying all the mayhem going on around you. Breathe wherever is convenient on 'See him run' (bar 94 onwards); the words have become merely part of a melismatic decoration.

Appendix – Editions and Publishers

In this list of the songs appearing in the last section of the book (168 in all), I have used the following abbreviations:

B&H = Boosey & Hawkes
MB = Musica Britannica (Stainer & Bell)
NE = Novello English
S&B = Stainer & Bell
Banks = Banks Music Publications
Century = A Century of English Song – Thames
Heritage = A Heritage of 20th Century British Song – B&H
Imperial = New Imperial Edition – B&H
Kagen = Kagen's Purcell editions – International Music Company
Leonard = Hal Leonard
Mayhew = The Singer's Collection – Mayhew
OUP = Oxford University Press
Recitalist = The Junior Recitalist – Stainer & Bell
Thames = Twenty English Lyrics, two books

For Purcell:
  OUP = Timothy Roberts's edition in two books
  S&B = Peter Wishart's edition in three books
  Novello = Fifteen Songs, two books
  Kagen = Forty Songs, four books
  PS = Solo Songs, four books, ed. Margaret Laurie
  Schott = Songs ed. Tippett and Bergmann, single copies and five books

Purcell

There are many editions and many keys for most of Purcell's songs. I have underlined the original key, but it is worth bearing in mind that the pitch in Purcell's time was probably as much as a tone lower than it is today. I have also given each song its original gender, though there is nothing to stop the opposite sex singing it provided the text is appropriate. Britten's editions should be considered as separate pieces in their own right, given the extent of his realisation of the accompaniments. They can be extremely effective when the accompanying instrument is the piano, and I recommend anyone to try them. The following information comes from *English Solo Song, vol. 4 – Purcell* by Michael Pilkington (Thames 1994).

1. Fairest Isle (f)
>high (Bb)   *OUP 1, Britten Seven Songs B&H*
>high (Ab)   *Novello 1, Kagen 1*
>med. (G)   *OUP 1*
>low (F)   *Novello 1, Kagen 1, Britten Seven Songs B&H*

2. Let the dreadful engines of eternal will (m)
>low (F)   *Britten (Faber)*
>low (Eb)   *Schott, Imperial 5*

3. Ye twice ten hundred deities (m)
>low   *Imperial 6, Kagen Six Songs for Bass*

4. Sweeter than roses (f)
>high (Cmi)   *Novello 1, Kagen 1, OUP 2, Britten Six Songs B&H*
>high (Bmi)   *Schott 1*
>med. (Ami)   *Novello 1, Kagen 1, S&B 1, Britten Six Songs B&H*
>low (Gmi)   *Schott 4, OUP 2*

5. If music be the food of love (final setting) (f)
>high (Gmi)   *Kagen 1, OUP 1, PS 4, Britten Seven Songs B&H*
>med. (Emi)   *Kagen 1, OUP 1, Britten Seven Songs B&H*

6. From rosy bowers (f)
>high (Cmi)   *Novello 1, Kagen 2, Schott 2*
>high (Bmi)   *S&B 2*
>med. (Ami)   *Novello 1, Kagen 2, Schott 4*

Arne

1. Jenny (m)
>high   *S&B 12 Songs 1, ed. Pilkington*

2. O come, o come, my dearest (f/m)
>high   *S&B 12 Songs 1, Leonard, ed. Pilkington*
>low   *Leonard, ed. Pilkington*

3. The fond appeal (f)
>high   *S&B 12 Songs 2, ed. Pilkington*

4. The timely admonition
>high   *S&B 12 Songs 2, ed. Pilkington*

5. Where the bee sucks (f)
>high   *S&B, B&H, Novello, Imperial 1, ed. Northcote*

Linley (snr)

When a tender maid (f/m)
>high   *S&B Songs of the Linleys, ed. Pilkington*

Linley (jnr)

O, bid your faithful Ariel fly (f/m)
>high   *Imperial 1, ed. Northcote*

Pinto   *Musica Britannica vol. 43, ed. Bush and Temperly*
1. Invocation to Nature (f/m)
    med.
    + *Tuneful Voice (ed. Roberts), Recitalist 2 (ed Bush and Temperley)*
2. From thee, Eliza, I must go (m)
    med.   + *Tuneful Voice*
3. Eloisa to Abelard (f)
    high

S S Wesley   *Musica Britannica vol. 43*
1. By the rivers of Babylon (f/m) med.
2. Collect for the third Sunday in Advent (m) low

Sterndale Bennett Musica Britannica vol. 43
1. Gentle Zephyr (m)
    med.
2. To Chloë in sickness (m)
    med.
3. The Past (f/m)
    med.

Parry   *Musica Britannica vol. 49, ed. Bush*
1. My true love hath my heart (f)
    high   + *NE 1*
2. No longer mourn for me (f/m)
    high   + *NE 2*
3. To Lucasta, on going to the wars (m)
    med.   + *NE 3*
4. To Althea, from prison (m)
    low   + *NE 3, Thames 20/1*
5. Why so pale and wan (m)
    med.   + *NE 3, Thames 20/1*
6. Bright Star (m)
    high   + *Century III, NE 4*
7. And yet I love her till I die (m)
    med.   + *NE 6*
8. Love is a bable (m)
    low   + *NE 6, Thames 20/1*
9. Sleep (f/m)
    low   + *NE 7*
10. Nightfall in winter (f/m)
    low   + *NE 8, Thames 20/1*
11. From a City Window (f/m)
    high   *Century I or NE 10 <u>not</u> MB 49*

Stanford

1. La Belle Dame Sans Merci (f/m)
   med.   *MB 52, S&B*
2. Golden Slumbers (f)
   high   *MB 52, Heritage 1*
3. Prospice (m)
   med.   *S&B 6 songs* or *MB 52*
4. Crossing the Bar (f/m)
   high   *MB 52*
5. Songs of the Sea (m)
   med.   *B&H Songs of the Sea*
5.1 Drake's Drum + *Heritage 1*
5.2 Outward bound + *Heritage 1*
5.3 Devon, O Devon, in wind and rain
5.4 Homeward bound
5.5 The Old Superb + *Heritage 2* or *B&H*
6. A Soft Day (f/m)
   low   *S&B, Banks* or *MB 52*
   high   *S&B*
7. The bold unbiddable child (f/m)
   low   *S&B 6 songs* or *MB 52*

Delius

1. To daffodils (f/m)
   high   *B&H Album, B&H 16 songs, Heritage 2*
2. I-Brasîl (f/m)
   high/med.   *OUP 19 songs*
3. The nightingale (f/m)
   high   *OUP 19 songs, OUP*
4. Twilight fancies (f/m)
   high   *OUP 19 songs, OUP*
   low   *OUP Solo Contralto*
5. Young Venevil (f/m)
   high   *OUP 19 songs*

Somervell

A Shropshire Lad
   med.   *B&H. A Shropshire Lad*
1. Loveliest of trees (f/m)
2. When I was one-and-twenty (f/m)
3. There pass the careless people (f/m)
4. In summer-time on Bredon (m) + *Heritage 1*
5. The street sounds to the soldiers' tread (f/m)

6. On the idle hill of summer (f/m) + *Heritage 1*
7. White in the moon (f/m) + *Heritage 2*
8. Think no more, lad (f/m)
9. Into my heart an air that kills (f/m)
10. The lads in their hundreds (f/m) + *Heritage 2*

Wood
Ethiopia saluting the colours (m)
  low   *Century II*

Bantock
1. A Feast of Lanterns (f/m)
  high   *Century III*
2. Adrift (f/m)
  high   *Century I*
3. Song to the Seals (f/m)
  low   *Century IV*

Vaughan Williams
1. Songs of Travel (m)
  high and <u>low</u> *B&H Songs of Travel*
1.1 The Vagabond low + *Heritage 2*, high and low *B&H*
1.2 Let Beauty Awake
1.3 The Roadside Fire low + *Heritage 1*
1.4 Youth and Love low + *Heritage 2*
1.5 In Dreams
1.6 The Infinite Shining Heavens
1.7 Whither must I Wander low + *Heritage 2*, high and low *B&H*
1.8 Bright is the Ring of Words
1.9 I have trod the Upward and the Downward Slope
2. The New Ghost (f/m)
  med.   *OUP Collected 2 & Century I*

Holst
From the Rig Veda (f/m)
  med.   *Chester Vedic Hymns*
1. Ushas
2. Varuna
3. Maruts

Quilter
1. Now sleeps the crimson petal (f/m)
  high & <u>low</u> *B&H*, high *Imperial 4*
2. Love's Philosophy (f/m)
  <u>high</u> & low *B&H*, high *Heritage 4*

3. Three Shakespeare Songs
   high & _low_   *B&H 3 Shakespeare*
3.1. Come away, death (m)
3.2. O mistress mine (m) low *Imperial 5*, high *Heritage 3*, high and low *B&H*
3.3. Blow, blow, thou winter wind (f/m)
4. Drink to me only with thine eyes (f/m)
   med.   *B&H. Arnold Book of old songs, B&H*

Bridge   B&H. Frank Bridge Songs
1. E'en as a lovely flower (f/m)
   high & med.   + high *Imperial 4*, med *Mayhew 1, B&H*
2. Blow, blow, thou winter wind (f/m)
   med.   + *B&H Shakespeare*
3. Fair Daffodils (f/m) med.
4. Come to me in my dreams (f/m) med.
5. My pent-up tears (f/m)
   med.   *Thames 5 early songs, _not_ B&H*
6. Love went a-riding (f)
   high   + *Heritage 3, Banks, B&H*
7. What shall I your true love tell? (f/m)
   high

Ireland   *S&B Complete Songs in five volumes*
1. Sea Fever (m)
   low   *Complete 2, 11 songs S&B*, + higher keys *S&B*
2. The Trellis (f/m)
   high   *Complete 1, 11 songs S&B*
3. The Encounter (f/m)
   high   *Complete 1, Land of Lost Content*
4. Three Hardy Songs   *Complete 3*
4.1. Summer Schemes (f/m)
   med.   + low *Cramer*
4.2. Her Song (f)
   low   + high and med *B&H,* med. *Cramer*
4.3. Weathers (f/m)
   low   + high and med. *B&H*

Bax
1. Cradle Song (f)
   high/med.   *Century V, (Chappell)*
2. In the Morning (f/m)
   med.   *Century II, Thames 12 Songs*

Farrar
Brittany (f/m)
    med.   *Century IV*

Butterworth
Six songs from A Shropshire Lad
    med.   *S&B. A Shropshire Lad*
1. Loveliest of Trees (f/m) + *Mayhew 1*
2. When I was one-and-twenty (f/m)   + *Mayhew 2*
3. Look not in my eyes (f/m)
4. Think no more, lad (f/m)
5. The lads in their hundreds (f/m) + *Mayhew 1*
6. Is my team ploughing? (m)

Browne   *Thames Six Songs of W D Browne*
Epitaph on Salathiel Pavy (f/m)
    high   + *Century 3 & Heritage 1*

Gibbs   *Thames Ten Songs*
1. The Fields are Full (f/m)
    high   + *Heritage 4 & B&H*
2. Silver (f/m)
    high   *Heritage 4, B&H, not Thames*
3. Titania (f/m)
    med.
4. The Splendour Falls (f/m)
    med.
5. Philomel (f/m)
    high

Gurney
1. Spring (f/m)
    high   *B&H Five Elizabethan, Heritage 1*
2. Sleep (f/m)
    <u>high</u>   *Five Elizabethan, Imperial 4, B&H*
    med.   *Heritage 1*
3. Severn Meadows (f/m)
    low   *OUP 20 Favourite, (Songs 5)*
4. Thou didst delight my eyes (f/m)
    low   *OUP Songs 3*
5. The Scribe (f/m)
    med.   *OUP 20 Favourites, (Songs 2)*
6. Black Stitchel (f/m)
    med.   *OUP 20 Favourites, (Songs 1)*

Bliss
The return from Town (f)
    high   *Century V*

Burrows
Mistress Fell (f)
    high   *Century V*

Howells
1. King David (f/m)
    med.   *Thames: A Garland, B&H Songs, Heritage 4 & B&H*
2. Gavotte (f/m)
    high   *Century I, OUP Soprano & OUP*
3. Come sing and dance (f)
    high   *OUP*

Warlock
1. As ever I saw (m)
    med.   *Thames songs 2, B&H Songs*
    high   *Mayhew 1*
2. Lullaby (f/m)
    med.   *Thames 2, B&H Songs*
3. There is a lady sweet and kind (m)
    med.   *Thames 2, B&H Songs*
4. Captain Stratton's Fancy (m)
    <u>med</u>.   *Thames 3, S&B 13 songs, Mayhew 2 & S&B*
    low   *S&B*
5. Sleep (f/m)
    med.   *Thames 3, OUP baritone & OUP*
6. Three Belloc Songs (f/m)
    <u>med</u>.   *Thames 7, OUP 2*
6.1. Ha'nacker Mill
6.2. The Night
6.3. My Own Country   + high *OUP*

Gill
In Memoriam (f/m)
    med.   *Century II*

Head
1. Sweet Chance, that led my steps abroad (f/m)
    <u>high</u>   *Heritage 4, B&H Album 1, B&H*
    med.   *B&H*

2. The Estuary (f/m)
      med.   *Heritage 3*

Finzi
1. Let us garlands bring
      med.   *B&H Let us garlands bring*
1.1. Come away, come away, death (m)   + *Heritage 3*
1.2. Who is Silvia? (f/m)
1.3. Fear no more the heat o' the sun (f/m) + *Heritage 3*
1.4. O mistress mine (m)
1.5. It was a lover and his lass (f/m)
2. Earth and Air and Rain
      med.   *B&H Earth and Air and Rain*
2.1. Summer Schemes (f/m)
2.2. When I set out for Lyonesse (f/m)
2.3. Waiting Both (f/m)
2.4. The Phantom (f/m)
2.5. So I have fared (f/m)
2.6. Rollicum-Rorum (f/m) + *Heritage 4*
2.7. To Lizbie Browne (m)
2.8. The Clock of the Years (m)
2.9. In a Churchyard (f/m)
2.10. Proud Songsters (f/m)

Poston
Sweet Suffolk Owl (f/m)
      high   *Century V*

Britten
Winter Words (f/m)
      high   *B&H Winter Words*
1. At Day-close in November
2. Midnight on the Great Western
3. Wagtail and Baby + *Heritage 3*
4. The Little Old Table
5. The Choirmaster's Burial + *Heritage 4*
6. Proud Songsters
7. At the Railway Station, Upway
8. Before Life and After

Cox
Fine English Days! (f/m)
      med.   *Century IV*

Hopkins
A Melancholy Song (f)
    high   *Century I & Chester*

Hugh-Jones
1. Futility (f/m)
    high   *Century III*
2. Remember (f)
    high   *Century V*

Butt
Virtue (f/m)
    high   *Century IV*

Roe
Satires of Circumstance (f/m)
    med.   *Thames*
1. At a Watering Place
2. Outside the Window
3. In the Restaurant
4. By Her Aunt's Grave
5. At the Altar-Rail
6. In the Moonlight

Hold
Song at Night (f/m)
    <u>med</u>.   *Century IV, Banks*
    high   *Banks*

Williams
Reading Scheme (f)
    high   *Century V*